S0-AEJ-314

Democracy's Dilemma

Democracy's Dilemma

Environment, Social Equity, and the Global Economy

Robert C. Paehlke

The MIT Press
Cambridge, Massachusetts
London, England

This book was set in Sabon by Graphic Composition, Inc., using QuarkXPress 4.1. Printed and bound in the United States of America.

Library of Congress Cataloging-in-Publication Data

Paehlke, Robert.
Democracy's dilemma : environment, social equity, and the global economy / Robert C. Paehlke.
p. cm.
Includes bibliographical references and index.
ISBN 0-262-16215-6 (hc. : alk. paper)
1. Democracy. 2. Globalization. 3. International economic integration. 4. Environmentalism. 5. Social justice. I. Title.
JC423 .P222 2003
306.2—dc21

2002038071

10 9 8 7 6 5 4 3 2 1

Contents

Preface

Many have a sense that governments are increasingly out of control, that elections have less and less influence on the social, environmental, and economic conditions we face every day. It seems that just as formal democracy is spreading into new corners of the world following the collapse of communism, the effectiveness of many longer-lived democracies is subtly, or perhaps not so subtly, declining. Civic involvement and even voting are less entrenched than they were as recently as the 1970s, and political cynicism is all too normal. Political life seems to most people to be dominated by media and money. Why?

The answer for some is expressed in the single word *globalization*. Single explanations are of course always too simple, but a widespread desire to be globally competitive can lead to abrupt changes in productive capacity (and to political acquiescence in such initiatives). In turn, the innovative expansion of social programs and quality public schools is frequently deemed unachievable, and environmental protection is frequently seen as impossibly expensive, even in the richest nations in the world.

At the same time, decisions made in nonelected and essentially closed global trade organizations have been known to override hard-won environmental initiatives in democratic nations or communities. It is little wonder that trade integration, like government as a whole, is often met with a kind of resigned suspicion, if not open hostility.

Global economic integration, however, is part of a centuries-long trend that almost two centuries ago saw economic markets grow beyond regions and principalities and thereby foster the growth of nation-states. It was in those jurisdictions that democracy ultimately flourished. Moreover, today's *global* economic integration has been fostered and accelerated by computers, media, and communications technologies that have in turn aided the spread of democracy to the former communist nations and elsewhere. The combination of these factors has also likely promoted overall economic expansion that in turn could help to sustain both democracy and social progress.

Thus the realities of global economic integration are far more complex and multifaceted than simply involving a rise of global corporate actors to political dominance, as some believe. Democracy, formal if not necessarily effective, *is* spreading to more nations as global economic integration proceeds. Trade offers positive benefits of many kinds, from product diversity to economic growth. The frequent and rapid movement of people and information within globalization exposes more people to a wide array of cultures.

At the same time, however, the process of expanding global interaction is overwhelmingly dominated by economic considerations. This is indeed the core problem. The expansion of markets beyond local borders in the nineteenth century was followed by the expansion and intensification of political life—geographically to the scale of the nation-state and structurally to encompass all classes, males and females alike, and all manner of burgeoning social and political organizations. Basic political rights were universalized in many nations. Democracy established itself at a scale comparable to the newly expanded economic marketplace.

Now, through global-scale communications, computerization, and travel capabilities, we are moving toward worldwide economic integration in forms and styles that never existed previously. But politics cannot easily follow economics to this new scale of operation. The notion of global government is almost universally distrusted. Faced with it, we yearn more than ever for local government, for the decentralization of authority. But absent politics, global governance proceeds as if all that mattered were economic considerations. In a word, at the global scale there is no semblance of democracy and no semblance of balance.

Economic considerations overwhelm all else. What might be called "economism" is triumphant. We pretend that at the global scale we can build a structure of economic rules and leave all else to the sovereign nation-states and other levels of government. This is nonsense. The reason communism failed was that it was fundamentally undemocratic and fundamentally economistic. It let economic considerations overwhelm environmental considerations and denied citizens the opportunity to defend their own social rights through rights-based laws or through independent social and economic organizations, including trade unions and religious and community organizations. There was no effective balancing of economic, social, and environmental factors and interests.

That same reality is close to existing at the global level. Private corporate actors and their many and varied associations are there in force, but almost no other voices are heard. No other considerations enter the arena of trade-treaty creation and trade-dispute resolution. Environmental and social considerations are addressed elsewhere perhaps, but not comprehensively and not effectively. Environmental problems are systematically exported from rich nations to poor and to the margins of all nations. Social problems are not adequately addressed (and cannot be within any nation at risk of being economically uncompetitive). Social equity is in retreat worldwide. In the absence of deliberate balancing at the highest level where economic decisions are made, this result is almost inevitable.

To compound the problem, this pervasive economism is everywhere reinforced by commercially oriented, increasingly global electronic media. Today's media convey a dream world in which all problems are solvable through the purchase of goods and services. Economism is again ascendant as these media become increasingly the central means by which information moves within societies. Balance is thus lost not only in the processes of political life but in everyday communications as well.

In this new world of global, electronic capitalism we must develop new ways to restore the balance we once had in the domestic politics of many nations, a balance among at least three aspects of societal life—economy, social equity, and environment. The task at hand is to resolve democracy's dilemma at the global scale, not withdraw within autonomous national, ethnic, religious, or even local bastions. Too much potential would be lost in doing so. It is also not clear that we could do so even if we wanted to. Through a myriad of inventions and activities, humankind has been moving toward global integration for centuries. Global economic integration calls for more effective democracy—democracy that attends to human economic, social, *and* environmental needs on all levels from the global to the local.

President George W. Bush, commenting in May 2002 on the possibility of normalizing relations between the United States and Cuba, spoke of a need for "the substance of democracy, not its hollow empty forms." This is a challenging standard to which *all* nations might now be held.

1

The Challenge of Global Economic Integration

Today's emergent postindustrial, post–cold war socioeconomic order is characterized by increased global economic integration, cultural dominance of very large, privately owned media organizations, and automated and/or offshore production of goods. Many find this new world dynamic, exciting, and full of promise; others, even before September 11, 2001, found it threateningly insecure. This new order is also clearly, in many of its important dimensions, undemocratic. It is all of these things; both the promise and the perils are real. The processes of global integration are seemingly inexorable—economically, politically, culturally, socially, and environmentally. We are all more and more bound together by integrated production, transportation, communication, investment, and politics. This book argues that this integration, in both process and outcome, has been inequitable, environmentally unsustainable, and undemocratic, but that this result is neither inevitable nor inherent in the fact of globalization.

This book, then, is neither a celebration of the technological wonders of the new digitally integrated age, nor another ethical/political "alarm bell" over globalization. I seek an analytic and balanced, yet provocative perspective on global economic integration, in an emerging era that carries both enormous challenges and enormous potential. The central challenge is to imagine politically plausible ways global society can realize its positive potential more fully. We are a long way from doing so. One reason for this failure is precisely the global character of the emerging society and our understandable and appropriate discomfort with the very idea. Another is the structure and nature of its principal means of organization and communication. As Bill McKibben has argued so persuasively, ours is increasingly an age of "missing information" wherein our old ways of learning and communicating are replaced in large measure by global media, an inferior substitute in many ways.[1]

Democracy's Dilemma

Democracy's dilemma is this: global economic integration virtually requires some form of corresponding political integration, but the very notion of global government in any form is worrisome, especially perhaps to those with strong liberal democratic instincts. The response to this dilemma among most of those who advance freer global trade and investment opportunities (and the expanded integration of media, communications, travel, and immigration that are bound up in the process) is often a disingenuous denial. They imagine, assert, or proceed as if the world can be integrated ever more tightly economically, while each nation at the same time is "free" to establish its own rules regarding social equity, environmental protection, and all manner of other "domestic" policy concerns and outcomes.

This is simply not the case. Global economic integration provokes an array of lowest-common-denominator socioeconomic and policy tendencies, usually bound up with an ongoing political and economic search for "competitiveness." Economic integration without established global social and environmental standards, while not always a race to the bottom in terms of social equity, environmental protection, taxation, and wages, does comprehensively shift the balance of political pressures. As economic integration advances, absent systematic countervailing pressures and/or regional environmental and social standards, many nations have difficulty enforcing existing environmental standards and face great challenges in establishing any stringent new initiatives. Moreover, work conditions such as maximum hours worked involuntarily, or the proportion of the workforce in involuntary forms of part-time, low-benefit employment, as well as the relative wage position of low-income individuals and families, are prone to deterioration even in very wealthy nations. In addition, all manner of public social programs suffer retrenchment (conceived as updating), and gone entirely is the once-normal promise of ever-improving programs.

There are, of course, also countertendencies of several sorts. The European Union (EU) has sought to harmonize many social and environmental standards and has generally done so in a way that harmonizes upward (though it has not often established the highest possible standards as a EU-wide norm). The EU has, in effect, created since the early days of the European Coal and Steel Community a half-century ago, a partial political integration to complement the deliberate, and widening, economic integration of the continent. A second modest countertendency has occurred in the unusual circumstance in which something approaching full employment has arisen (as in the United States from the mid-1990s into the new millennium). In those rare instances, pressures arise to improve low-end wages, and the very fact of full employment may raise the relative economic circumstances of the poor as a whole. Finally, there are particular circumstances in which jurisdictions can urge, or even force, higher environmental standards on other, reluctant jurisdictions. This outcome, however, may require a particular and uncommon set of circumstances.

More frequently, production within jurisdictions with lower environmental standards has an advantage, and political pressures are thereby created within jurisdictions with higher standards. These pressures push governments to at least tread softly with enforcement lest local manufacturers fail to remain competitive. They also pressure governments to be less responsive to public preferences for more stringent standards of all kinds and toward lower levels of taxation, especially for globally mobile corporations and wealthy investors. The positive side of downward pressure on taxation is that it may urge greater efficiency on the public sector. However, without minimum social standards, or at least expectations, the result may be more often marked by a deterioration of health, education, and infrastructure than by true increases in efficiency.

So pervasive and powerful are these pressures to achieve a capacity to compete globally that it can be argued that democracy itself is undermined by global economic integration. That is, the new economic realities of mobile capital and production capacity pressure elected governments to ignore or manipulate public opinion toward what they perceive to be economic necessities. Domestic policy is thus systematically skewed by conscious creation of economic integration without social and environmental minima. This new reality alters the array of democratic political forces within every participating nation. Also utterly undemocratic are the processes of trade-related decision making growing outside the nation state. Both contexts might be characterized as economistic—they now proceed as if economic gains always and automatically produce cost-free gains in all realms, including the social and the environmental realms. This is patently false.

In the realm of economistic global institutions, where the creation and ongoing management of the global economy take place, democracy's dilemma is most starkly visible. The only way to pretend that comprehensive global governance has not already been established is to pretend that the decisions made are technical and somehow solely and wholly "trade matters." Accordingly, virtually all inputs into the decision processes come from technicians and from those with a demonstrable interest in trade outcomes: industries, industry associations, investors, financial institutions, governmental agencies, trade organizations, and perhaps a few well-established labor unions. An intricate web of trade treaties and organizations established to maximize trade and cross-border investment opportunities is established, but the highest environmental standards are not imposed on all participants, nor are *any* minima with regard to wages, domestic social equity, or social policy such as pensions or even the legality of trade unions.

These rules have been established through processes largely closed to the public and even the media. They are carried out by participants virtually united in their economistic presuppositions and invariant in terms of their backgrounds and interests. These forums are, in essence, global government that refuses to claim the title or to behave according to any semblance of democratic selection or participatory processes. But to acknowledge this seemingly places one in a position of advocating actual and acknowledged global government or at least governance—the establishment of processes that reject economism and seek to establish the environmental and social minima necessary to rebalance and democratize the outcomes associated with the global economic integration before us. Yet what democrat among us does not see the difficulties of distance and scale and defense of national interest that this would imply? This combination almost seems to fly in the face of democratic possibility. This is democracy's dilemma in the age of globalization.

Capitalism and Democracy in a Global Age

This book takes as a given that at present, and perhaps for the indefinite future, there is no politically viable alternative to markets as the central structure through which a great proportion of socioeconomic activity is organized. Governments, however, should and do still urge economic markets in one or another direction (even if they deny, or fail to recognize, that they are doing so). However, markets themselves—contemporary mythology notwithstanding—are neither neutral nor autonomous. The worst excesses of "accumulation-maximizing" markets, operating on a global scale, may harm human well-being as much as they enhance it, threaten nature, and at times undermine their own stable functioning. Guiding "free" markets, then, is not a contradiction in terms, though it is a considerable challenge.

One must assume (or at least hope) that effectively functioning markets do not *require* radically unequal income distribution and environmental destruction. This assumption seems to run contrary to contemporary elite opinion, especially in North America.[2] And one must also assume that democratic governments, even in an elite-dominated era, will in timely fashion find the wisdom to steer economic production away from the environmentally nonsustainable trajectory on which it presently seems to be locked. Such redirection will not be universally popular, but there is every reason to hope that democratic intelligence will learn to focus on longer-term human well-being, especially because contemporary tendencies are going to make that new focus more and more necessary.

One significant political error of the 1990s was the understandable, but erroneous, view that the abysmal failure of command economies somehow demonstrated that "unfettered" markets were the only way to economic and all other forms of societal success. There are at least three problems with this view. First, all markets are "fettered" in one way or another. Second, markets without an effective and active democratic state are every bit as prone to systemic failure as are states without effective markets. A world of low-wage economies, for example, has no customers. Also, bankers are not prudent by nature; it is not their money. Moreover, the only firms that can enforce their own contracts are monopolies and the Mafia. Third, economic success without success in terms of human well-being and environmental quality is not only all but worthless, but radically unstable on its own terms. Employees with environmentally induced illnesses may have low productivity. If there are no fish, there are no fish products to sell.

One further introductory caution remains. Given the emerging structure of a globally integrated capitalist economy, "taming" or "guiding" the market would seem a more prudent, feasible, and desirable goal than "managing" or "controlling" it—given democracy's dilemma as described above. Thus this book is market-sympathetic and market-sensitive enough that it takes as a fundamental task a careful search for tools of intervention that will restrain the worst excesses and steer the market in better directions but that do not presume to dictate one market behavior for all. Moreover, the book seeks tools that will "tame" without requiring legions of public employees to monitor the details of production and consumption. At the same time it asserts that public service is essential, and even still a higher calling. This book is, then, politically middle of the road though some will see it as either surreptitiously "left" or "right."

I also begin with two other, deeper, assumptions. The first is that some values are more important than economic values and need to find more effective expression within both democratic affairs and everyday life. The second is that the economic realm is based on principles and practices that are not easily directed in detail. We might wisely render unto Caesar, but societies, if they are to be societies, also need to place some values above short-term monetary outcomes, and to intervene in the economic realm accordingly.

The New Age of Global Integration

One way to understand the form of global society that is emerging is to understand where it comes from. Today's society is a global and uniquely media-dominated capitalist system that has arisen out of mass industrial society, which in turn developed from an earlier industrial (agriculture and craft-based) society. Prototypical products of craft society were food, furniture, clothing, and other household goods. Prototypical products of mass industrial society were automobiles, radios, televisions, and appliances. Prototypical products of today's global capitalism are software, computers, movies, and mutual funds. Craft societies bridged a transition from feudal, agricultural societies to capitalism. Mass industrial societies were highly contested in terms of socialist and capitalist forms of socioeconomic organization. Craft societies were primarily rooted in communities, cities, and regions. Mass industrial societies arose in tandem with, and were essentially managed within, nation-states. The new society, it would appear, will be dominated by privately owned, global-scale economic organizations. It is an open question as to whether states will act cooperatively and effectively to countervail the domination of those global corporations.

The global organization of the economy and the global mobility of investment discourage economic intervention by single states, unless those interventions are promoted by, or necessary to, nationally resident branches of global firms. Charles Lindblom's observation that citizens hold governments responsible for economic stability and well-being still largely holds, but the reality now is that few governments, singularly, have the power to impose their will on one or several large firms, or even on some groups of high-income individuals.[3] All of these actors are now free to invest as, when, and where they choose with ever-fewer restrictions and ever-greater protection of their capital. This power can be all but overwhelming politically unless governments can cooperate either regionally or globally to achieve an agenda different from that which these corporations might prefer. Thus far, however, there have been few attempts at concerted action, other than actions taken to accelerate and intensify the process of globalization.[4]

The evolution of the new global capitalism has been overseen by corporate managers chosen from within corporations and adhering to their values. To make the point starkly, the autonomous political realm has been all but eclipsed throughout the world. It is not that nations are suddenly bereft of capable political leadership. But their positions are suddenly bounded by a new logic. The position "political leader" has been reengineered; democracy has been constricted. The incumbents in political positions operate within a more delimited space, with fewer ideological and policy options. The bottom line of global competitiveness is defined and enforced largely outside what remains of the political process. Bottom-line performance, measured solely in terms of gross domestic product (GDP) and profit, is judged day by day "on the markets," whereas elections resolve differences in telegenic style and polling competence (resulting in minor adjustments in sound bites and policy mix). In the global era, though possibilities for significant adjustments in the global rules of the game still exist, noneconomic voices have been largely confined to the back pages.

The electronic media (which have now subsumed much of the world of print in style, content, and integrated ownership) are the voices most frequently heard, and they are increasingly integrated and monopolized by large corporations. Diverse voices remain within some segments of public discourse (in books, in universities, on the Internet), but mindless and systematically uncritical infotainment increasingly prevails. It is no accident that public affairs often seem indistinguishable in content from soap opera and film. Media attention, for the most part, focuses on the trivial and the personal because actual politics have all but left the electronic stage. The great issues of our time are rarely spoken of in public, and serious matters such as poverty and the environment appear tedious to many.

The Ironies of the Global Age

The age of global economic integration is rife with ironies, both obvious and subtle. Among the more obvious are rising poverty in the face of an enormous surge in productive capacities, declining leisure time in the face of increasingly automated industrial production, and reversals in environmental protection in the face of advancing environmental knowledge and high levels of environmental concern. The negative effects of globalization on wage levels and working conditions in some industrialized countries have also been widely noted. Also widely discussed are the effects of a possible "race to the bottom" in terms of taxation levels and social programs among nations competing for investment, further undermining the lives of the economically disadvantaged.[5]

George Soros and James Goldsmith, highly successful international investors, have both raised questions about the need to balance corporate power in the age of globalization. Soros argues that laissez-faire capitalism "holds that the common good is best served by the uninhibited pursuit of self-interest. Unless it is tempered by the recognition of a common interest that ought to take precedence over particular interests, our present system is liable to break down."[6] Goldsmith is more direct in noting that "forty-seven Vietnamese or forty-seven Filipinos can be employed for the cost of one person in a developed country, such as France. Until recently . . . 4 billion people were separated from our economy by their political systems, primarily communist or socialist, and because of a lack of technology and of capital. Today all that has changed. Their political systems have been transformed, technology can be transferred instantaneously anywhere in the world on a microchip, and capital is free to be invested anywhere the anticipated yields are highest."[7]

Goldsmith then comes to rather unexpected conclusions. He draws a "finger-in-the-dike" conclusion openly opposing further European integration. He might more reasonably have advocated widespread political integration matched to the scale of economic integration. In this strategy the European Union might be seen as a beginning. Ultimately some form of integration might develop that could lead to the gradual harmonization upward of wages in poorer nations rather than the rapid driving down of wages in rich nations that he seems to fear.

Another irony of the global age is perhaps even more surprising. Despite significant gains in industrial and financial-sector automation and corporate "delayering" and "reengineering," all resulting in productivity gains, average work time, especially outside Europe, is actually increasing. In some poor nations, conditions in plants producing for export markets closely resemble conditions in the sweatshops and satanic mills of nineteenth-century Europe and North America. Hours there are extremely long. In wealthy nations as well, even when unemployment rates are high, average hours worked have frequently increased. Since 1980, the percentage of employed people working more than fifty hours per week has increased 19 per cent. Bruce O'Hara, an advocate of reduced work time, has concluded that work-time reductions occurred from 1800 through 1950, but since that time the conversion of some productivity gains to increased leisure has been reversed.[8] The increase in work time is compounded from a family-centered perspective, considering the sharp increase in the proportion of women in the workforce in this same post-1950 time frame. The staggering irony is that precisely when time away from work is most needed (because of transformation in gender-based work patterns), and is most possible in terms of automation and productivity breakthroughs, the reverse trend is gaining ground.

Environmental protection in the global age is also fraught with both irony and complexity. Clearly there may be some correlation between increased total economic activity and increased threats to the global environment—a correlation far from one-to-one, but a correlation nonetheless. To the extent, then, that there is a race to the bottom the environment might gain when that race constrains wages (and thereby buying power), but will almost certainly lose when conducted in the realm of environmental regulation.

However, other possibilities must also be considered. Low-wage workers may produce more per dollar of wages, and what is not spent on wages will be spent either on such things as private corporate jets or on automated production capacity. In such cases the environmental costs of wage restraint may be higher. Moreover, rising GDP may well correlate with increased pollution-abatement expenditures. And economic insecurity is often (though not universally) associated with poor resource-use decision making and management.[9] Simply put, then, both poverty and wealth can result in either environmental damage or environmental improvement. The challenge is to balance social, economic, and environmental needs, to optimize gains in all three realms in a balanced way.

Complexity has frequently been used as an argument against attempts at coordinated public action. This view presumes that humans are less likely to learn when they are trying to do so. F. A. Hayek presumed that the "invisible hand" of market decisions was wiser and more capable than the self-conscious, collective rationality of democratic decision making.[10] The market is, however, both highly structured in terms of access, and monolithic in terms of values. The rules under which markets operate—and the absence of rules regarding some matters—are established and enforced by governments and could be different than they are. Moreover, within electronic capitalism more and more contested matters, ironic or otherwise, are left to marketplace resolution (or inattention). The process of globalization urges individual governments to intervene less on behalf of nonmarket—redistributive or environmental—values. It is, however, increasingly clear that governments must act collectively, perhaps even in the best interest of the market system itself and certainly in the interest of human societies as a whole, as well as nonhuman species.

Thus we have entered an age of high irony. We work ever harder, when automation and labor-saving technologies abound. Moreover, some societies are prone to rising unemployment at the same time that many individuals work increasingly longer hours. Global and domestic poverty grow even as production capacity and actual total output expand rapidly. We seemingly love nature more, but appear unable to slow its destruction. Yet, in an age when we have never needed political activity more, citizens seem even less interested in such initiatives. And the greatest irony of all, perhaps, is that we do not need less globalization, but more (albeit in different forms and in a different spirit).

The capacity to influence markets has always been a near-perfect function of wealth and income. The capacity to influence governments' relationship to markets is a function of both political and economic variables (including everything from political activism to media visibility to the capacity to invest or to influence interest rates, or governmental bond values, or currency exchange rates). Wealth and income of course influence government, although it is hoped that this influence is at least in part offset by such things as voter autonomy, rational argument, and public preferences for values other than strictly economic growth or rising profit levels. The question is to what extent and in what ways the array of changes considered in this book have altered the balance between democracy and markets. Many analysts, writing from a variety of perspectives, have contributed to our understanding of this patterned change.

The Academic and Popular Critique of Globalization

Criticism of global economic integration has emphasized possible job losses within wealthy economies, increased economic instability, increased economic inequality, cultural homogenization, environmental deregulation, and constraints on democratic effectiveness. The latter are seen to arise when global economic competitiveness overwhelms domestic politics and from the closed nature of global decision processes.

The leading critics of globalization, and what Dan Schiller has called digital capitalism, include Robert Frank and Philip Cook, who see a winner-take-all society arising out of the nature of new electronic products and global production capabilities and markets; Jeremy Rifkin, who has misperceived the new era as an end of work; William Greider, from *Rolling Stone,* and John Gray, the renegade British Tory, both of whom see a global economy as a less stable economy; Hans-Peter Martin and Harald Schumann, reporters for *Der Spiegel,* who describe an "80–20" world wherein majorities (80% even in rich nations) are economic losers; and Linda McQuaig, a Canadian who in *The Cult of Impotence* berates today's governments for making a fetish of their own self-created powerlessness in the face of global competition. Also notable are Schiller, who critiques a society rooted in computerization and communications, and Benjamin Barber, whose 1995 appraisal in *Jihad vs. McWorld* now seems frighteningly prescient.[11]

Table 1.1
Average Unemployment Rates

	1965–1969	1970–1974	1975–1979	1980–1984	1985–1989
United States	3.7	5.3	7.0	8.3	6.2
Japan	1.2	1.3	2.0	2.4	2.6
Germany	0.9	0.9	3.8	6.1	7.7
France	1.8	2.6	5.0	8.1	10.2
United Kingdom	1.7	3.1	4.7	9.6	9.7
Italy	5.5	5.7	7.0	8.8	11.6
Canada	3.9	5.7	7.6	9.9	8.9
Average	2.7	3.5	5.3	7.6	8.1

Much in these assessments is valid, but it does not appear that there is a systematic decline in employment opportunities nor does a global economy seem any less economically stable. Unfair perhaps, but not necessarily less stable unless and until environmental and resource nonsustainability comes into play in a major way.

North American concern with the effects of globalization on employment took hold in the late 1970s and early 1980s, when imports rose sharply and North American productivity was stagnant. In particular, Japanese management, that nation's extreme appetite for work, and its emphasis on savings and just-in-time production were widely promoted as vastly superior. The North American response was a rationalization of production codified in trade agreements. We can see in hindsight that Rifkin and others overinterpreted the repositioning of the North American economy as a permanent decline of work opportunities. Such a conclusion would be easy to draw from the data in table 1.1, but the 1990s and since have not held to the pattern. Similarly, the Asian monetary crisis of 1998 was overinterpreted by others as the instability of a global economy.

More accurate is Martin and Schumann's assessment of the systematic corporate reporting of profits in low-tax nations, helping to drive down business tax rates everywhere. Global tax havens have not been widely challenged even in the face of growing global terrorism (other than for terrorists). Martin and Schumann identify 100 global centers where deposits are immune from taxation either because banking records are secret or because citizens of larger nations also hold citizenship and/or maintain residence in these bastions. The amounts of wealth involved are considerable: "According to International Monetary Fund (IMF) statistics, a total in excess of 2000 billion dollars is managed under the flag of various off-shore mini-states, beyond the reach of the countries in which the money was made."[12] Martin and Schumann's other notable contribution is the argument that the solution to many of globalization's problems lies not in less economic integration, but in more political integration, through the World Trade Organization (WTO) or a strengthening and spreading of the European Union model.

Without some form of global governance at a scale matching the evolving economy, some envision a global society where all is dominated by the reward structure of entertainment and sports—where thousands compete, most unsuccessfully, for a very few positions with a very high level of reward. In sports, performance differences of hundredths of a second distinguish between fame and obscurity, between vast wealth and the need to find another way to earn a living. This shift is already dramatic within the mass media, where reproduction costs are almost zero and markets are more and more global and homogenized. The incomes of live local performers often decline at the same time global media stars attain staggering wealth.

The winner-take-all phenomenon is pervasive in today's economy and applies to goods as well as information. Frank and Cook assert that whenever there are significant economies of scale, there is a natural tendency for one product to dominate the market. Getting an early edge can be crucial, and thus small differences in performance result increasingly in large differences in reward.[13] In Frank and Cook's words, "To be a player in the tire market in northern Ohio it was once sufficient to be the best tire maker in that part of the state. But the well-informed consumers of northern Ohio—like their counterparts everywhere else—now choose from among only a handful of the best tire producers worldwide."[14] This new reality is one source of an increased bargaining power for a small number of top managers and marketers, and provides the basis for the intense drive to lower production costs.

One result is a continuous skewing of income distribution. Frank and Cook note a 104 percent rise in the upper 1 percent of U.S. incomes compared to a 7 percent rise in median incomes between 1977 and 1989. At the same time that income increases skewed in favor of upper incomes, marginal U.S. tax rates declined from 91 percent to 28 percent between 1961 and 1989. These increasing income disparities are not unlike the concentrations that occurred in the early days of the industrial revolution, when vast fortunes were made in steel, railroads, oil, and lumber. Despite declining unemployment in the 1990s, on a global scale at least income skewing has continued.

The United Nations Development Programme (UNDP) has documented increased global disparity. At the turn of the millennium it reported that the wealth of the world's 200 wealthiest individuals more than doubled, from $440 billion in 1994 to $1.042 trillion in 1998.[15] This wealth is equal to the combined annual incomes of 41 percent of the human population (over two billion individuals). In another example, the incomes of corporate CEOs as a group were 100 times that of the average industrial worker in the 1960s; now they are 350 times. This historically rapid rise in inequality, one might reasonably argue, is a central defining characteristic of today's economy.

Another result of economic integration is homogenization, a decline in cultural, social, and environmental diversity. In response there has been a growing organized resistance to the inclusion of "cultural industries" in trade agreements. One early attempt at defending cultural autonomy is noted by Schiller, and cultural autonomy was one of the points on which the Multilateral Agreement on Investment (MAI) treaty foundered.[16] Some nations limit cultural homogenization by subsidizing domestic publishing, filmmaking, and music because extreme savings of scale in cultural industries sometimes determine majority cultural preferences.

Economic concentration and specialization (and fewer sites for the extraction and production that may accompany this change) can also have a variety of environmental and social effects. Environmentally, concentrated production can lead to concentrations of pollution beyond nature's local assimilative capacities (though it may also lower the per-unit cost of pollution abatement in some cases). Plant monocultures (whether forests or farms) increase the need for chemical fertilizers and pesticides and generate other ecological costs. For example, global-scale hog and chicken production have resulted in pollution problems in the Carolinas and Arkansas respectively. Socially, one effect is the restriction of occupational choice in particular locales or even nations. On this point, Herman Daly has noted that the strong comparative advantage of Uruguay in sheep and cattle production frustrates local ambitions other than to be shepherds or cowboys.[17]

Daly observes that personal fulfillment, community, and nationhood all require economic diversity—the opportunity to have local banks, universities, medicine, and symphonies, not just ranches. Environmentally, without a "local" symphony one must expend fuel (and generate air pollution) to bring in a visiting orchestra (or have a nation or region forgo the experience of live symphony performances). Narrow economic assessments of comparative advantage and savings of scale miss much of this.

Schiller articulates the reach of global homogenization in both the economic and cultural realms (especially communications, media, and education). He sees this transformation as going hand in hand with the evolution and rapid growth of networking and the systematic deregulation and privatization of telecommunications. He calls this new reality *digital capitalism,* and he links global economic integration and the evolution of computer networking. He notes, for example, that the rise of the Internet, the rapid post-1970 growth of telecommunications, and the rapid expansion of transnational corporate operations outside of the wealthy nations were simultaneous and not coincidental.[18] Important and related aspects of the transformation to digital capitalism are, for Schiller, the commercialization of the Internet, the privatization and deregulation of the worldwide telecommunications, and the rapid movement of large corporations into the sphere of education.

Schiller's insights are essential to an understanding of the new global political economy. My own preference of a descriptive term for what has emerged is, however, *electronic,* rather than digital, *capitalism.* One reason for this preference is that the global and information economy preceded the digitalization of dominant media. Indeed television, film, and print media established global markets and branding before PCs or the Internet were widely available. Moreover, "electronic" capitalism implies an important role for some noncommunications technologies in the contemporary transformation (automation and a wide variety of measurement technologies, for example).

The more important point regarding either digital or electronic capitalism—whatever one prefers—is that instant global communications make global economic integration technically possible, and the private, near-monopoly, and highly commercial character of that emerging communications system has created today's cultural, economic, and political outcomes. Cultural and even linguistic homogenization is but one aspect of this evolution. Another is an enormous political imbalance in that I call *economism* (and Benjamin Barber calls *economic totalism*)—a systematic and continuous dominance of social, cultural, and environmental concerns by narrowly defined economic objectives.

Barber sees this secular commercial world, McWorld, as locked in a titanic dialectic struggle with various forms of spiritualism, traditionalism, and tribal localism that he calls "jihad." He links McWorld with "manufactured needs, mass consumption and mass infotainment" and sees both it and tribalism as rejecting moderation and democratic guidance. Accordingly, he fears a future where the only available options are blood brother or solitary consumer. Like Martin and Schumann, he notes a dearth of effective global rule making.[19]

National governments often welcome visible external pressures as a means of diverting blame. McQuaig's phrase "the cult of impotence" describes governments that are all too happy to be powerless in the face of global economic forces. These same governments have put in place, largely within closed bargaining sessions, trading rules and regimes that seemingly force them to do unpopular things. Whether or not today's national (or state and local) governments have more options than they pretend to have, there is no denying that nations could *collectively* choose to establish wage, environmental, and social policy standards as part and parcel of global economic integration. They might do this through the trade-agreement process, but to date they have not.

The democratic dilemma, then, is multidimensional and rooted in part in economism and a belief that GDP growth will lead linearly to all manner of social good, as well as to consumer goods. Social programs are cut back so that taxes can be reduced so that economies are more competitive so that economic growth may occur and thereby obviate the need for social programs. The logic is impeccable, unless one is an unemployed cancer victim or a child in a poisonous inner-city school. A similar logic and unfortunate outcome often apply to the restraint of environmental protection. Barber captures this nicely in observing that both jihad and McWorld are at best indifferent to democracy and that "it is not capitalism but unrestrained capitalism counterbalanced by no other system of values that endangers democracy."[20]

Getting Beyond Easy Assumptions Regarding Economic Growth

Economic growth is, then, the overriding objective of globalization, but there could ultimately be barriers to that growth—or at least there is cause to believe that economic growth in some forms carries a considerable environmental, and perhaps a social, price. Many believe, however, contrary to a major theme of this book, that there is a systematic and virtual one-to-one correspondence between economic wealth and societal well-being. Aaron Wildavsky, for example, has made the case that the wealthier the nation, the healthier its people. He makes his case well enough to give pause regarding easy assertions that the costs of economic growth beyond a certain level threaten to exceed the "real" gains. Another question worth asking here, a question not often raised by many critics of globalization, is the following: Might global economic integration not promote competition for positive environmental and social performance as well as economic efficiency? David Vogel argues that this is the case, at least in some circumstances. Julian Simon and Herman Kahn go further and argue that virtually all of the possible limits to economic growth are more imagined than real.

Simon and Kahn's edited 1984 volume *The Resourceful Earth* (funded by the conservative Heritage Foundation) offered a wide-ranging rebuttal to the Global 2000 Report to the President published in 1980. It remains one of the more comprehensive "cornucopian" statements.[21] The central assertion of this work is that for the most part the world's resources are not threatened and should not become a significant constraint on future economic growth. With hindsight, it is clear that the thesis of the Global 2000 report was, in fact, overstated in some respects. It also needs to be said that many of Simon and Kahn's assertions were well taken. In particular, some of the cautions offered regarding the prospects for renewable energy as a replacement for fossil fuels are pointedly correct—a systematic dependence on forest biomass as an energy source, in the phrase of a cited source, "would mean operating a worldwide herbarium."[22] This is not to say that some proportion of present energy use could not derive from such sources, but that "soft-energy" advocates do need to be reminded that the higher that proportion the greater the environmental price in terms of, for example, erosion and loss of nonhuman habitat.

Ironically, however, the Simon and Kahn volume is at its worst regarding the question of habitat and wilderness issues. As chapter authors in this volume, Simon and Wildavsky handle this in an interesting way, but for the most part miss the point of environmental analysis. They seem to take the absence of certain evidence of a sharp rise in extinctions of species to be sufficient grounds for minimal concern regarding deforestation or declines in wild habitat. They may have been correct regarding alarmist estimates of extinctions over the period 1980–2000, but both they and those they critique are wrong to focus excessively on extinctions per se. If habitat-conservation action requires proof of mass extinction, surely little can be done after the fact. More important than extinction is the question of the rate at which viable large-scale ecosystems have endured or large, healthy populations of classes of species continue to exist in the wild. What proportion of old-growth coastal forests in North America remain? What proportion of coastal saltwater marshes? What is the trend in the wild population of tigers? Parrots?

Simon and Wildavsky are plainly unwilling to value nature intrinsically, or even highly, as the following assertion suggests: "One should not propose saving all species in their natural habitats, at any cost, even if it were desirable to do so, any more than one should propose a policy of saving all human lives at any cost, for the cost is counted in human welfare forgone because limited resources were devoted to lesser uses. Certainly we must try to establish some informed estimates about the social value present and future of species that might be lost."[23] The only possible value is taken to be "social value." Moreover, they consider only active acts of saving, rather than the possibility of passively permitting, wild existence. Conservationists are making the point that virtually all nonhuman habitat is under threat or may be in a matter of centuries or even decades. Simon and Wildavsky presume that humankind somehow has a right to choose which species it will, or will not, eliminate.

In brief, looking back from beyond the year 2000, this volume and the report it criticized are both (as one might expect) unevenly successful on many counts. Simon and Kahn offer some warranted cautions regarding the assertions of environmental science. They were generally correct regarding the future of nonfuel minerals. They were generally wrong about the future of the world's fisheries, which has turned out in many cases to be at least as bad as anyone had predicted and far worse than this volume seemed to be claiming. But "cornucopianism" of this vintage was never so wrong as in the tone of its assertions regarding climate warming. The 1990s turned out to be warmer than Global 2000 had worried the decade might be. Hans Landsberg, in a chapter in Simon and Kahn, is generally judicious in his criticisms of Global 2000's climate worries and correct regarding the general benefits of reforestation, but almost certainly wrong in assuming that more warmth would necessarily benefit agriculture in northern climes and that polar melting was not likely to be problematic.[24]

Overall, sustainability concerns are still with us despite Simon and Kahn's lack of concern. More interesting, however, is Wildavsky's attempt, in *Searching for Safety,* to systematically link wealth and health.[25] Whatever the flaws in the details of his argument (an argument that cannot account for health outcomes in some nations both rich and poor), Wildavsky's broadest point is well taken. Richer is better, especially in terms of potential. Many critics of globalization dismiss overall net gains in global GDP because the larger share of the wealth increment has thus far gone to the rich, especially the rich in rich nations. I obviously am in strong sympathy with this general view, but would not dismiss the desirability of economic growth per se. After reading Wildavsky, it is harder to reject additional increments of economic growth out of hand. To the extent that electronic capitalism actually delivers growth in the right form and to the right people, it likely would add increments of well-being, including improved human health.

However, it is much better to demonstrate well-being gains directly, and to see economic growth as a means rather than an end. The proper end is human (and nonhuman) well-being. These must be measured independently and not simply assumed to follow from rising total societal wealth. To his credit Wildavsky sought to demonstrate a correlation, and while he overinterpreted his general finding, the matter of possible linkage was for him an important and complex question rather than a mere assumption. The economy is an intermediary means; the ultimate means is the array of living beings (flora and fauna), materials, and energy that comprise nature. Nature, and human ingenuity and prudent intelligence, are the ultimate means. The question is not simply how humankind can maximize GDP, but how we can maximize well-being per "dollar" of GDP and how we can get the most GDP per extraction from, and imposition on, nature. Richer is likely better in terms of well-being, but in the age of electronic capitalism we must also ask: Which nations are achieving all that can be achieved environmentally and socially at any particular level of wealth? And why are they, or are they not, achieving all they can?

Where Wildavsky is an unabashed advocate of economic growth (even if there are environmental costs), Vogel is generally inclined to trade as a means of achieving growth, and is open to the possibility that trade can also deliver environmental benefits (over and above the health benefits Wildavsky might see as resulting from growth). Vogel also sees many protective regulations as intentional nontariff trade barriers. He attributes the possible environmental gains associated with increased trade to what he terms the "California effect." As he puts it, as trade increases, "a number of national consumer and environmental regulations exhibit the California effect: they have moved in the direction of political jurisdictions with stricter regulatory standards."[26] In other words, there is sometimes a tendency for a "race to the top" in terms of environmental and other regulations. The particular case in point regarding the name given to the phenomenon involves the higher standards regarding automobile emissions in the state of California. These higher standards are made necessary by high population density, heavy automobile use (associated with urban sprawl), and climatic conditions favoring severe inversions and associated air-pollution events.

This is an important outcome that shows some of the complexity of the relationship between economic integration and environmental outcomes. It will be helpful to keep this in mind throughout this book. There are a number of possible negative effects as well that will be discussed from time to time whose limited nature is not, in my view, as easily demonstrated empirically as Vogel asserts. However, Vogel's explanation for why the California effect occurs is much more important than the question of whether the positive or negative effects of trade on environmental regulations are greater: "The California effect requires both that political jurisdictions with stronger regulatory standards be rich and powerful, and that non-state actors in rich and powerful political jurisdictions prefer stronger regulatory standards. California's impact on both American and European regulatory standards is a function of the size of its 'domestic' market."[27] Vogel goes on to assert that Germany has had a similar positive effect within the European Union because it is not Portugal, as California is not Delaware (bigger and richer are also cleaner in both cases).

This conclusion could not be more important. What Vogel may have missed, however, is that the preference for higher environmental standards usually results from environmental effects within the borders of the wealthy jurisdiction. That is, all the cars in question operate within California. It is also in Californian's interest that the requisite mines and mills that make the steel that makes the cars and the power plants that provide electricity and the logged forests that go into its newspapers come from somewhere else. The environmental consequences of these activities generally do not affect California residents personally (though pollution, in some cases, is mobile). More important, nonstate actors must have a consistent capacity to affect domestic and/or global policy outcomes. These concerns aside, the California effect remains a significant hope. Many Californians think as global citizens and, if informed, do not like using phone books made from British Columbia's old-growth forests. I am convinced that on the global scale, to which electronic capitalism is rapidly moving economically, culturally, and politically, the United States—with other big rich nations—must somehow attain the wisdom to help to establish a California effect in a wide variety of policy realms. This has decidedly not happened thus far.

Trade Agreements: Structuring Globalization

Brian Mulroney, Canadian prime minister at the time of the intense Canadian debate over passage of the Canada-U.S. Free Trade Agreement (FTA), the predecessor to the North American Free Trade Agreement (NAFTA), asserted that the FTA posed no threat to Canada's cherished social programs. He also asserted that the FTA's failure to say anything about the environment would not, as environmentalist opponents asserted, affect Canadian environmental standards. This is a trade agreement, he said, not an agreement on social policy or the environment. Something akin to paranoia on the part of opponents of free trade was the implication of his assertions. Mulroney won a parliamentary majority in the "FTA election" of 1988 (with 43 percent of the popular vote in a three-party race). The FTA was signed by Canada and the United States in 1989 and was followed by the NAFTA in 1993.

Immediately following the FTA agreement there was a massive economic restructuring that saw several hundred thousand industrial jobs lost in Ontario, and to a lesser extent in other Canadian provinces, and a rapid rise in provincial budgetary deficits as high unemployment had an impact. In the wake of this increased insecurity, in 1995 Ontario voters elected a government that radically rolled back provincial social programs and decimated the provincial Ministry of the Environment. Through the late 1990s and into the beginning of 2001, though not necessarily as a result of neoliberalism in Ontario, there was a strong economic recovery (though Canada's unemployment rate has remained well above the rate in the United States, despite a sharp fall in the relative value of the Canadian dollar). The absence of significant clauses in NAFTA regarding social programs, and even the positive language regarding environmental protection in the so-called "side" agreements, did not prevent or soften these outcomes—which were "freely" chosen by the voters of Ontario when faced with the alternatives (declining credit ratings and/or significant tax increases).

Trade agreements that result in the free movement of capital and goods all but guarantee a harmonization of the essentials of public policy. Autonomy is not eliminated, but it is severely constrained. Prime Minister Mulroney, a conservative, likely disingenuously pretended (or at least frequently asserted) that this was not the case. The policy adjustments will be incomplete and different in detail, but will almost certainly be in the direction of the options involving lower (tax-supported) costs. Resistance is not altogether futile, but is at best likely to be no more than marginally effective. John McMurtry perhaps overstates such realities when he asserts: "Under new international free trade agreements, businesses relocate to places where they do not have to pay [the] costs of protecting human life and the environment—for example, jurisdictions like Mexico where wages are a small fraction of what they are in Canada and the US, effective pollution controls are more or less nonexistent, and taxes for public health and education have been reduced or abolished."[28] Some businesses are not portable, pollution-abatement costs are not a high proportion of the expenditures of most firms, and many industries require skills and services not widely available in low-wage and/or low-tax nations.

However, extensive trade creates pressures on all (with some latitude for the wealthiest) jurisdictions to constrain relative work standards and benefits, environmental and safety regulations, public expenditures, and corporate taxes. Downward pressure is also exerted on wage expenditures, resulting in the continuous rationalization of employment within firms (downsizing), especially in high-wage nations. The process as a whole continually lowers the cost of producing goods. That is a good thing economically, as long as additional products are continually created and additional markets continually opened. Outcomes are not necessarily positive, either environmentally or socially. Free trade agreements other than the European Union, pointedly, have not thus far included effective minimum working conditions, minimum human rights, minimum environmental standards, minimum wages, or minimum levels of social, educational, or public health expenditures. Moreover, trade regimes have been used to directly undermine national regulations as in the case of Canadian or U.S. environmental regulations under chapter 11 of NAFTA, or through WTO rulings, for example, against European regulation of hormone-treated meat from North America.

As McMurtry puts it, "Only government intervention in the free market—for example, international minimum standards of rights and environmental protection in trade agreements—can prevent standards of life from falling to the lowest common denominator, which itself can keep falling."[29] That lowest common denominator has indeed been falling in Indonesia, Mexico, and Russia, for example. The tale of globalization's race to the bottom is familiar: "There are thousands of pages of rules to protect corporate and business rights, over 20, 000 pages of them in the most recent General Agreement on Tariffs and Trade (GATT), but no rules protect human rights or the quality of the environment."[30] GATT (WTO) actually does disallow trade in products manufactured by prison labor (for fear, presumably, that some nations might proceed to imprison a proportion of their populations in search of some increment of competitive advantage).

There is, however, more to the story than this view allows. While globalization places downward pressure on wage rates in rich nations, there may be an uneven but modestly upward pressure on wages in at least some poor nations. Average wages in South Korea, for example, rose considerably between 1970 and 1997. Even impoverished India has seen the creation of a significant middle class, a possibility that would not have been widely predicted in the 1960s. Moreover, global production has lowered the price of some manufactured goods and agricultural products in wealthy nations, partly offsetting slow (or negative) industrial wage growth. In addition, inflation would appear to have been less of a threat in the 1990s than at any time in the recent history of industrial capitalism (other than during recessions and depressions). The decline of inflation is not surprising given that an increasing proportion of production, wage rates, and employment are now in competition either with offshore-production options in low-wage nations, or automation, or both. Clearly gains as well as losses are associated with global economic integration. But how does one evaluate in a balanced way the complex of net costs and benefits?

Conventional economics is not enough. Life does not improve if one's employment is preserved only by virtue of lower wages or the privatization of health care and a deteriorating educational system. GDP growth may also come (temporarily) through the exhaustion of natural resources or the pollution of the atmosphere. Moreover, one must ask how the benefits of increased productive efficiency are distributed and what unintended costs are associated with that growth. Are public goods and services increasing or decreasing, absolutely or as a proportion of the economy as a whole? And what of even more direct measures—life expectancy, infant mortality, social cohesion, crime, water quality, recreational opportunities, even subjective measures such as happiness and a sense of security? All of these factors and many more are part of societal success and failure. Just because a nation has a greater economic capacity does not ensure, or even suggest, that it will have a superior environmental and social performance, either absolutely or per unit of economic capacity. The success or failure of any economy or society—whether local or global—must be independently measured in at least three dimensions: social, environmental, and economic.

Toward Three Bottom Lines: Economy, Society, and Environment

A globally integrated economy may be prone to economic instability in some situations, but thus far it has seemed remarkably resilient. Globalization likely contributed to two notable "bubbles" in recent decades—the Japanese urban-realty bubble of the 1980s and the dot.com stock bubble of the late 1990s. Neither, however spectacular in character, fundamentally disrupted the global economy as a whole, and it is not clear that such bubbles would not have arisen within a global economy structured in a somewhat more autarkic manner. Nonetheless, it is also fair to say that judging overall system performance by GDP and profit levels is not enough. Systems of social and economic organization must be evaluated in terms of a variety of values, measures, impressions, and judgments.

Some proneness to social inequity and instability has been widely discussed. The systematic employment and economic contractions of the early 1990s, for example, likely helped to promote militias and some increase in other social problems in the United States as well as rising racial intolerance in Europe. In this regard, Gray, the British conservative analyst, is particularly harsh in his assessment of the United States. As he puts it, "In the United States free markets have contributed to social breakdown on a scale unknown in any other developed country. Families are weaker in America than in any other country." He continues: "Free markets have also weakened or destroyed other institutions on which social cohesion depends in the US. They have generated a long economic boom from which the majority of Americans has hardly benefited."[31] Other commentators would add that the institutions on which society rests, community and family, are continuously undermined by the very system and technologies championed by those who warn of threats to family life as if they were wholly moral in origin.

Yet it might also be objected that Gray is rather silent on how, specifically, globalization and free markets undermine family. One outcome that harms families are declines in public expenditure on schools as well as on other community and social services. A second problem is the increase in the proportion of young families where both parents must work given that real wages have declined for many people. Also threatening is the extent to which competitive pressures and downsizing create situations where parents of young children have to work long and irregular hours, or to change jobs frequently. A third possible threat to social well-being is the continuous extra effort, extensive travel, and frequent relocation demanded of executives or aspiring executives. A fourth is the isolating character of such contemporary realities as television and suburban living patterns (frequently involving long commutes). Clearly we must find ways to evaluate the quality of social and community life by measures other than basic economic statistics, both in social scientific and personal terms.

Another complication that has been discussed less frequently involves the environmental costs directly related to global-scale market organization. Environmental quality is in effect a crucial third bottom line—where the first is economic, primarily measured by "traditional" means, and the second is social, measured in terms of income distribution, the well-being of children, the quality of education, the level of crime, and health outcomes, as well as broader measures such as social equity and social cohesion. Environmental quality is in turn itself three dimensional—habitat and biodiversity being one dimension, pollution and environmental health the second, and resource sustainability the third.

Much is added to our understanding by an integrated consideration of all three "bottom lines" (economic, social, and environmental)—a three-dimensional analysis and measurement of societal performance. Adding social and environmental measures raises questions about the quality of life delivered by contemporary economic developments. However, looking at three bottom lines at once complicates realities considerably. The process reveals any number of negative aspects of the contemporary realities of global economic integration. But it also suggests that these realities are not straightforwardly and monolithically negative—and not, then, an outcome appropriately to be resisted by all right-minded global citizens.

In my view an overall, three-dimensional evaluation suggests that seeking systemic redirection may be more appropriate than resistance to global integration (whether or not such resistance is futile). That is, while global economic integration is not without economic benefits, it could enhance those benefits and deliver them in a far more balanced and equitable manner. Moreover, a case can be made that such added benefits, well distributed, are an essential component in helping to reduce the vulnerability of an integrated global economy to environmental degradation and social inequality and—as a longer-term complement to military, juridical, and diplomatic efforts—to international terrorism. Simply put at this point, however, to optimize three-dimensional outcomes societies must first collectively and systematically engage in three-dimensional analysis. In contrast, the analysis that presently has the ear of the media and governments, not to mention corporations and investors, might be best characterized as one-dimensional "economism."

Naming the Contemporary Era

Several analysts have emphasized the media and/or digital-industry component of the emerging global political economy. Schiller, indeed, used the apt name *digital capitalism* to describe this new era and system. As noted, I prefer *electronic capitalism,* but would be pleased to see the wide adoption of either term to identify the emergent system of political economy characterized by increasing global economic and financial integration and increasingly dominated politically, economically, and culturally by the use of electronic media and computers. As noted above, not all media are wholly digital—neither television nor film has even yet been fully digitized (though they soon likely will be). It is also not certain that this digital nature will endure, but it is harder to imagine this world as other than electronic. In any case it is less the digital character of these technologies than their pervasiveness and importance that characterizes and makes possible the new age. In the end I opt for *electronic* simply because it is the broader term. There is no doubt that the age is appropriately called *capitalist,* whether in celebration or with concern.

The digital/media/electronic aspect of the globally integrated capitalist economy is sufficiently distinctive that it urges not only a new name for the system as a whole, but also some reinterpretation of the past to gain a fuller understanding of the present. Suffice it to say here that this new era is as qualitatively different from nationally based mass industrial society as that society was from the primarily community-based craft/agricultural era. The global scale of the new socioeconomic era threatens to overwhelm national governments much the same way that industrial production overwhelmed feudal barons and local craft-based production. The earlier transformation to mass industrial society and the contemporary transformation to electronic capitalism both simultaneously involved great promise and significant costs. The challenge is to comprehend both the promise and the costs in a balanced way. Such analysis must begin with definition.

In discussing globalization, Gray offers two parts of the definition of electronic capitalism. The first puts the focus on the "electronic" aspect, identifying globalization as "the spread of new, distance-abolishing technologies throughout the world."[32] Those technologies are primarily media, telecommunications, and computers, but also include container ships, oil

Box 1.1
The Central Features of Electronic Capitalism

1. Globally integrated production systems and the rapid international movement of information, currency, capital, employment (but not, to the same extent, labor), markets, technologies, and products prevail. Such movements lie almost exclusively within the management and control of large private corporations.

2. Extensive automation of industrial production as well as the rapid, widespread, and continual elimination of once-essential workplace tasks occurs. This results in systematic reductions in production employment through transformations known variously as downsizing and reengineering. Some production work is also exported from high-wage economies to low-wage economies and/or is converted to part-time, temporary, or seasonal tasks.

3. Computing, automation, and communications technologies permit, and all but require, the global micromanagement of subsidiaries, global component outsourcing, and the continual removal of middle-management layers throughout organizational structures in both the public and private sectors.

4. Electronic media are a dominant industry in their own right and the principal means by which all other products are branded and sold globally. The ownership of communications capacity is increasingly centralized within large private corporations and is a rapidly growing component of wealthy economies. Global competitiveness, communicated pervasively through the media, threatens to become a universal core sociopolitical value.

5. Capital investment is all but guaranteed by elaborate trade treaties. These treaties generally ignore social and environmental policies and realities. International loans, however ill-advised, are guaranteed by the power of the International Monetary Fund and other agencies and organizations to require that national governments impose the costs of any excesses on a broad social basis within receiving nations.

tankers, and low-cost air travel. The result, when combined with trade liberalization, is an increased regional and global mobility of capital, market access, and production technologies. Gray speaks as well of "policies whose ultimate objective is to incorporate the world's diverse economies into a single global free market."[33] This latter project, he believes, is neither desirable nor possible. Gray's doubts aside for the moment, the process and project have gone hand in hand and have proceeded sufficiently that we can speak of "electronic capitalism" as an all-but-accomplished fact of the contemporary world. Box 1.1 incorporates much of the discussion in this chapter and sets out its central features.

Control of the international movement of investment, production, employment, and profits carries the power to influence, if not dominate, the political life of nations much of the time. Kenichi Ohmae, an analyst who celebrates the rise of the globalized economy and trade agreements, warns of governmental actions capable of "scaring away" the skittish decision makers of the global economy and resulting in turn in economic growth that proceeds at best "at a snail's pace."[34] Ohmae speaks specifically of China and the dangers to the economy of that nation implicit in human rights abuses, but he ignores the positive capital flows associated with human rights and labor union abuses elsewhere. He might also have noted that equal skittishness can arise in response to higher corporate tax rates and humane social programs deemed excessive by bond holders and other often-distant investors.

Putting aside questions of the relative ethical and social merits guiding the use of economic power, one is left with the importance of the power itself. The power lies in the fact that most national governments have assumed the demeanor of a South Seas cargo cult—looking skyward, or computer-ward, for the arrival of global investment, production technologies, and global market access for locally produced products. Moreover, Ohmae's skittishness may be an understatement as regards global capital. The miraculous peaceful transition of South Africa from a racist state counted for nothing in terms of currency stability only a few years later. Rising wages, social safety nets, and environmental protection standards can all be marks in the wrong column in the eyes of some anonymous international investors. Even the decades-long economic tiger status of Southeast Asia did not stand up well in the short term to the power of electronic currency speculation (in 1998). The power is there, and it is not unreasonable to suggest that it is not always appropriately used or appropriately countervailed and balanced by more democratic forces. Thus far there is virtually no organized and effective democratic power at the global level.

Electronic capitalism, as presently structured, places downward pressures on social equity and environmental protection initiatives, but it carries significant positive potentials as well. Increased trade has led to solid economic growth within many nations. Until the seemingly short-lived economic dislocations of the late 1990s, overall economic output in many poorer nations, even India and some African nations, was improving significantly for the first time in decades—led by increases in private investment and industrial employment. Moreover, to the extent that rich economies substitute the production and "consumption" of information for the production and use of goods, environmental impacts may well decline per dollar of GDP as economies become less energy and materials intensive. Finally, electronic capitalism has the technical potential to provide an increasing proportion of humankind with additional free time, with increasing freedom from tedious labor. The potentials implicit in these shifts may or may not be fully realized, or delivered to those most in need. However, the core reality is that there remains precious little that is inevitable about electronic capitalism. It is still possible that the considerable power associated with increased capital mobility can be, at least partially, offset.

The Scale Problem: Politics within a Globally Integrated Economy

It could be argued that the fear of globalization is akin to the fear of flying. It is widely known that it is far safer to travel by air than by automobile, yet few people fear driving while many fear flying. The reasons are clear—one has more influence over the outcome when driving (or even when riding in a car). In addition, many automobile mishaps are minor, while the survival rates in airline crashes are much lower. Similarly, influencing global political or economic outcomes even in the most trivial way is beyond the imagination of most citizens. Global competition, as noted, is now widely perceived as an inevitable determinant of many dimensions of national public policy. This lies at the heart of democracy's dilemma. Effective global-scale democracy is beyond the contemporary imagination even though the need for it, in some form, is increasingly plain.

Few contemporary political figures or media commentators are prepared to argue that anything is more important than the international competitive position of one's particular nation. How, other than this lack of extranational efficacy—even among political leaders in the most powerful nations—can one explain the almost complete absence of any effort to promote, or even permit, any semblance of democratic political life above the national level? Most people instinctively fear globalization, but, even after the events in Seattle in 1999 and elsewhere thereafter, most citizens and elected political leaders were prepared to leave global governance to invisible, largely economically self-interested, "pilots" in the closed cockpits of global trade organizations.

The globalization process is widely distrusted on many concrete and specific grounds, but these concerns have thus far found few, if any, institutionalized political outlets. Many trade unionists see globalization as resulting in the export of employment and limiting increases in employment and income or selectively driving down industrial wages. Many public-sector employees and politically progressive citizens see it as an excuse for shrinking the size and scope of the public sector and reducing taxes on corporations and the wealthy. Many environmentalists see global restructuring as a means of enhancing the power of polluters to restrain, or avoid the enforcement of, environmental regulations. Many social policy advocates see a parallel race to the bottom in terms of social programs hard-won during the era of mass industrial society. Others see global capitalism as highly unstable economically, especially as a result of excessive currency speculation and short-term, nonfixed investment. Yet others argue that economic development in poor nations is radically distorted by massive external debt burdens, IMF impositions of austerity, and the power of transnational corporations to keep wages within poorer regions extremely low—through continuous mobility among local subcontractors and nations.

There is much truth in each of these concerns, but until recently no effective political response had arisen at any level—political participation regarding such issues so far has been largely limited to street protests. One reason is that there is little citizen politics at the global level. Rumors of an emerging global civil society are much exaggerated unless the emphasis is placed on the word *emerging*.[35] Global governance, thus far, is about negotiations among government and corporate representatives charged with the responsibility of defending national and corporate economic interests. Government representatives are chosen for their ability to skillfully trade off weaker domestic economic interests for the stronger, if necessary. That is the assigned task of those involved in trade negotiations and it is a weighty and complex assignment.

There has been no meaningful place in trade processes for other interests or considerations, and the participants in the process are unqualified with regard to, and largely uninterested in, other matters. Some seem at times quite unaware that there even are any other interests or considerations of any consequence. Wage rates, working conditions, union rights, human rights, and environmental protection are simply presumed to remain as "domestic concerns." Trade negotiators, like Prime Minister Mulroney, may imagine (or pretend to imagine) that these other matters can and will continue to be effectively dealt with elsewhere. Moreover, "their" trade discussions are held behind closed doors, effectively excluding any and all other voices (including weaker domestic economic interests). Like airline pilots, trade negotiators do not wish to be distracted. However, unlike airplanes there is no chance that trade treaties (even when proceeding as they should) will not significantly alter everything around them including society, environment, and all aspects of what was formerly the domestic policy arena.

Thus, what has emerged at the global level is a one-dimensional politics, and that dimension is economic. The sole issue at hand within the effective (nonmilitary) structures of global governance (WTO, NAFTA, IMF, and so on) is the harmonization and balancing of domestic economic interests as if such an outcome affected nothing else. The globalization process is led by corporations and by appointees of various national governments, the latter often backed by an elaborate process of consulting with domestic firms and trade associations. From time to time there are also, of course, separate environmental negotiations that have resulted in a number of global or regional environmental treaties. These are well intended for the most part, but so far these environmental treaties are only sometimes effectively enforced. A few have had positive results, but these results pale compared to the influence of ongoing global pressures on domestic environmental regulation and enforcement. The environmental race to the bottom is less defined by the removal of existing regulations in wealthy nations than by the outmigration (or simply the expansion) of problematic activities (such as mining) in more or less regulation-free settings (e.g., Indonesia, Mexico, Kazakhstan, or Guyana).

Poverty and/or the lack of domestic democracy explain why these and other nations resist effective environmental protection at both the domestic and the global level. But what accounts for the absence of effective resistance to the negative social and environmental effects of globalization in wealthy nations (such as Canada, New Zealand, and elsewhere, including the United States), where hard-won wage levels, social programs, and environmental protection have been undermined? Many contributing factors are involved; four partial explanations are offered here: (1) the control and use of electronic media; (2) the changing shape of workplace structures; (3) the changing need for employees within many large corporations (resulting in a process of continuous downsizing and a general political timidity); and (4) the competition-driven "race to the bottom" between and within nations (the latter resulting in part from the decentralization of environmental decision making). Each of these assertions requires brief elaboration.

1. In his lucid explanation of why it was that proletarians were more politically oriented than were peasants (though both were poor and exploited), Marx talked about how the individual cottages of each isolated peasant family looked out at the fields they individually worked. In effect, the peasants related to the world as individuals and simply had no effective "window" on the complex realities of social and economic organization. Their lives were neither urbanized nor sufficiently collectivized within production situations. They also resided at a distance from their neighbors; community thus was (in Marx's view) minimal. Television screens, arguably, are not unlike the peasants' window on the fields. They provide a glimpse (in this case a consciously controlled glimpse) of a small part of the world, but also isolate existence, reduce community, and narrow experience, both intellectual and actual.[36]

Television rarely asks questions about the desirability and importance of consumption, or about the structures of society (or media ownership patterns). It just "entertains" in a mildly addictive sort of way, filling silences and providing a substitute for community institutions. It supplies amusing and undemanding friends and highly skilled athletic activity without the need for effort or the risk of injury or personal failure. It is also the ultimate selling machine for both goods and politics. In most developing nations it is, in effect, the advanced guard of globalization—it is at the heart of global-scale economic integration. Access to the airwaves (other than very locally) is all but unavailable to citizens, or to organizations without millions of dollars to spend.

2. Social science has extensively investigated the process of politicization and few have bought this work together more insightfully than Seymour Martin Lipset in his influential study *Political Man*. In this classic work,

Lipset surveys the early decades of empirical voting-behavior research seeking an answer (in an industrial-age context) to the (probably industrial-age) question of who votes "left" and why. One segment of his analysis is particularly pertinent here (assuming that questioning the effects of globalization is a "left" perspective). Lipset concludes that "perhaps the most important condition is the presence of good communication among people who have a common problem."[37]

Lipset marshals, for example, evidence of higher left voting and class-conscious political activism, in many different nations and contexts, among industrial workers employed in larger rather than smaller factories. Other very politicized groups had "a social structure favorable to intra-group communications and unfavorable to cross-class communications." Lower-income white-collar employees who worked within smaller groups "scattered among higher-level managerial personnel" were proportionately less inclined to politicization.[38] Particularly highly politicized were workers who not only worked within larger assemblages, but who engaged in activities (such as rolling cigars) where they continuously conversed among themselves while engaged in production activities.

The workplaces of the contemporary ("postindustrial") economy tend to have fewer employees in any one location. Moreover, many contemporary "industrial" jobs involve the largely isolated task of monitoring of automated processes.[39] Contemporary work typically places employees one on one with computer screens or a set of dials and gauges. Fewer people work in industrial settings; those who do are often engaged closely with supervisory personnel. Indeed employees are now so often and so thoroughly engaged with computer screens that they directly engage with fellow workers only irregularly, and some workplaces are no longer places at all.

The largest exception to this is the service sector, involving working behind counters alone or with a small number of other employees. These employees typically work an elaborate set of varying part-time shifts for local franchisees rather than directly for a large corporation. Other non-screen-oriented employees work in small, nonunionized factories (which may in turn supply large corporations). The workplaces of electronic capitalism are thus less conducive to a class-based political sensibility and—as Robert Putnam's analysis suggests—voluntary community organizations of all kinds are also in decline.[40] All in all, one-way media communication has partially replaced workplace and other forms of two-way and direct communication and community.

3. Lipset also notes that those who had experienced an extended period of employment insecurity seemed to feel disadvantaged and to be more politically active and class conscious. This possibility may not apply, however, in a contemporary context, where employment insecurity is often the norm even when the unemployment rate is low. Unemployment may be less politicizing when virtually everyone has recently had one or more such experiences. The experience of losing a job, most report, is upsetting and even demeaning, but there is no contemporary evidence that it still promotes political engagement (of a "left" character).

The reality of downsizing, outsourcing, and offshore job migration is now more widely accepted as a "part of doing business" and even "how the economy advances." Indeed in some contexts job losses may arouse a dislike of "unfair" foreign competition or of foreign immigrants—not of management. When management indicates that a plant will only remain open if certain concessions are made or if the whole of an industry (e.g., television production or steel) gradually loses out to foreign competitors, the conclusions drawn by employees, and their friends, neighbors, and relatives, are frequently the opposite of Lipset's "politicization." The result is often a buy-in to the rules of global competition and/or a sense of personal failure.

4. There is a wide perception that citizens, however well organized and active, cannot alter outcomes at a global level. And, given that few governments now are willing to enact policies that do anything other than "enhance national competitiveness," more and more citizens are put off politics altogether, presuming it to be a realm beyond their control. The result is a deep cynicism, a decline in political activism, and a disdain of all politicians—a result, ironically given its leading global position, nowhere more pronounced than in the United States. The irony is that, at the moment, the United States is the one nation that sets the standard of global competitiveness—having regained a technological edge, having driven down relative industrial wage levels in the late 1980s and early 1990s, having reduced its already-minimal social policy standards, and having, throughout the early and mid-1990s, downsized its way to great productive efficiency. Historically prone to extreme overwork, Japanese business

elites are now outworked by North American managers and a growing army of well-paid "microserfs."

Thus, the global competition is established. The leading nation, experiencing the benefits of full employment and massive capital in-flows, does not wish to change and few other nations can easily avoid adopting the worst excesses of the current "leader" (just as America adopted Japanese management and overwork, New Zealand, Britain, and Canada have slashed public spending). As Gray puts it, "Within the view of the world that is dominant in our time economic efficiency has been disconnected from human well-being."[41] There are no established social and environmental minima within which global competition presently takes place and no effective democratic politics or governance at the global level to redress the imbalance. Accordingly, checks and balances at the national level are washed away in a sea of cash within the leading nation(s) of the moment, and in a tide of desperation and high unemployment in many others.

Little wonder political life has not easily moved to the global level when the reality is that many citizens are hard pressed to identify the nations of the world on a map, let alone imagine how they, as citizens, might contribute to global political outcomes. It is thus hardly surprising that there has been no global citizen's movement demanding a global minimum wage or globally enforced antipollution regulations (with the understanding that this might make domestic protections more defensible). Ironically, perhaps as a reaction to increasing complexity and scale, there has been in many jurisdictions (including the United States and Canada) an increased *decentralization* of decision making. For example, many aspects of environmental regulation have been passed down from the national to the state or provincial level.[42] The result, arguably, is some potential for "internal" domestic competition regarding restrained enforcement. The principal reason for declining standards in this decentralized context is the greater relative power of particular industries within smaller jurisdictions (e.g., the power of the copper-smelting industry in particular Western states compared to its power within the United States as a whole, or the power of the forest industry within British Columbia as compared to Canada as a whole).

The decentralization of public policy and governance results in part from a general disillusionment with government, a false sense that units of governance are so unresponsive that they must be too large. Yet new global-scale economic entities are being created every day. Every enterprise yearns to produce for the global market lest it perish. Every backwater economic entity on the planet (the IBM ads have told us) must engage in global e-commerce. Yet, ironically, commerce at a regional and global scale, without governance at a comparable scale, results in governance that is often little more than the humoring and wooing of investment. The only way to reestablish active governance, to provide effective balancing competition for those who would prefer to only humor and woo, is to enact and enforce at a higher scale. Only then will there be any real prospect for collective and secure global social and environmental minimum standards—and a resolution of democracy's dilemma.

Industrial mass production—the age of steel and rail and telegraph, marked by teeming cities of immigrants from the countryside or other lands, and involving the birth of the assembly line—required and helped to create the political nation-state. Political scale followed economic scale and saw to the continued, if uneven, development of industrial society—softening, compromising, and smoothing its worst contradictions, excesses, and ironies. Economic globalization similarly requires political globalization in some form. It is perhaps the greatest of ironies that only though securing social and environmental minima at a global level can national, state, and local governments regain the space within which a positive democratic politics is possible. To understand this necessity more fully, we need to recall the process by which agricultural, craft, and early industrial societies were transformed into mass industrial societies and consider how this change is different from the contemporary evolution of global electronic capitalism.

2

A Tale of Two Transitions

The politics of electronic capitalism, such as it is, takes place as much within trade negotiations, trade-dispute resolutions, and battles for media ownership and influence as within the world of electoral politics. This new "politics" is about the globalization of production and consumption and about control of communications systems and networks. Democratic and electoral politics is marginal to this larger political process. A globally integrated economic elite, mostly organized within corporate and personal techno-fiefdoms, now conducts its business and resolves its differences all but unimpeded by governments, communities, employees, customers, or even shareholders (so long as an ever-growing return on investment continues). In addition, as is now already a commonplace, the revolution in communications and computer technologies has transformed work patterns and work relationships worldwide. The digital revolution and globalization are also, though in less direct and obvious ways, bound up with the rise of neoliberal ideology and the widespread contemporary revulsion toward politics and government. Most complex, and even less fully understood, are the connections between the rise of electronic capitalism and the rise of environmentalism as a way of seeing and valuing the world.

Our understanding of these and other contemporary connections can be aided by the construction of simple models of the evolutionary stages of past and present societies. We can understand today's system best through seeing where it comes from and what it is not. These models are ideal types in Max Weber's sense and are meant to highlight and render more visible systematic societal similarities and differences. Only by looking backward and utilizing concepts can we gain a sense of what is historically distinctive about the emerging era. We can then begin to imagine (or guess) how it will evolve or, with the aid of value and policy analysis, how societies and polities might collectively choose to modify and/or adapt to the evolving patterns. Many analysts have identified varying numbers of industrial revolutions, or stages in socioeconomic history. It is sufficient for the argument of this book to put those other models aside and to keep our evolutionary model relatively simple and straightforward. The history of industrial society can, for our purposes, be effectively captured in three distinct stages.

Craft Society, Mass Industrial Society, and Electronic Capitalism

Electronic (or "digital" or "globalized") capitalism can be understood as a socioeconomic mode different from all previous modes—as a third type of industrial society. The evolutionary model here distinguishes craft (early industrial) society, mass industrial society, and now electronic capitalism—a global, industrial, and postindustrial society increasingly dominated by digital, communications, and automation technologies. These three types of industrial society are differently organized and patterned—technically, economically, socially, culturally, and politically. To be clear from the outset, today's new technologies could (and likely will) promote and sustain many different forms of socioeconomic organization. That is, few aspects of contemporary social reality are technologically determined. The societal structures and patterns of electronic capitalism will evolve considerably over time and in ways that cannot be predicted. Marx, obviously now, was decidedly wrong regarding his prediction of a technologically determined sociopolitical fate for mass industrial society. The possibilities for electronic capitalism are likely even more open ended.

In a three-mode typology, craft and early industrial societies, at the beginning of industrial manufacturing, were often yet dominated by rural and small-city settings. Even in Europe and North America, a large majority still earned a living in agricultural pursuits or activities that supported such pursuits. It was, however, soon to be an age of experiment and expansion, invention and urbanization, steel and steam engines, railroads and telegraph wires. These early industrial societies inflicted considerable damage on nature, particularly through deforestation, soil erosion, and air and water pollution from mines and mills, but the overall scale of ecological impact was relatively limited prior to the extensive development of heavy industries.[1] Mass industrial societies, however, launched accelerated and massive mechanized extraction of raw materials from nature, the creation of hydroelectric projects and coal-fired thermal electric plants needed to support large-scale and assembly-line production facilities, and later the mass production and use of petrochemicals.

Socially, early industrial society did not lead very quickly to any improvement in the everyday lives of most individuals. In England and Scotland, where industrialization first took hold and where arguably the only industrial *revolution* took place, life for most in the early mines and mills was truly horrendous. But that horrendous life followed on decades of emiseration of former peasants through the Enclosure Acts, the Speenhamland period (1795–1834), and the Poor Law Reform of 1834. The Enclosure Acts drove many nonowning agriculturalists from common lands. This was followed by the not-so-tender, more or less well-intentioned, pauperization associated with a decision of the local rural justices (all landowners) of Berkshire meeting in Speenhamland, near Newbury, England, on May 6, 1795. These notables, in the words of Karl Polanyi, "in a time of great distress, decided that subsidies in aid of wages should be granted in accordance with a scale dependent upon the price of bread, so that a minimum income could be assured to the poor *irrespective of their earnings.*"[2] In other words, wages were subsidized from local tax revenues up to an amount sufficient for bare survival.

The result was that actual wages for the unskilled fell very near to zero, but given the need to be on a local roll in order for the family to survive (there was a small allowance for each family member), there was no labor mobility. In effect, employers fell back on the local treasury to keep employees and their families alive. The so-called right to live "effectively prevented the establishment of a competitive labor market. Whatever limited assets, skills and positive work experiences rural workers had once had were soon lost to them and to society."[3] Polanyi described the result of this system, stating that "under the Speenhamland Law a man was relieved [supported] even if he was in employment, as long as his wages amounted to less than the family income granted to him by the scale. Hence, no laborer had any material interest in satisfying his employer, his income being the same whatever wages he earned. . . . Within a few years the productivity of labor began to sink to that of pauper labor, thus providing an added reason for employers not to raise wages above the scale. For, once the intensity of labor, the care and efficiency with which it was performed, dropped below a certain level, it became indistinguishable from 'boondoggling' or the semblance of work maintained for the sake of appearances."[4]

The "liberal" (free-market, centrally administered) Poor Law Reform of 1834 abolished this system and created a national labor market, pushing rural families desperately seeking some means of survival into cities. Thus widespread poverty was replaced primarily and abruptly by widespread hunger and homelessness. The first modern, industrial labor market was created in this truly ruthless fashion, and early industrial capitalism was born. Again, in Polanyi's words, "If under Speenhamland the people had been taken care of as none too precious beasts deserved to be, now they were expected to take care of themselves, with all the odds against them. If Speenhamland meant the misery of degradation, now the laboring man was homeless in society. If Speenhamland had overworked the values of neighborhood, family, and rural surroundings, now man was detached from home and kin, torn from his roots and all meaningful environment. In short if Speenhamland meant the rot of immobility, now the peril was that of death through exposure."[5]

The conditions in the mines and mills and factory towns of nineteenth-century Britain are, of course, legendary and terrifying. One need merely recall the novels of Dickens, or paintings by Daumier, to conjure images of the unspeakable squalor of urban and factory life. Young children worked in mills for up to nineteen hours a day on very little to eat. Others found no work at all. As Robert Heilbroner has noted, "It was a grim age. The long hours of work, the general dirt and clangor of the factories, the lack of even the most elementary safety precautions, all combined to give early industrial capitalism a reputation from which, in the minds of many people in the world, it has never recovered."[6] Living arrangements in Glasgow were described at the time as consisting of "a labyrinth of lanes, out of which numberless entrances lead into small square courts, each with a dunghill reeking in the centre." Fifteen to twenty naked humans to a room slept on the floor: "Their bed consisted of musty straw intermixed with rags. There was generally little or no furniture in these places; their sole article of comfort was a fire. Thieving and prostitution constitute the main sources of revenue of this population."[7]

Only decades earlier England's industrial cities did not exist, or were no more than villages. Poverty was not uncommon, but work for many was seasonal. Those with craft skills were organized into guilds and earned a living wage. Many had some means of access to a small allotment of fertile land. They also had the skills and access to the tools necessary to produce and maintain much of their own subsistence. This relative autonomy was lost in a generation or two of industrialization and to date, arguably, has not been recovered—except in remnant form in the handyman and gardening hobbies of contemporary suburban life. Thus, even today many long for, and go to great lengths and expense to recreate, an imitation of such relatively unalienated forms of productive, self-maintaining, and family-centered, work. This apparent lack of fulfillment notwithstanding, industrial society was, as it turned out, a great (if imperfect) gift to all humankind from these desperate former English peasants and their immediate descendants (and of the driving entrepreneurs and inventors who directed them). It is too seldom recognized that most of those who unknowingly gave the gift of future prosperity got less than nothing in return themselves.

Robert Heilbroner asks a crucial question in his wonderfully insightful book *The Making of Economic Society.* "Why," he asks, "did the Industrial Revolution originally take place in England and not on the continent?" He offers three primary reasons. First, England was relatively wealthy and that wealth was distributed broadly enough (to a commercial class as well as to royalty and nobility) to develop demand—a consumer market. Second, "England was the scene of the most successful and thorough-going transformation of feudal society into commercial society. A succession of strong kings had effectively broken the power of the local nobility and had made England into a single unified state."[8] Third, there was a national enthusiasm for scientific farming, science, engineering, gadgetry, machines, and invention. Other important factors included the already-noted Enclosure Acts and Poor Law Reforms that resulted in a desperate and thereby compliant and low-cost industrial working class. They also included a patent system designed to stimulate and protect the act of invention and finally, and generally underestimated, the ready availability of significant resource reserves—in this case especially iron ore and coal.

The importance of these factors is plain enough. There are also important parallels, to be drawn below, for the contemporary transformation to the global economy of electronic capitalism. Two of these factors in particular should be noted here. First, resources, and especially the energy necessary to extract, process, transform, and transport, were crucial to the transition to mass industrial society—and remain every bit as crucial within today's transformations. As Heilbroner notes, "The output of coal increased tenfold in forty years; that of pig iron leaped from 68,000 tons in 1788 to 1,347,000 tons in 1839."[9] Second, there is the question of trade-offs between the accumulation necessary for capital investment and social justice. Heilbroner dwells on this, and rightly so. He comes to an important conclusion—the industrial revolution began within what amounted to a "scarcely-better-than-subsistence" society. During the first transition the standard of living of the broad mass of society could not have been raised without increased production of all goods. This was achieved, in effect, by reducing the wages of the poor to, on average, below subsistence (unless all family members including children worked long hours). It then took three generations (from the late eighteenth-century until about 1870) for any significant distribution of output other than in the hands of an elite to arise.

On this point Heilbroner is clear: "There was simply not enough to go around, and if somewhat less lopsided distributive arrangements might have lessened the *moral* indignity of the times, they would not have contributed much to a massive improvement in basic economic well-being. Even assuming that the wage of the city laborer and the income of the peasant could have been doubled had the rich been deprived of their share—and this is an extravagant assumption—still, the characteristic of rural and urban life would have been poverty."[10] This is true, but several additional points might be made. As noted above, we all now owe a great debt to those who lived and died in squalor then. Also, their sacrifice only makes the moral sense Heilbroner attaches to it to the extent that the "share" of the rich could be usefully, and actually was, reinvested in productive capacity. Such reinvestment and expansion of productive capacity—as we are now finally beginning to learn—is also continually dependent on the availability of resources and the capacities of nature. Finally, societies will not often redistribute wealth or reduce work time on an uncontested basis—even when, as in the 1870s, it is in the interest of the very productive system that they helped to build, which at some point needs a market larger than a small wealthy elite.

There is no mistaking that by the 1870s an expanded need for consumer demand existed in England. The expansion of productive capacity was breathtaking. In the eighteenth-century cloth production in England grew by 3,000 percent, most of that growth taking place after 1780. The wealthy of many nations wore layer upon complicated layer; the physical producers of the cloth in England wore rags throughout this period and well past it. But the most spectacular gains came after early trade union and political struggles (including the expansion of voting rights beyond the owners of land, capital, and property)—and, most dramatically, on another continent, North America. Where the "first" stage of industrialization (in England) had emphasized agriculture, iron, coal, and textiles, the "second" stage in the United States (in the midnineteenth century and thereafter) involved "a clustering of industrial inventions centering on steel, on railroad and steamship transportation, on agricultural machinery, and chemicals." And, more was to come quickly: "By the early years of the twentieth century there was a third wave of inventions: electrical power, automobiles, the gasoline engine."[11] By 1900 there were 18,500 internal combustion engines in the United States, the capacity of which had increased for a single engine by thirtyfold between 1893 and 1900. The automobile was invented in 1892; by 1905 there were 10,000 employees in 121 firms producing them.[12]

Three observations are necessary here, the first harking back to a reason on Heilbroner's list of why England was the seat of the original industrial revolution. That reason is the prior organization of the whole of England into a single market with a single government through the dominance of a monarchy over the nobles whose power was locally based. The United States also quickly became a large single market, with a single economically dominant government (rooted in large measure in the rather prescient interstate commerce clause of the U.S. Constitution). Germany and Italy were not unified politically until nearly a century after the United States gained independence, and arguably their industrialization required unification. Locally rooted power tends to slow the expansion of commerce and the development of industry in many ways. For example, local powers may favor one producer over another owing to political and personal factors rather than productivity, quality, and price. Local fiefdoms may, for instance, charge monopoly-based tolls on roads or bridges, slowing the expansion of markets. But most important, perhaps, there is the absence of a state that can expand demand by creating or supporting crucial social institutions, by helping to stabilize employment and incomes and by preventing, at least in part, some of the excesses and instabilities to which capitalism is notoriously prone.

There has never been any doubt, except among overexuberant capitalists (and hypereconomistic intellectuals), that capitalism needs frequently and continuously to be saved from itself—from the overblown egos and arguably necessary greed of its dominant figures. These tendencies (and personalities) are thus both inherent in and often essential to the system, and prone to excess. That is, not only do capitalist systems tend to generate morally doubtful social outcomes; without political guidance, they tend to be better at expanding supply, the capacity to produce, than at expanding, distributing, and maintaining the capacity to consume. Governance, then, as Polanyi makes clear, has had a central role to play all along in the establishment and ongoing functioning of industrial economies—it protects property (and sets rules that reward invention), smooths the way to a geographically expanded market for both labor and goods, and often forces redistribution through minimum wages, defense of trade union rights, and the countercyclical social-income-provision schemes necessary to absorb and sustain the operation of existing productive capacity.

On the European continent the unification of the nation-state and the beginnings of the development of social well-being went hand in hand. In Polanyi's words,

> Italy and Germany arrived only during the second half of the nineteenth century at that stage of unification which England achieved centuries before, and smaller Eastern European states reached even later. In this process of state building the working classes played a vital part. . . . In the industrial age such a process could not fail to comprise social policy. Bismarck made a bid for unification of the Second Reich through the introduction of an epochal scheme of social legislation. . . . The Continental worker needed protection not so much against the impact of the Industrial Revolution—in the social sense there never was such a thing on the Continent—as against the normal action of factory and labor market conditions. He achieved it mainly by the help of legislation, while his British comrades relied more on voluntary association—trade unions—and their power to monopolize labor. Social insurance came, relatively, very much sooner on the Continent than in England.[13]

On the continent unification of the nation-state, liberal democracy, the weakening of feudalism, and the beginnings of broad-based consumer demand were fused. However it happened in various locations, a market the size of a substantial nation-state and the nation-state itself were essential to the continuous creation and recreation of mass industrial society.

Second, mass industrial society in all its stages and variants was, and yet is, based in a fundamental and material way on the availability of fossil fuels. Coal and the steam engine gave rise to the age of textiles and iron. Coal and oil and gasoline begat the age(s) of railroads, steel, automobiles, the assembly line, and petrochemicals as much as did English, continental, and American inventors, entrepreneurs, and factory workers. One of the fundamentally different things about the transformation to electronic capitalism is that within this second fundamental transformation, the energy basis of the first transformation and the entire history of industrial society thus far must somehow be superseded. This is true for a number of reasons, including climate warming and the imminent peaking of fossil-fuel supplies and output. Industrial and postindustrial production organized on a global scale and existing primarily within urban configurations that presume a high degree of physical mobility will not make such a shift any easier. Nonetheless, it is important and a great mercy that some of the technological transformations, and potential social transformations, associated with electronic capitalism may provide, in part, the means for achieving such a shift. That is, a significant and growing proportion of the output of electronic capitalism is exactly that: electronic. More specifically, it consists of electronic devices and especially electronic communications—almost dematerialized outputs that can be delivered instantaneously and at very low per-unit cost throughout the planet and, for that matter, beyond.

Third, the transformation from mass industrial society to electronic capitalism allows us to see the stages of mass industrial society as a unitary piece. The age of textiles and iron, the age or railroads and steel, the age of automobiles and oil—whatever the subgrouping of the differing forms and patterns of mass industrial society—seem more of a kind with each other than with what preceded (agricultural-craft society) and what has now followed. Today's capitalism is already distinctive in several ways—its global organization of production and markets is thoroughly integrated, its communications systems are growing in range and scope and are increasingly centrally owned, and the capitalist organization of economic life is now essentially uncontested. Moreover, the core political structure—the nation-state—is already in a process of eclipse. As the scale of market organization is transformed, so too eventually will the dominant site of politics and governance change. As national economies required national governance, so global economic organization requires some form of global governance (however disturbing the possibility).

A Picture of Craft Society, Mass Society, and Electronic Capitalism

Economically, the craft era was dominated by agriculturalists and by producers of handmade goods, with early industrial output, primarily in textiles and small manufactured items, as a promising addition. Most clothing and household items were still produced at home from flax or sheep or trees. Most craftspeople created whole products using a considerable range of skills and took personal pride in their output, whether using the product themselves or offering it for sale. The majority of adults and children devoted most of their time to food production and rural life. Cities were built on trade in goods and were the seat of most early manufacturing. This was an era characterized by the design and production of farm machinery, coal extraction and modest-scale steel production, early trains and carriages, some factory-produced cloth and clothing, dishes and pots, and some elementary communications devices. There was no assembly-line mass production. Almost no one, save large-scale landowners, was wealthy and life for most people was often insecure. Uncontrollable disease outbreaks were not uncommon—for rich and poor alike.

Workplaces, markets, and communities were modest and manageable in scale. Few people traveled great distances frequently, most never did. Communication was by post and telegraph. The majority were illiterate, but possessed an array of personal survival skills—most could grow crops, build modest houses with whatever raw materials were at hand, make and repair tools, hunt, fish, make their own clothing with few tools, and breed and care for domesticated animals. They could do for themselves most of the things needed for their own, and their family's, survival. Trade was mostly limited to barter or sale in the nearest village market—and even that only on an occasional basis. Specialized labor was limited to such professions as priest, metalsmith or other craftsperson, teacher (for the children of landowners), musician (mostly in the service of royalty, or working in a traveling company), and a small number of physicians, bakers, and innkeepers.

The mass industrial age changed all that. Products were produced for regional and national markets in large factories by vast assemblages of

Table 2.1
Sociopolitical Characteristics of Three Economic Eras

	Craft	Mass Industrial	Electronic
capital/job	low	medium	high
workspaces	shop	factory/office	workstation
family	extended	nuclear	one parent
scale of governance	community	nation-state	global
workforce adjustments	closure	layoff	downsizing
work pattern	job	job/career	wide use of contract and part-time work
social structure	local hierarchy	middle class	repolarizing
dominant ideology	liberal/tory	liberal/socialist	neoliberal
residential pattern	rural/town	city/suburb	suburb/mobile

people, each engaged in repetitive tasks that fit together in a collective whole. Few individuals independently produced goods of any kind and the time and ability to do so were soon lost for most urban industrial workers. Output, and to a lesser extent incomes, increased, as did the range of goods produced by society. Labor unions developed and accelerated the redistribution of factory-produced goods by raising wages and reducing work hours. Urban populations increased at a rapid rate, and the range of activities assigned to government grew rapidly as the proportion of the population employed by government grew.

Most important, the industrial revolution (and especially the assembly line) radically altered how humans worked and what (and how much) they produced. It also obviously altered everything else about society and everyday existence. As we have seen, most of the changes were, on balance, for the better once past the first generation or so of the transition. The second transition, still now in progress, is likely to prove every bit as dramatic in many ways. Again, in the early days of change to electronic capitalism not all of the social changes are positive and there is every reason to suspect that social improvements will be far from automatic. Whether the net results will in time prove to be positive remains to be seen. Some of the basic dimensions and characteristics of the three societal modes are summarized in tables 2.1 and 2.2. For each of the items in the left column of table 2.1, the table indicates a typical or dominant mode for each of the

Table 2.2
The Three Eras of Industrial Society: Some Trends

Continuous decline: craft to mass to digital
Labor/unit output
Materials and energy/unit output
Accelerating decline in unit costs
Continual rise: craft to mass to digital
Capital/unit output
Output/unit of energy and material
Rising craft to mass; declining mass to digital
Public-sector employment
Social aggregation within workplaces
"Left" politics
Corporate taxes
Wages (in many sectors)
Declining craft to mass; rising mass to digital
Distributional inequity
Rural/small community living (potentially)

three societal types. Table 2.2 identifies some central trends of the whole period under a number of broad headings.

Thus, as mass industrial society developed, workplaces increased in size in both factories and administrative bureaucracies, public and private. The rise of left politics ensued. In addition, politics was soon overwhelmingly organized within sovereign nation-states. Most people came to reside in large cities (rather than in rural or small-town settings) and, with the mass availability of automobiles, within both cities and suburbs. As electronic capitalism evolves, however, residential patterns may become increasingly open ended if telecommuting options increase. These patterns have already become unstable—residential moves and extended commutes are frequent owing to downsizing and other forms of, mostly involuntary, career and employment shifting. Contract work is an expanding pattern in electronic capitalism, far more common than it was in mass industrial society. Suburbs (edge cities) now dominate the North American landscape, though city-core living remains significant. One-parent families are not quite at majority level, but have increased enormously in recent decades and may be the future norm.

As noted, in electronic capitalism work is increasingly isolated. One cannot easily converse while manipulating words or data on a screen. Few jobs do not involve the extensive use of computer terminals or tasks where terminal use is mingled with often essentially anonymous face-to-face contact with customers. The Internet and e-commerce, as well as call centers, continue to reduce the directness of this contact. Modes of employment where employees do not almost constantly interact with a terminal are often found only in relatively isolated situations, as in the case of truck driving, farming, and resource extraction. Some manufacturing employment and teaching still have significant collective and nonmediated interactive dimensions. However, the proportion of persons engaged in manufacturing is in decline and even teaching may increasingly be offered via the Internet, separating teachers and students. The net sum of these changes may be one source of the significant decline in left politics and in what Robert Putnam calls social capital (see the discussion in later chapters).

Isolation, however, is probably not the most important outcome of the changes in the nature of work. Marx was wrong about much in economics (not to mention politics). But he was right about the extent to which human satisfaction derived from work and about the extent to which something real and important had been lost in the transition from craft production to industrial production. He spoke of "alienation" of the producer from the product. He attributed this loss to capitalist ownership of the means of production and capitalist control of the product—what was produced when and how, as well as what it was sold for and to whom. The shift from craft production using one's own tools to industrial production using someone else's is certainly alienating, especially if there is no participation in production decision making, and especially when the products themselves are unaffordable and unattainable for the producers. Industrial society was fundamentally different from craft production of goods essential to oneself and one's family or neighbors.

Marx, however, as we now know, underestimated the extent to which this alienation was a result of the industrial nature of production, rather than merely being a matter of the ownership of the means of production. Eliminating private ownership does not eliminate the alienation associated with mass industrial production. Moreover, shorter hours, early retirement, and higher incomes, regardless of the matter of ownership, certainly go a long way toward compensating for alienation. The increasing output of mass industrial society made such things (time and money) possible and rendered socialist revolution all but impossible. But still, throughout the history of mass industrial society, there has been a persistent sense of something missing, some failure of happiness and comfort for many people regardless of income. Employees, of course, can and do identify with the output of "their" factory or ministry or firm, but even these possibilities are in decline under electronic capitalism (given the increasing fragility of workplace tenure and employment stability). And the pleasures of work can and do still abound away from working for a living.

In the end, it is hard to deny that two centuries after the rise of mass industrial society, humans still get their greatest pleasures from meeting their own needs directly and from directly helping others to meet theirs. We still also very much enjoy wholly creating something of use—whether produced from materials or activities or ideas. In contrast, electronic capitalism takes alienation to another stage—automating production, detaching even sales personnel from customers, and destabilizing most work settings. At the same time, however, electronic capitalism has the potential—not yet widely perceived—to allow us to recover much of what was lost in the first industrial revolution (not so much to capitalism as to industrialization and bureaucratization).

The new stage of alienation involves industrial automation: the systematic removal of more and more people from industrial workplaces, from the collectivized and alienated industrial production process. Fewer and fewer people are involved in the production of anything tangible. Machines can make things with relatively little human assistance; they even now make other machines. Electronic capitalism involves the dispersal of production out of any one factory into a process scattered around the planet. Few worksites now make automobiles; they make hubcaps. The dominant work task of more and more people, especially in wealthy societies, is not to extract, grow, or make anything; it is to facilitate purchases of goods and to convince (often unseen) people that they need or want something they would not otherwise realize they needed or wanted. To some extent this is a task of imagining and designing things that might be needed, but mostly it is a task of getting the attention of, or manipulating, other people.

As Marx might have said, automation and globalization also involve "creating the material conditions" for recapturing in the second transition (to electronic capitalism) some of what was lost in the first. But despite qualitative material change, society seems a long way from anything like a new social transformation. The key to achieving this potential dealienating social transformation is a fundamental value shift. The shift, almost wholly speculative at this point, would in turn lead to a widespread view that time and satisfaction were at least as valuable as money and goods. Greater industrial productivity in this scenario might lead as often as not to something other than greater industrial production. There are some signs that such a shift is possible, but there are other signs that we are moving further from the possibility every day. This is but one of the central ironies of the new stage of capitalist social organization as it has evolved thus far.

From the Age of Iron to the Age of Irony: The Second Transformation

More than two centuries have now passed since the early days of the industrial revolution in England. Even early on amidst the squalor and desperation of nineteenth-century English mining and industrial cities there were glimpses of better times to come. Early in the industrial revolution, Robert Owen and others established socialist, anarchist, and/or religiously based productive communities that delivered greater material comfort to many of their members. A small number of other employers, not ideologically committed to transforming the lives of the poor, nonetheless created workplaces that were both socially superior to those surrounding them and a step up for employees in comparison to their prior lives as rural peasants. Josiah Wedgwood, of chinaware fame, was one such capitalist employer.

The climb from the horrifying slums, the seemingly endless hours of work in dangerous settings, and the hunger, disease, and short lives of nineteenth-century Britain to the typical lives of industrial workers and the middle classes in the rich nations at the turn of the twenty-first century has been a spectacular achievement. Comfort for a majority of society's members had rarely existed in earlier periods of history (though there were some exceptions among hunter-gatherer and agricultural societies).[14] What contemporary majorities now have has not come easily, of course. Only rarely were significant gains in equity made without political and trade union struggles. Long, bitter strikes, imprisoned labor leaders, police attacks on factory workers, and democratic and not-so-democratic efforts to attain control of governmental agendas and objectives were the norm for many decades. These efforts were combined with a great expansion of productivity and total production as well as with the creation of arrays of products and services once unimaginable.

This once-familiar tale (still familiar to labor historians, but to few others) was intermixed with the periodic collapses of production and employment to which capitalist systems are still prone. Mass industrial society was thus characterized by boom and bust and by political contestation over the equitable division of the benefits of labor, invention, and output. For more than a century trade unions and other organizations slowly drove hours down and wage levels up and gradually improved working conditions. With the help of others, they also established social minima in terms of income protection, pensions, education, and public health services, which helped to soften the effects of, and alter the actual occurrence of, depressions and recessions. Societies where citizens owned comfortable homes, consistently ate well, owned automobiles, and had a vast selection of clothing and appliances did not arrive quickly, consistently, or automatically. The most astonishing part of the story is, however, being told in the present. As observed above, the ultimate historical irony has overtaken even some wealthy nations—many of the things so painstakingly won are again under intense political attack, eroding even as collective wealth continues to expand.

In the past decade especially, a century following the sacrifices of the poor of England (or the coal miners of Pennsylvania and West Virginia), poverty and insecurity were widely renormalized. In some locations some aspects of this shift backward were temporary, but it appears in some places and ways to be a permanent part of the transformation to electronic capitalism. There has been a simultaneous acceleration of the rate at which wealth is becoming more concentrated. As noted, wage levels for industrial workers in many sectors and nations have been falling for more than a decade, despite overall economic growth. Moreover, a significant proportion of the world's clothing is now again manufactured under conditions not vastly different from those in early-nineteenth-century mills in England or in late-nineteenth-century mills in New England. Homelessness has also increased in most of the major cities of North America, even those so brutally cold in winter that death is a common result.[15] In some North American cities, even tuberculosis has returned, a measure of the decline of both working conditions and cutbacks in public health expenditures.

It is, however, more difficult to explain any of these tragic contemporary ironies on the grounds that Heilbroner proffered regarding early-nineteenth-century England—developments perhaps justified by a need for rapid capital accumulation in a society of general scarcity. There is now no shortage of capital or industrial capacity in wealthy nations. On the contrary, as Greider and others have documented, there is a vast and (possibly) growing industrial overcapacity worldwide and the world is all but awash in mobile capital. One indication of this is the obvious fact that, in the 1990s, stock prices came to bear no relation whatever to the actual value of firms. At the same time that this "excess" of dollars are "productively invested," many billions are also annually pumped into an endlessly growing variety of electronically managed gambling opportunities. Capital shortage is thus not a problem in the second transition. Nor is there any shortage of labor (worldwide) willing to work for low wages—it is not as if additional poverty were somehow needed as an incentive to work. There may be a billion humans in the world who want and need work but do not have it.

At the same time, of course, machines now make machines and economic production (could be) automated and otherwise conducted with far less human effort than has been the case thus far. Rifkin's error was to assume that just because work was increasingly unnecessary in terms of the production of goods and services, it might become increasingly unavailable. As noted in chapter 1, per-capita work time among full-time employees is again increasing, especially in North America, where it is moving to rival the levels that were the norm in Japan in the 1970s and 1980s. Those levels were known then to be unhealthy. We are not just "working smarter," as contemporary mythology would have it; those who have employment are working more and harder as well. Some will see this change as wholesome and healthy, the one means by which economies can be more competitive. What is not clear is competitive for what purpose and with what overall net social and environmental effects.

The need for radically increased production in the eighteenth and nineteenth centuries was obvious and constituted a strong argument to justify ensuing social sacrifice. Though want still abounds as the second transition advances, there are several fundamental differences between then and now that give one great pause. While the textile workers of England in 1800 or 1840 wore rags and most of the cloth they produced found its way to the wealthy of London or Paris, much of today's globalized output is purchased by a much broader proportion of the global population, whose level of material well-being is considerably higher than that of the elites of the nineteenth century. That is arguably a social advance, but given massive equity differences on a global scale, the price for which today's goods are sold is totally out of relation to the actual cost of production. Part of the difference is the cost of transportation of products, but the larger part goes to marketing, advertising, endorsements, publicity, media image making, and profit—activities, other than profit, unknown at the time of the first transformation. In effect, as noted, a larger cost of the product today is devoted to convincing potential buyers that they have a need for the product—a need that might not otherwise enter their consciousness. Many of the goods so casually acquired are hardly used and the loss of some of them would be of only passing consequence to purchasers.

Moreover, production is now increasingly organized on a global basis, in global firms. The political prospects for an eventual alteration of conditions of work and society are fundamentally different. There may now be little chance of bringing governance into line with global economic realities, whereas in the nineteenth century, movement to governance in nation-states was rapid. The Poor Law Reform of 1834 dissolved local responsibility for social protection throughout England. In Germany, Bismarck sought the support of the urban industrial workers for a national government through the early passage of social insurance. Unions in the United States were, for the most part, national unions—within, for example, the *American* Federation of Labor. However social reforms were achieved in various nations at various times, they were almost always achieved nationally—within jurisdictions that were coterminous with the scale of the market that existed at the time. There is now only an inkling of a global civil society, no democratic political forum at the global level, and no effective global-scale unionization (indeed unions are illegal or ineffective in most of the nations where global production is increasing most rapidly—e.g., China, Indonesia, Mexico, and elsewhere). It is not clear how, or if, the sacrifices of the present will lead to a changed social reality in the future, especially in the locations where the greatest sacrifices are presently being made.

There is as well, arguably, a second order of sacrifice being made—a global environmental price is now paid for each increment of additional industrial production. These environmental costs are detailed in chapter 4. Suffice it to say that while neither the mines nor the factories of early industrial Britain or the United States were environmentally benign, the world is now fundamentally different. Today's environmental effects and problems are at a global, not a local, scale and ecological costs can now overwhelm or undermine social and economic gains on a wider scale—save for those who are sufficiently wealthy to buy their own ecological reality, or so poor that the alternative to severe environmental damage is short-term hunger and death.

If that were not sufficient, it is also now arguable that there are not enough of some essential resources (energy and wood, for example) to deliver additional wealth to all on an equitable and sustainable basis (see chapters 4 and 5). If this is true (and obviously this is a complex matter), there are many implications for the ongoing, and probably now unstoppable, transition to global electronic capitalism. In brief, there are enough environmental warning signs to alert the prudent to the possibility that contemporary North American/European lifestyles cannot be replicated globally on a long-term basis—certainly not without radically modifying the character and methods of industrial output everywhere, and possibly even with such changes.

There is no doubt, however, that those North American/European lifestyles are what most humans are now imagining for themselves or for their children or grandchildren. This perhaps illusory possibility is being sold hard and readily accepted throughout the world—electronic images of the "good life" are, alas, far easier to deliver than are the physical realities. There will likely soon be ten billion humans in the world. It is important to ask now whether that many humans can live in comfort on this planet for very long. This is not a straightforwardly negative assertion. The fact that it makes sense to even ask such a question bespeaks a great advance in human possibilities. The even better news is that the new technologies of electronic capitalism may provide the technological basis for rapidly globalizing the industrial revolution. The bad news is that our social and political institutions and moral sensibilities are not keeping pace with this possibility and that even the present level of industrialization cannot likely be sustained without a significant and simultaneous alteration in material expectations, production techniques, and societal and individual priorities. That is, to put the same point more positively, the electronic images beaming across the planet cannot be realized, but what could be might be as good, or better.

Many of the possible changes become more visible with a clearer sense of the past as viewed from the present and from the perspective of these possible futures. Some things lost in the first transition—such as a more broadly distributed access to land and greater opportunities for unalienated (not necessarily waged) work—could be at least in part regained within the second. We can begin to see these possibilities, first by comparing the two transitions (from agricultural/craft to mass industrial society and then from mass industrial society to electronic capitalism), and then by setting out within this context some of the positive and negative features of electronic capitalism as it has unfolded thus far.

The Two Transitions: Identifying the Similarities and Differences

Above we began a discussion of some of the differences between the two transitions (to and from national-scale mass industrial society), and we will return to that discussion shortly, but just as interesting are the similarities. Five similarities stand out: (1) new, rapidly expansive economic sectors signal, in both transitions, fundamental economic change and produce vast concentrations of wealth that rapidly eclipse the fortunes of prior wealth-holders; (2) in both transitions, most older economic sectors continue to increase output at a moderate pace, doing so with an ever-decreasing proportion of the workforce; (3) in both transitions the organization of production expands geographically well beyond the scale of existing political and social organizations and structures; (4) the economies in both transitions remain subject to the booms and busts of the business cycle, including the excessive exuberance to which capitalist orders are periodically prone; and (5) both transformations are driven by new technologies. In all of these ways, and others, the two transitions are remarkably parallel. These parallels are important for an understanding of how we might accelerate the positive aspects of the second transition, while at the same time softening the social costs and steering clear of the greatest risks. Each of these similarities requires brief elaboration.

1. In the nineteenth and early twentieth centuries, especially in the United States, vast fortunes were accumulated by the "captains of industry," also known as robber barons, a term first applied to the legendary railway

tycoons by Kansas farmers in 1880. Matthew Josephson, the great 1930s chronicler of the rise of Vanderbilt, Rockefeller, Frick, Gould, Carnegie, and Morgan, drew a conclusion typical of the decade in which he wrote: "And during the long years of industrial lethargy, while grass literally grew upon the floors of magnificent factories, the lesson would finally be driven home of the fearful sabotage practiced by capital upon the energy and intelligence of human society."[16] The rail, steel, and oil fortunes resulted in splendid mansions lining Fifth Avenue in New York City, and in "cottages" that still stand, some open as tourist attractions, in Newport, Rhode Island, and elsewhere. One such Newport cottage, Marble House, is one of the world's truly stunning displays of opulence; some of these cottages had up to 100 domestic staff. The fortunes of these families were accumulated in but a few decades as the then-new industries of mass industrial society emerged in North America.

The parallels with contemporary realities are stunning—the great new fortunes of electronic capitalism have been made in computer software, microchips, sports and gaming, telecommunications, filmmaking, pharmaceuticals, and the effective use of these technologies in other industries, including retail (Wal-mart, Amazon.com, Virgin, Nike). The greatest fortunes of electronic capitalism have, of course, been associated with computers and software (Microsoft, Apple, Compaq, Dell, Oracle, Cisco Systems, Nortel, Intel), and despite some losses many individuals who launched or invested early in these firms remain extremely wealthy. "First in" usually wins big, in both transitions—sometimes via a new product, sometimes by especially effective promotion of an older product or service with newly available means. The fortunes suddenly created within a fundamental economic transition are only rarely achieved so readily at any other time. From Vanderbilt and Rockefeller and Ford to Gates and Dell and Walton and Ellison—individuals showing imagination, initiative, effort, and perhaps just a touch of ruthlessness have their moments in economic history. The speed of both change and wealth accumulation in both transition periods has been simply breathtaking.

2. The original industrial revolution required more than new machines and products; the new factories required a mass of workers. In 1800 those workers could only come from rural areas; most would only opt to be factory workers if they were no longer needed as agricultural workers (in part since they were not to be well paid within the new industries). Sharply

improved agricultural productivity was thus an essential underpinning of industrialization. In the United States, where at the time of mass industrialization potential agricultural land still seemed boundless, both agricultural and industrial workers were imported—as industrial immigrants, settlers, or slaves. In North America there was a rapid movement to agricultural mechanization (beginning with the famous cotton gin of Eli Whitney), and the result was a continuous domestic supply of labor that supplemented immigration. Agricultural output continued to rise while agricultural workers fell from a strong majority to well below 10 percent of the workforce through the twentieth century. Similarly, post-1970, the workforce in heavy (mass) industry has undergone a contraction nearly as dramatic, often with no loss of total industrial output.

Needless to say, some industries are utterly eclipsed by economic transformation. The automobile replaced the manufacture of carriages and buggy whips. Computers have replaced a wide variety of business machines and typesetting devices (and employment), as well as much of the production of business forms. Other industries—clothing and shipbuilding and to a lesser extent steel manufacture, most notably—have migrated almost wholly to lower-wage locations. Some of these are not necessarily traditional smokestack industries: consumer electronics migrated within a matter of decades of its rise to economic significance. Nonetheless the broad point holds true; in electronic capitalism traditional manufacturing output has not declined, but its share of the workforce in advanced economies has. Whether as an activity it will decline in terms of a proportion of the workforce to quite the extent that agriculture has is uncertain at this point, but that may prove to be the case. In this narrower realm Rifkin may have been somewhat more accurate in his prediction of an end of work.

3. Heilbroner has observed that one of the principal reasons the industrial revolution first proceeded in England was that earlier English kings had forged a nation-state—the basis for a market for labor and goods large enough to allow industrial-scale production to occur rapidly. Elsewhere in Europe, industrialization caused the market and the organization of both production and political life to expand beyond local boundaries, in effect creating and reinforcing the nation-state and overwhelming local economic and political decision making. In North America, industrialization

and especially the railroad and telegraph allowed the rapid creation of continental-scale nation-states. The parallels to the present day are again stunning. As Susan Strange has noted, "Today it seems that the heads of governments may be the last to recognize that they and their ministers have lost the authority over national societies and economies that they used to have. Their command over outcomes is not what it used to be. Politicians everywhere talk as if they have the answers to economic and social problems, as if they really are in charge of their country's destiny. People no longer believe them."[17] The nation-state that grew hand in hand with industrialization is now in some ways in a position analogous to the feudal fiefdoms at the rise of the industrial era in continental Europe.

4. It was once imagined that Keynesian economic interventions would reliably soften the business cycle, and indeed they did do that in some contexts (and might continue to do so in a limited way). For the most part, however, governments proved largely unable to run surpluses or even to balance budgets nearly so often as they were open to extended deficits. Moreover, Keynesian interventions proved all but powerless in the face of "stagflation" introduced by the abrupt rises in oil prices in 1973 and 1979. One cannot stimulate and restrain simultaneously. Keynesian stimulation within any given domestic economy is also obviously relatively ineffective to the extent that that economy is dependent on imports and exports. So too are tax cuts, the neoliberal variant of Keynesianism, more rapid than public revenue growth. Monetary control is another lever that is partially effective, perhaps more effective in a global era if coordinated internationally (as inevitably it must be to some extent to control excessive capital flows). Indelicate monetary interventions can, however, have brutal social results, the avoidance of which one assumes was the very reason to stabilize economies in the first place.

Some now contend that globalization and automation—core dimensions of the new age—will result in a long-term respite from the business cycle through extended productivity increases (and corresponding downsizing) and thus the continuous restraint of wage-based inflation (and thereby the need to induce recessions through monetary intervention). The most severe contractions of the 1990s in Mexico (1994), and later in Indonesia, Malaysia, Thailand, Korea, Japan, and Russia, would seem to belie such a conclusion—the business cycle is still with us, even if perhaps the richest of nations are getting just a little bit better at engineering soft landings. It might also, on the contrary, be argued that the more globally integrated the economy becomes, the more vulnerable it is to global-scale disruptions. We stand or fall together once thoroughly integrated on a global scale. This is another basis for arguing that a global economy requires global governance and policy levers—in the economic as well as the social and environmental realms. What has been considerably underestimated, one fears, is the extent to which social and especially environmental problems can trigger economic and political failures.[18]

5. Finally, technology has been a driver of economic and political evolution in both transitions. The steam engine and power loom promoted early industrialization and large-scale industrial production. The railroad and telegraph promoted political and economic coordination over vast expanses. Modern telecommunications, containerized shipping, low-cost air travel, accelerating automation, and related efficiencies based on computerization promote global-scale production integration, investment, and micromanagement. The new technologies and their economic effects have all introduced tendencies toward wider cultural and political integration and homogenization, as well as the possibility of achieving rising economic output with a significantly smaller workforce. The new technologies also create the possibility of simultaneously larger human populations and economic output that in combination increasingly threaten the natural world, including the very energy sources that create and sustain agricultural and industrial capacity.

The second transition is also, however, distinctive in a number of ways. Six differences are discussed here: (1) environmental limits are a greater potential restraint on economic growth now than they were at the time of the first transition; (2) there is the potential for a partial "dematerialization" associated with many of the new products typical of electronic capitalism; (3) there is potential for a considerable, and again unique, geographic delinking of residential location and employment location; (4) there is also now, however, a deeply embedded habit of induced consumption that has been accelerated and globalized by electronic capitalism; (5) there is also, potentially, a clear alternative to the endless promotion of products that is unique in human history—a simultaneous freedom from both want and work for a significant proportion of the population; and (6) missing in the second transition is any obvious route through which to rematch in scale contemporary forms of economic and political organization. In combination, these differences define both the positive excitement of the contemporary era and the very real array of risks.

1. Since the beginnings of industrialization, there have been assertions regarding environmental costs and resource limitations. Warnings regarding the health effects of air pollution date to the seventeenth century and earlier. Energy shortages were first predicted in 1865.[19] What is different now is that there is scientific evidence of global-scale environmental impacts (detailed in chapter 4), and there has been massive growth both in the human population and in the average volume of energy and material throughputs per person. There is also a capacity and intent to accelerate global economic resource use, even in cases where sustainable supplies are clearly limited (as in the case of wood fiber, fish, and fossil fuels). Environmental impacts per unit of economic output, as well as the resource use per unit, have likely improved, but not as rapidly as economic growth has proceeded. Many crucial questions remain: Will resource-use efficiency advance more quickly in the future than the global economy grows? How significant are the entropy factors operating here? That is, even if resource use gains in efficiency faster than it expands with expanding GDP, are there not resources that are running down in any case and for which we are unlikely to find suitable substitutes? Since this latter question is inherently unanswerable with certainty, what is the appropriate level of prudence?

2. As noted, one dimension of great promise in electronic capitalism is the fact that many of its dominant new technologies and products are produced with significantly less energy and resources per dollar of GDP. There is probably enough inefficiency in electricity use in most economies to power, if rectified, all of the telecommunications equipment being added for a considerable period of time.[20] For example, substituting communications for transportation saves significant amounts of energy, as in the case of teleconferencing in lieu of face-to-face meetings or electronic banking in lieu of a trip downtown. Telecommuting can help to reduce office space and result in longer life for vehicles, effecting both energy and materials savings. In brief, the economic drivers of the second transition are significantly less material and energy intensive than the drivers of the first

transition. The question is, are we wise enough to take full advantage of these possibilities, or will we allow the new economy to be just an add-on to continuing unsustainable growth in products and processes that demand excessive energy and material per dollar of economic output?

3. Another potential of electronic capitalism—the possibility of an increased detachment of residences from the site of employment—also has important social and environmental implications. This is the exact opposite of the effect of the early evolution of mass industrial society that drew human populations into cities and into direct proximity to industrial worksites (given fourteen-hour days and poverty, no one "commuted" for long). In contrast, now—especially when work lives are organized through a mix of successive and overlapping contracts—living near to one's place of work may be difficult if not impossible. Increasingly, however, employees can deliver work output and access all information necessary to complete tasks from anywhere at any time, since few "new economy" jobs involve the handling of physical things. There are few compelling reasons, for example, why more schooling, especially at higher levels, could not be delivered this way (as some already is)—physical meetings, when necessary, could be handled within a specific time frame (perhaps during a few days of the week or weeks of the year). There is even a potential for a partial reintegration of home and work, a recapturing of one of the real social losses from agricultural/craft to mass industrial society. Broadly, where the first transition pulled people out of the countryside and set them within easy walking distance of industrial worksites, electronic capitalism opens all options—including some redispersal into more rural or distant urban or scenic settings.

4. Advertising and marketing were hardly necessary in the early days of the industrial revolution. Little activity of this type existed in specialized form prior to the twentieth century. No one needed to be convinced, beyond the barking of the occasional snake-oil salesmen, that they truly needed something they were unaware they needed. Prior to the existence of real market saturation for some commodities and the onset of a declining marginal propensity to consume, needs for products were ordinarily obvious. Life with or without lightbulbs or a refrigerator is different enough that advertising need not scream, if it was needed at all. Chapter 3 will consider this issue in depth; suffice it to say that it is now almost impossible to lead a life

on much of the planet without being continually confronted by advertising. The average North American or European is exposed to thousands of advertisements every day. To limit oneself to mere hundreds of such exposures requires either a considerable effort, or a strong disinclination to all media forms, or both. Arguably, the worldwide electronic promotion of products is the very essence of electronic capitalism. The organization of production and production itself are now of secondary importance to global firms in comparison with marketing, promotion, and branding.[21]

5. On the other hand, it is possible that advertising's excesses carry the seeds of its own demise. Overhyped consumers may even have subversive political potential in the contemporary age. That is, just as the industrial working class altered the trajectory of the first industrial revolution, the targets of the endless stream of advertising may grow weary of the role in which they have been cast today and take action. There is some evidence that more people are seeing the possibilities of alternative lives achieved not so much through political organization as through downshifting, voluntarily reduced work time, early retirement, or just a comfortable sense of sufficiency. Such options, discussed extensively in later chapters, are most available to the well off in wealthy economies, but would produce more "trickle down" to the less well off (through opening preferred work opportunities) than would the alternative, the continuing acceleration of consumption (met increasingly by largely automated plants). The possibilities here have only been glimpsed thus far—electronic capitalism has the potential to deliver simultaneous freedom from both (real) want and (unwanted) work. This is not, however, a transformation that can be delivered easily—socially, politically, economically, culturally, or psychologically.

6. Finally, and central to our discussion in chapters 6 and 8, when during the first transition, the organization and scale of economic output burst through the geographic boundaries of political structure, the nation-state was born through national unification (Italy and Germany), or thrived (England), or physically grew (North America). The possible path or paths to democratic global governance are, however, far from obvious. There remain fierce national loyalties and significant political resistance thus far to any legal and structural steps toward global political integration, other than within a realm somehow imagined to be "purely economic." Global economic integration is presumed to be inevitable, while global political

integration is widely presumed to be fundamentally undesirable. Arguably, the vacuum so created undermines national and local political democracy through the substitution of one-dimensional global rules conducted on the basis of economistic precepts and market whim.

In the world of global trade decision making there is at present neither transparency, nor public debate, nor democratic political accountability. The relevant agreements and decisions effectively determine ever more of the formerly domestic political agenda, either directly or indirectly. It is simply assumed that public services and hard-won labor protections must diminish in the name of competitiveness. At the same time, global environmental treaties are duly signed with considerable fanfare, but few are effectively enforced. National governments of every existing political stripe simply represent domestic economic interests in international forums as if they were the only interests for which they speak or by whom they were elected. Almost no one objects, save what neoliberals see as a ragtag collection of anticapitalists, radical environmentalists, and unionists, as conservative commentators have been known to put it. There is as yet no institutional structure from which democratic global rule making can emerge, nor any obvious prospect for such an initiative.

Thus the age of electronic capitalism has costs and benefits, positive potentials and negative risks, to which we now turn. Following that discussion is a fuller assessment of some of the more interesting societal possibilities inherent in electronic capitalism, including a closer look at the possibility of recovering in the second transition some of what was lost in the first.

The Transition to Electronic Capitalism: Positive and Negative Trends

As noted, globalization and the transition to electronic capitalism are alternately viewed as a pathway to a prosperous, technologically exciting, free-trading, democratic heaven and the earthly birth of a hellish nightmare of greed, poverty, and environmental destruction. Both views are, of course, caricatures—either wholly disingenuous and self-serving or relentlessly depressing and on the edge of paranoia. There is little doubt, however, that one view has prevailed politically thus far. The negative take on electronic capitalism, while frequently articulated, has virtually no forum outside of books, a limited number of newspaper columns, and some university classrooms, environmental organizations, union staff meetings, or gatherings of church-based intellectuals (and of late the streets of Seattle, Quebec City, and Genoa). The positive take is expressed systematically through the electronic and print media, often by the publicists of well-funded conservative think tanks, at corporate gatherings, in the power centers of most governments, and through virtually all the means also available to the negative side. Both views are, nonetheless, far from the mark.

A more balanced evaluation might begin like this. Much that can be said about electronic capitalism was also said about the capitalism of the first transition—it is dynamic, creative, and has the potential to vastly improve the economic aspect of the human condition in the short run and perhaps the long run, too. Like its predecessor, however, it also tends to exaggerate and even at times to celebrate human greed. It is prone to social and economic instability, and unchecked and unbalanced by public-spirited democratic wisdom, it regularly results in, or contributes to, great harm. Yet, that said, governmentally managed economies are also prone to self-serving excess and abuses of power in the name of the public good. Such governmental excesses are particularly pronounced within many, though not all, attempts to replace markets with "public" bureaucracies. Bureaucracies do not manage well when expected to manage detailed activities across broad sectors of the economy. This does not mean that some public services of an economic nature are not appropriate and superior to private-sector ownership or management—or especially that public and private (as well as nonprofit, nonpublic) enterprises could not or should not all participate in the broadcast media, health-care, education, transportation, utilities, or for that matter any other sector in the economy.

Mass industrial society worked best when private-enterprise dynamism and exuberance was continuously offset, balanced, softened, and, from time to time, controlled by competing social, political, and economic forces and institutions. Without trade unions, public education, the public provision of health-care services, unemployment insurance, environmental regulations, national and other parks and wilderness areas, public provision of utilities especially in poor places or hard times, public health services, workplace safety and health controls, banking and securities regulations and controls, public broadcasting and support for the arts, and a plethora of other innovations, life under capitalism might, for many people, be little changed from life in early-nineteenth-century England.

Public enterprises have been, however, as often unsuccessful as successful, but even at its worst the public provision of housing, for example, has been and remains vastly superior to widespread homelessness, which seems to be the alternative. Arguably, the public postal service has, for instance, outlived its usefulness (and has been largely reduced to a low-cost means of circulating universally unwanted advertising flyers without public recourse to a right of refusal), but even here, in remote locations, those without electronic mail might see postal costs rising sharply. Nonetheless, a more appropriate contemporary question might be whether there should be wider public provision of Internet access.

The broad point here is that *unchecked* capitalism does not serve society well and is not even very good at consistently delivering (either through time or throughout all of society) what it delivers best—goods and services. The real bottom line is that there is, or should be, much more to life than that which can be better delivered privately and at a profit. To reiterate a point made earlier, government's proneness to excess and error often needs to be checked by the marketplace, but the market's proneness to inequity and instability also needs to be offset by the ongoing actions of democratic government rooted in an attentive and informed public. To be fully effective, democratic government—or at the very least enforceable and openly developed public policies—must exist at each and every jurisdictional level at which market and economic organization and decision making take place. The absence of such initiatives all but guarantees that global-scale electronic capitalism will present to humankind trends full of positive promise, but dominated by negative consequences.

Boxes 2.1 and 2.2 summarize the consequences (negative trends) and potentials (positive trends) specifically associated with electronic capitalism so far. Some of the argumentation and evidence for the assertions in these summary lists have already been presented, but in a few cases additional explanations and elaboration follow the appropriate box.

The first of these evaluative assertions is perhaps the most controversial, and all would likely provoke considerable disagreement in some circles. Conventional economic wisdom would argue that the job losses of the early 1990s, especially in North America during the Reagan years and following the FTA and NAFTA, were a short-term correction and rationalization that restored economic competitiveness and allowed the growth and low unemployment in the United States in the late 1990s. Now that

Box 2.1
Some Negative Trends within Electronic Capitalism

1. The evolving patterns of unemployment may reflect a new noncyclical instability in employment within some economies. Greater insecurity in employment now exists at most income levels and throughout both the private and public sectors, superimposed on cyclical unemployment. The proportion of part-time, temporary, unstable, and unpredictable work options has increased within many contexts, as has (with notable exceptions) the overall level of unemployment.

2. Governments are increasingly unable to tax corporations or mobile high-income individuals, and there may be a long-term tendency toward declining public revenues (as a proportion of GDP—reversing a decades-long trend).

3. An initial tendency toward high governmental deficits has given way to declines in public expenditures and social transfer payments in some nations.

4. There has been a declining ability and inclination within governments to regulate or to protect the environment, again reversing a trend of several decades standing. There has also been rising pressure in some locales to do environmental damage in the name of employment opportunities.

5. There has been a declining individual loyalty to, and involvement in, community life and social organizations and a declining sense of loyalty and commitment within corporations to employees or to any locale or nation within which firms have operated over time.

6. There is widespread family breakdown and declining family formation where young-adult unemployment is high or employment stability is otherwise limited.

7. There has been a significant rise in income disparities, especially for the highest percentiles and often for the highest quintile relative to all others.

8. There has been a trend toward increased global speculation and short-term investment and the potential for increased capital mobility, also called capital flight, and continuing economic volatility and instability.

Box 2.2
The Positive Potentials of Electronic Capitalism

1. One potential may be (or would be if realized) one of the greatest achievements in human history—the possibility of freedom from the need for almost all humans to engage in subsistence and/or wage labor for most of their lives.

2. There is a continuing potential for modest and sustainable gains in material comfort (limited "only" by environmental choices and resource sustainability) for present numbers of humans.

3. The opportunities for instantaneous, low-cost, global communication are unprecedented.

4. There is the potential for developing the time availability, gender equity, and workplace organizational flexibility essential to seeing *both* parents effectively combining career and family. That is, there is, in wealthy societies especially, considerable potential for resolving the growing gender tensions and family disruptions.

5. The is also a potential availability of the work time essential to environmental protection in such labor-intensive areas as ecological agriculture, sustainable forestry, recycling, public transportation, and building renovation.

6. There are increased opportunities for people to choose where they live largely unrelated to employment opportunities—thus the potential to reestablish greater community or neighborhood stability through the substitution of communication for transportation.

7. Global economic integration appears to create greater restraints on inflation.

that time has passed, it would be said, low taxes and free trade maintain low unemployment and thereby provide considerable net social benefits. Labor market flexibility is the key to this competitiveness, it would be argued, which in turn is the key to prosperity. High unemployment is not a consequence of the changes that have occurred in the global economy, but is best avoided by accelerating and universalizing those changes (smaller government, trade agreements, deregulation, low wages for the less productive, and low taxes for all).

Only time will sort out that debate. Clearly unemployment rose widely and sharply a decade ago in a pattern not unrelated to the rationalization associated with North American and global trade integration. Employment levels indeed recovered in several economies, most dramatically in the United States. But equally clearly downsizing, with or without mergers, is here to stay, and stable work histories are less the norm now than they were thirty years ago. Involuntary exits (as distinct from temporary layoffs) from positions are far more common than they were twenty or thirty years ago (especially in the form of mass downsizing even in the face of corporate health and high profits), and so too is part-time and temporary employment. Clearly this has been a boon to corporate profits, so much so that there was almost no surer way to drive one's stock higher a few years ago than to announce that one's firm was dismissing a significant proportion of its employees (where that was once a clear sign that a firm was facing economic difficulties). That is one major difference between mass industrial society and electronic capitalism.

Whether or not, overall, people's lives have improved is another question. Debatable too is the question of whether society as a whole could benefit more from efficiencies gained from global economic integration and rationalization than it has thus so far. We will look more closely at such concerns in chapters 4 through 8.

Regardless, rationalization in the digital sector is relentless. No sooner are jobs created in thousands of video rental establishments than the ownership is in the hands of a few franchise operations, and even they and all their employees are likely slated for oblivion as we move to interactive television, which will be all but devoid of employees. Movie theaters no longer need even one technician. The cashless society is a bank teller-less society. What we cannot yet see clearly is that this is not necessarily as problematic as it might appear socially, but it is more problematic than it might appear environmentally. An economistic society is, however, all but incapable of thinking clearly about either of these realms.

The potential for a renewal of historic reductions in work time is undermined by excessive global competition and, in some jurisdictions, excessive per-employee taxes, costs, and charges. The global nature of competition in electronic capitalism has restrained reductions in full-time work that otherwise might occur as labor-replacing technologies and techniques are introduced. Japan's success in the 1970s and 1980s was achieved in large measure through the efficient organization of production and obsessive work habits, sometimes called "Japanese management."[22] The United States reemerged as the dominant global economy during the 1990s in good measure through the imposition of continual downsizing.

Moreover, the application of very large costs (unnecessarily) on a per-employee basis drives firms to increase hours per employee (or to avoid reducing hours) and to reduce the number of (full-time, benefit-eligible) employees.

Economism in nondominant economies is much like a modern-day cargo cult, holding on to the view that if market conditions (deficit levels, inflation, taxes, and wage levels) are right, private investors will suddenly come from somewhere. "They" will produce new products for some unidentified market and employ large numbers of people. This is nonsense. It really is, in effect, the equivalent of a postmodern, postindustrial cargo cult. Ever lower corporate taxes and ever-fewer regulations in the digital age means more profits that mean more investment that just as likely means *fewer* jobs. The world has changed. Economism has blinded us to fundamental changes in society and economy. We could produce most of what we have time to consume, or that nature can sustain, in far less time than we presently are expected to work. For many reasons, it is time to bury economic "man."

Not the least of those reasons is an urgent need to restore and further enrich community life and civil society. In chapter 3 and elsewhere this need will be considered through the groundbreaking work of Robert Putnam and others.[23] So long as we imagine life as essentially fulfilled by the successful achievement of economic success in terms of increased GDP, we put aside all the potential of political life to turn electronic capitalism toward its rich potentials. We now consider some of those potentials. These potentials implicitly include the basis of the restoration of civic life (time and an ability to see beyond the media-induced assumption of the desirability and inevitability of economism), but also require it.

Electronic capitalism has many positive potentials that have been missed or ignored by most critics as well as by its proponents. That is, some of the positive potentials listed in box 2.2 might only be achieved at some cost to short-term profit maximization and/or would require the restoration of a more positive and active role for governments. Among the rarely noted positive features are the reopening of real prospects for work-time reductions; the possibility of an acceleration of the "dematerialization" of economic inputs and outputs (at some cost to resource industries); increased cross-cultural interaction (threatened by one-way media flows and cultural homogenization); and the technological capacity to reduce, or even eliminate, human poverty (limited by the combination of inequitable economic distribution, overpopulation, and possible resource and environmental limitations).

One dilemma of electronic capitalism not unrelated to the democratic dilemma becomes apparent when we consider these two boxes simultaneously. We humans now have for the first time the technological capability of producing enough for all, but unless the neediest among us get a disproportionate share of the increased output, our living planet may not be able to create or sustain this new potential for shared prosperity. Therefore we can no longer assume that everyone, especially the rich, can continue to get even proportionately more until the poor have what is sufficient for them. Thus far, electronic capitalism has provided the already rich with *dis*proportionately more. As McKibben puts it, "If we could block out the assumption that economic expansion will fill our lives with sunshine—then perhaps we could talk realistically about our predicament. Because it is a predicament—on the one hand continued economic growth threatens the environmental stability of the planet, but on the other hand the system we've rigged up requires constant acceleration or else it produces unemployment, misery, want."[24] Contemporary societies seem to require that several dollars be put in rich pockets to allow the placing of one dollar in the hands of the poor.

The bald truth is that the overwhelming majority of humankind has yet to gain significant benefits from the first industrial revolution, let alone any share of the benefits of electronic capitalism. The increased output that can come from a global division of labor and automation is crucial to the impoverished majority of humankind—those billions of humans whose annual incomes in total fail to equal the fortunes of a few hundred wealthy individuals. The prospects for that majority to gain the lion's share of the increase in output would seem remote at best. To hope that they will get a share proportionate to their share of total production, that is, that they might stop losing relative ground is optimistic, given the performance of electronic capitalism thus far. The problem is, just to be completely clear, and as I will show in succeeding chapters, that the planet earth cannot produce enough goods for the projected number of humans to ever all live in minimal comfort if the poorest among us do not get something like that impossible lion's share of all future gains, starting very soon.

At the same time, while we are excited by the possibilities inherent in contemporary technologies, we yearn for many aspects of earlier times. We sense that something important has been lost. Both neoconservatism and environmentalism have sought to articulate that something. That something is a greater control over our everyday and immediate personal, family, and community circumstances; it is a more direct sense of participation in production and contact with nature; it is also a greater sense of identity, simplicity, and security. It is escape from, or at least a reduction in, stress. It is having more time. It is a more and more intense, and less and less fulfilled, desire to personally make something of lasting value. It is, as well, what might be called "family values" (hopefully in a nonbigoted form).

In the 1970s this yearning found fulfillment for some in the back-to-the-land movement. More recently, the yearning has more often been a vague wish that things might be different, somehow better and more secure. It is also the accelerating interest in gardening and "cocooning," and—especially among the young—in the creative arts, an interest that seems to grow in direct proportion to the endless hype and economic rewards associated with the study of computer science, systems engineering, accounting, and financial management.

The widespread yearning for aspects of a lost past, the enthusiasm for the arts, and the fascination with the technologies of the future may be connected in a significant way. The growing economic insecurity for some and accelerating pace of work for others have led many people to recognize (perhaps only in a semiconscious way) that a global, digital economy has the capacity to extricate more and more people from lifetimes of tedious work. The yearnings and the fascination could find a common resolution. There actually is the possibility that many, many people could spend much of their lives creating something directly, or could have more time, not less, for domestic and family responsibilities and pursuits. "All" that is missing, at least in wealthy nations, is a firm democratic commitment to equitably redistribute employment on a continuing basis and a wider and more frequent recognition that time is worth more than money. While environmental sustainability may also require a widespread ethos of, and structured opportunities for, some moderation in the consumption of materials and energy (in effect, a redefinition of prosperity), electronic capitalism could take humanity to an altogether different place than the one toward which we have recently been heading headlong.

A final question is why the negative consequences have prevailed so far? Why do so few even imagine, let alone collectively and democratically achieve, the positive potentials of the digital age? In part, it is because we are only beginning to realize that something qualitative and permanent has recently happened to our society, economy, and politics. The widespread disrespect for politicians of all viewpoints suggests perhaps that the population recognizes that the world has changed fundamentally and that none of the old answers (left, liberal, right, or neoright) is the correct answer.

An alternative explanation for the distrust of all political leadership and for the general failure to more fully perceive the positive potentials is more ominous. The alternative explanation is that most information sources are controlled by the dominant economic forces of the digitalized/globalized society—perhaps more centrally controlled than they have been since the invention of the printing press. Discrediting things political discredits the societal institution most capable of countervailing the pure economic power of ownership. This media concentration and its increasing dominance of contemporary politics and culture make democracy's dilemma even more difficult. Citizens learn of the challenge of globalization, but are left to see, through the eye of the electronic media, the choice before them as one between essentially unfettered economic integration and street rampage.

Today's print media are increasingly of a blandly neoconservative bent, though a small number of high-quality, politically centrist outlets remains. Electronic media, perhaps owing to their very nature, systematically avoid intellectual content in favor of good visuals. Media owners on the whole subscribe to a narrow economism. They are blind to the broader potential of the society they are helping to create because such insight might require seeing the necessity of a significant diminution of their own power in the interest of achieving effective democracy. It is to this world of centrally controlled, and hype-driven, media that we now turn.

3

Electronic Capitalism as Media Monolith

Electronic capitalism has a media mind. As a result, it is at times dangerously mindless, a social order suffering from a collective attention deficit disorder. Readers of this book need not worry personally. You would not have gotten this far (or, for that matter, likely ever found this book) if you yourself were severely affected by what might be called the media absorption of culture and information. But there is no escaping the fact that we are all affected. Our view of the world is constructed by what we see and hear, and what we see and hear more and more of the time is media. Media recognition and acknowledgment has become for many something akin to a measure of value, if not reality. The media are so central to the functioning and structure of today's society that it is no exaggeration to say that they are at once the driving force of our economy, the core of our culture, and the sine qua non of all successful politics and politicians.

It has often been said that our economy is increasingly dominated by transactions involving information and services rather than material goods. One of the earliest comprehensive assessments of the sociological implications of this shift was Daniel Bell's *The Coming of Post-Industrial Society.* For Bell, a central feature of postindustrial society was the majority status of white-collar workers (from 1956 in the United States) and the large and ever-growing proportion of professional, technical, and scientific workers. He also noted that "postindustrial society emphasizes the centrality of theoretical knowledge as the axis around which new technology, economic growth, and the stratification of society will be organized."[1] He would not have said that postindustrial society was simply a "service society" or a "knowledge society,"[2] but he did argue that while energy was the central technology of industrial society, information was the central technology of postindustrial society.

Electronic capitalism, as a conceptualization of contemporary society, differs from Bell's postindustrial society in at least three ways. First, both are models of a society in which knowledge has become an important organizing principle. But electronic capitalism is still first and foremost capitalist—its "axial principle" (Bell's term) remains economic growth, not as for Bell the "centrality of and codification of theoretical knowledge."[3] It is decreasingly also a society of "state or private control of investment decisions" and increasingly a society where such decisions are wholly private concerns. Second, the most important economic sector is not finance, as neo-Marxists might argue, or research or science, as Bell might argue, but media—a particular form and structuring of information and the key means of social organization, communication, value formation, and sociopolitical control. Third, Bell did not fully see the extent to which, and all of the ways in which, information might become a mass-marketed product in and of itself. Only in the last decade has a fuller range of these possibilities begun to come to fruition.

In electronic capitalism, then, both the means of production and the products are increasingly electronic. So too are the means of economic, cultural, ideological, and political communication and organization. In dollar terms, the most significant export from the United States to the rest of the world is not automobiles or airplanes, but Hollywood films. This "weightless" product results in export earnings in excess of $30 billion annually and promises considerable increases in the future (offset only by the expansion of "offshore" production organized through Hollywood studios, which continue to control both content and worldwide distribution). These films are on the whole ideologically loaded, both consciously and unconsciously. At the least they systematically convey as normal, when they do not openly celebrate, North American consumption habits and products—and, in general, violence.

Computer software and video games are equally important as products. They are typically even more violent and mindless, no small achievement. The Internet—and especially interactive television—promise to only accelerate the extent to which commercial values (and English-language culture) predominate. They will also speed up the process through which material goods can be promoted and "dematerialized" goods can be delivered worldwide virtually automatically (without employees once the "products" are initially produced). The Internet may be more than this as well, but it remains to be seen whether automated, dematerialized goods are truly significant culturally or politically. This matter will be considered further below.

In general, in electronic capitalism, many actual physical products are more (electronic) image content than physical content. A clothing item produced in Southeast Asia or Central America or the Caribbean may be manufactured for 10 percent or less of its sale price. A far larger proportion of the price will go to producers and conveyors of photographic and television advertisements, as well as to media figures such as athletes successful enough in their particular undertaking to display (through television) logos on their clothing or to model actual clothing items. Much of the rest of the cost goes to in-store presentation and to profit for "manufacturers" (of the image and brand) and retailers. The actual (subcontracted) "manufacturer" operates on modest margins, and the workers who make the items are fortunate if they earn enough to live in a dorm and have enough to eat. They almost never can afford the products they produce. The broad point here is that an ever increasing proportion of all physical products are information of a sort that Bell could not have fully foreseen but a few decades ago—information that is scientific only in the sense that a great deal of survey analysis often lies behind the images. Those images are not knowledge in Bell's sense and are often in fact literally wordless.

Many Pictures within a Single Frame

It is arguable that media dominance has created a society that is increasingly one dimensional. Contemporary media have many physical forms (radio, television, film, Internet, magazines, newspapers, books, and recordings). Yet in many ways the media as a whole speak with one predominant voice. This is in part because one form of media overwhelms all the others—television is far and away the most influential contemporary form of communication (probably even including face-to-face conversation). More important, most media are directed to a dominant objective—to increase, influence, and organize commercial transactions through advertising. Books and recordings are perhaps the only communications forms that have thus far avoided being largely subsumed by this single-minded purpose. Also, virtually all media (with the exception of university presses and public radio) are now owned by large private, for-profit corporations, or by extremely wealthy individuals. Many of the latter have a very conservative view of the world (though many corporate media executives are more moderate in their views).

Communications through the electronic media have certain characteristics. The seemingly endless varieties of visual and sound images are similarly framed. Some of this media framing is technically determined; some is ideologically determined. In either case, this framing shapes the way most people see the world most of the time. The largely technically determined rules of electronic media framing include the following: (1) entertainment must predominate, and ratings are the central goal; (2) for television, nothing is newsworthy if there are no visuals; (3) complex analysis is presumed to be beyond most viewers and listeners and likely to be impossible in any case (given 4); (4) a story cannot go on air without a good sound bite (thirty seconds is too long) and almost no story is worth more than a few minutes air time in total; and (5) every story must be "news"—there must be a new hook and some kind of story line with broad appeal. Taken together these aspects of framing help to create what might be termed a sense of "false immediacy." Substance is traded for alternately lighthearted and spectacularly and unusually tragic, but always brief, items. The overview provided, then, is ahistorical, nonanalytic, simple, visual, instant, and brief. Some print media are somewhat (but less and less) different, but they are only read reflectively and with care by a small percentage of the population.

The ideological determinants of framing are hardly necessary, given the power and effect of the technical determinants. Television news has been largely replaced by infotainment—"news" about media "personalities." So-called hard news has been increasingly dominated by a succession of real-life soap operas. All of this can be seen to be a conscious ideology of critical silence regarding any deeper changes or potential issues in modern life and society. It may, however, be more a reflection of the technical limits of the electronic media and the uncritical outlook of the wealthy creators and purveyors of media content. A survey in the *Columbia Journalism Review* reported that 40 percent of journalists admitted to "practicing self-censorship by not covering stories that might offend advertisers or the owners of their news organizations." Fifty-two percent avoided stories that were "too complex" and 77 percent did not pursue stories that were "important but dull."[4]

Nonetheless, there are at least two clear ideological dimensions to the framing of most media images and presentations, especially those delivered by large commercial organizations: do not offend any very large or powerful organizations or definable groups, and never question the desirability of growing prosperity, the importance and fundamental usefulness of most products, or the "obvious" and fundamentally unlimited linkage between happiness and consumption. A third dimension is a bit less rigidly "enforced": only rarely and ever so cautiously question (the justice of) the existing distribution of wealth in society or the world.

Obviously there are occasional exceptions to these rules, but these exceptions rarely survive in the media. The North American television program "TV Nation" made a brief incursion onto network television in the United States, but did not endure for long. The host of the program, Michael Moore, questioned the right of corporate executives to downsize employees in already-profitable firms while themselves living in increasing splendor. He also probed the ethics of unsolicited junk mail, a form of advertising not beneath the dignity of many large corporations that also advertise on television. He did so creatively, brilliantly at times, and always with good humor and entertainment value. He had a very short career in television and his film, in the same spirit, was not shown on many screens. His books have sold well, but needless to say have reached a smaller audience.[5] Outspoken viewpoints on the right seem to endure more readily in the electronic media world.

The Hypersaturation of the Culture of Hype

The primary focus and central purpose of virtually all media is advertising. This reality has evolved to the point where advertising is so pervasive that it arguably is the essence of contemporary culture. As Andy Warhol saw so clearly, by the 1960s iconographic product images had become the central and dominant images of contemporary life. Art can but replicate them. Our age seems to celebrate promotion and commercial image making; icons and corporate logos permeate the visible (thus far earthbound) universe. There are fewer and fewer noncommercial spaces of significance.

Indeed, it is almost impossible to communicate anything by any means (or to do anything or go anywhere) without the central, not incidental, presence of such images. One might reasonably wager at this writing that before this book is out noted celebrities will have corporate logos tattooed onto the exposed portions of their bodies and both church sermons and university lectures will have corporate sponsors (if they do not already). All public entertainment and sports venues have long since sold naming rights. Most universities and many other public institutions have in effect, if not quite explicitly, sold naming rights to most of their buildings—often room by room and chair by chair, if not yet brick by brick and course by course.

Even low-caliber amateur athletes are festooned with logos when participating at weekend events (on the T-shirts and banners commemorating the day). Most live performances have corporate sponsors, even when the cost of admission—as in the case of opera performances—is $100 or more. The presence of media, even local media, increases both the desirability and the cost of such sponsorships. Increasingly as well, commercial television (as well as the intensely logo-filled Internet and corporate-supplied text materials) is entering public school classrooms, as are licensed brand-based retail sites. And, in the United States, seventeen billion catalogs (sixty-four for every man, woman, and child) are mailed each year, equal to the total waste produced by 521,000 American households.[6]

Motion pictures have a long tradition of hidden commercials for smoking and any number of brand-name products, the most famous of which were the brand-name candies favored by the space creature in the film "ET." Motion pictures shown in theaters have added slightly sexed-up, TV-style commercials to the previews in lieu of the long-ago delights of cartoons; surprisingly, few paying customers seem to object. For that matter, few have objected to the implicit double billing associated with paying cable-television fees to receive commercially sponsored fare. Nor are suggestions even made regarding legislated protection against unsolicited telephone sales or surveys, or more effective protection against the hidden commercial sale of personal information to mass mailers. There may be other related issues on the horizon as well—for example, paid product placements in television programs as a means of circumventing ad-removing technologies or even paid product placements in novels. Even now, armies of advertising agents seek the placement of media "stories" of products as if they were news.

The broad point is that commercialization is more and more pervasive and invasive in today's society. Most North American children will be exposed to more than 100,000 TV ads before high school graduation.[7] Typical North Americans are exposed to 50 to 100 ads each morning before 9:00. What are the effects of this level of exposure? In terms of intentional effects, one can assume that Proctor and Gamble has studied with great care the results of its annual expenditures of $2 billion and concluded that it is getting value for its money. In broader terms clearly advertising expands the size of the economy and results in the sale of considerably more goods and services than might otherwise be sold. How much more in aggregate, it is impossible to say. However, the direct expenditures on advertising worldwide amounted to some $299 billion in 1997 (up from $237 billion in 1988 and $39 billion in 1950), and it is not unreasonable to assume that this expenditure stimulated aggregate economic activity (sales) equal to or larger than that amount.[8]

Why is this important? One can have ethical doubts about the extent of advertising from three possible vantage points: environmental, social, and cultural. Environmentally, one need not demonstrate that zero economic growth is, or ever will prove to be, essential or warranted to question on environmental grounds the desirability of a continuous stimulation of consumption by any and all means. One merely needs to conclude that economic activity typically carries a considerable environmental price. Even if a particular good or service carries only a small environmental price, its creation and sale may serve as a multiplier of less benign economic activity. That is, one's massage therapist may well be saving for a sports utility vehicle.

This is not to say that those concerned about the environment should not make every effort to take the environmental consequences of their choices as consumers into account. It is to say that marginally necessary (or utterly unnecessary) economic activity in an environmentally threatened world is truly wasteful. Both the high proportion of newsprint devoted to advertising and the induced purchases of products where no real need exists exact real and measurable environmental costs. This is not to say that induced purchases do not sometimes meet real needs and might not in the end be among the more useful purchases one makes. It is to claim that, at some level of ad saturation, this outcome would seem decreasingly probable.

One also might be concerned about what might be called the "social efficiency of consumption." That is, to what extent does advertising determine whether the mix of goods and services produced and sold is socially the best mix of goods and services? This is obviously an extraordinarily controversial line of inquiry in the age of electronic capitalism. The central underlying assumption in contemporary consumerist ideology is the view that advertising stimulates the economy and thereby increases the likelihood that all will benefit, that all (at least on average) will improve their prospects of satisfaction within the (growing) market.

However, automation, excess productive capacity, increasing productivity, downward pressure on wages in some times and places, and sharp currency fluctuations (among other characteristics of today's society) can affect this presumption. Such changes may lower prices, but they may also remove or reduce access to work or income and thereby goods. Both the collapse of some Southeast Asian currencies in the 1990s and the continual downsizing of employees with no loss of output—as well as the general shift of income from wages to profits—help to ensure that consumption is increasingly inefficient socially. Indonesian families more often go hungry, while North American families are induced by both relentless advertising and declining prices to hang clothes in their closets that they will rarely wear. The efficiency of production, in combination with advertising, promotes the "inefficiency" of inequitable consumption.

Socially and environmentally efficient or inefficient consumption makes sense if one assumes that there is some hierarchy to human needs and that there is at least some environmental cost associated with most production. As regards the notion of socially inefficient consumption, one does not need to assume that the capacity to consume (wealth and income essentially) should be equal or anything like equal. One need only accept that electric lights are somehow a more "meaningful" use of electricity than electric toothbrushes, and a meal for a hungry child more important than a larger-than-necessary meal for someone who is already overweight. The combination of environmental and social inefficiency of consumption is what is particularly problematic in ethical terms. Both the consumption and the costs of consumption are shared unequally. It is the conclusion that this combination exists that renders advertising's underlying assumption morally reprehensible. That twofold assumption is that all consumption is essentially of equal value and all additional consumption is good.

The core of the cultural argument against excessive advertising is that it can, through implicit repetition of particular messages, elevate this assumption to a status of central cultural precept. In effect, if a significant proportion of consumption is both socially and environmentally inefficient, then there is, in electronic capitalism, an ongoing and massive denial and moral silence. That silence is primarily an act of omission, an overwhelming of such considerations through the sheer repetition and volume of the all-consumption-is-equally-good message. It is also a function of the dominance of media forms that do not lend themselves readily to ethical debate—ethics is not easily rendered as a news bulletin, a form of entertainment, or a nontedious visual image. It is, however, a deliberate silence as well—a discussion forgone lest it put listeners and viewers off the message of those picking up the high cost of the presentations of the day.

A number of analysts—including William Leiss, Stuart Ewan, Alan Durning, Paul Wachtel, Fred Hirsch, Juliet Schor, and Michael Carley and Philippe Spapens—have thoughtfully considered these and closely related issues. In *The Limits to Satisfaction* Leiss, discussing the development and evolution of the market economy, observes that "the greater randomness of individual choices is not unstructured, for the cohesiveness of the whole is maintained through the ruling socialization pattern which encourages persons to interpret their needs solely as needs for commodities."[9] That ruling socialization pattern is, increasingly, delivered electronically. Even the satisfaction provided by the commodities themselves is diminished in this process.

For Leiss, "The individual must become increasingly *indifferent* to the fine shadings and nuances of both wants and the objects he pursues in the search for satisfaction." Why? Our complex needs (for feelings of self-worth, security, status, and actualization, for example) themselves are all increasingly commodified, even when they cannot be really satisfied with commodities. Moreover, the need for continuous production and replacement of goods requires a decreasing attachment to particular and particularly enduring goods. In Leiss's words, "This indifference to the qualities of objects, and the slightness of our attachment to them as we so readily replace them with 'new, improved' versions, is merely the other side of the developing shallowness and triviality in our articulation of our needs themselves."[10]

The source of this inherently unsatisfying quest lies in the transformation of industrial society through the rise of advertising. Ewan observes that "it was in the 1950s that the proffered dreams of the captains of consciousness [his term for *advertisers*], worked out in the twenties, really began to take concrete form. It was a period of monumental change. The commodity market parodied the patterns of 'conspicuous consumption' that Veblen had noted among the rich capitalists and middle-class imitators at the turn of the century, this time 'democratized' on a mass scale. The mass marketing of television (invented in 1925) carried the consumer imagery into the back corners of home life."[11]

Ewan discusses ideological consumerization as a deliberate substitute for the discontents of work in modern factories and the weakening of the bonds of rural family life. The family as consumption unit was sold as a replacement for the family as production unit—a replacement so vacuous and tenuous, especially for women, that it did not hold for long. Nonetheless, television and consumerism have survived all such disruptions and doubts. "Television," in Ewan's words, "became the common synonym for mass communications: a futuristic analogue to the hearth. Situated in the midst of the American household, TV became a vehicle for a consumerist mentality."[12]

Ewan examines the content of the classic 1950s sitcoms such as "The Honeymooners" and "The Life of Riley," as well as the messages of advertising. He concludes that

> consumption was inherent to the life style of 1950s television situation comedy. The comic impetus was often drawn from a consumerized context—the *wife* going overboard on a $40 hat was one of the all-time favorite plot devices. While a consumption-defined *middle-class* existence was proffered in shows and bolstered by the flashy beginnings of modern television advertising, working-class life was characterized chiefly by the laughable boorishness of the family breadwinner. . . . Were it not for the middle-class-minded wives—loyal consumers—the workingmen could hardly make it through the day. Over and over again, there was the spectacle of Ralph Kramden, the windbag bus driver played by Jackie Gleason, being "brought into line" by his wife, Alice, her arms forever burdened by the weight of omnipresent, recently purchased packages. In this and other such comedies, the normalcy of consumerism was defined and writ large in the living rooms of the American populace.[13]

Several analysts have attempted to relate the psychology of satisfaction and measures of happiness to issues having to do with commodification and the environmental costs thereof. Durning, for example, observes that "psychological data from several nations confirm that the satisfaction derived from money does not come from simply having it. It comes from having more of it than others do, and from having more of it than last year. Thus, the bulk of survey data reveals that the upper classes in any society are more satisfied with their lives than the lower classes are, but they are no more satisfied than the upper classes of much poorer countries—nor than the upper classes were in the less affluent past." He goes on to argue that "most psychological data show that the main determinants of happiness in life are not related to consumption at all" and quotes Freedman's observation that "above the poverty level, the relationship between income and happiness is really small."[14] Carley and Spapens argue that "expectations, fuelled by advertising and social pressures, rise with income, but satisfactions do not. So there is always an element of dissatisfaction which increased income cannot cure."[15] They refer to a Norwegian study that found that perceived well-being was constant between 1960 and 1993 despite a trebling of GDP and cite 1997 U.S. survey research concluding that many Americans were unhappy because they sought to meet nonmaterial needs with material goods.

Durning, in turn, examines the precepts of all major world religions and concludes that each has an insight similar to this finding based on survey data of social psychology. From Taoism's "he who knows he has enough is rich" to the Confucian "excess and deficiency are equally at fault" virtually every major spiritual creed would sanction the concept of "sufficiency" as put forward by Carley and Spapens and other environmentalists. Hirsch's classic *The Social Limits to Growth* links the dissatisfactions of prosperity to the declining utility of positional goods, goods that provide satisfaction only to the extent that they are scarce and held by but a few, or at least not a majority of, individuals.[16] This psychological quirk, of course, lies at the heart of advertising and marketing. It is inevitably, however, a source of frustration and accounts for why individuals will pay double or even tenfold what they need to pay for goods as long as those goods are visibly branded and known to all. It is worth mentioning, though, that having one very expensive watch or automobile rather than five or ten ordinary ones will impose less ecological damage.

For the most part, advertising, consumerism, and the exploitation of inherent dissatisfaction carry a considerable social, spiritual, and environmental price. Leiss sees the separateness of humans from nature as closely linked to these issues. In his words, "The ideology of human domination over nature is the most extreme version of this attitude. Its practical expression is the sort of pursuit of human goals in production and consumption activities that remains utterly indifferent to the impact of those activities on the viability of other life forms; the most extreme version is the social practice based on the doctrine of the insatiability of human material needs. In this social practice nonhuman nature is regarded as nothing but a means for human satisfaction." Both Leiss and Schor, as well as others considered below, regard part of the alleviation of what Schor calls "work-and-spend," and others might call the absence of a sense of sufficiency, as lying in more satisfying and creative, less alienating, work experiences—and in less organization of human lives within excessively long hours of unsatisfying work.[17]

Wachtel also speaks directly and with sympathy to Leiss's assertion regarding the alleged insatiability of human material needs (though he does not cite his work). As Wachtel puts it, "Defenders of growth and consumer values frequently argue that it is 'human nature' always to want more, to want the kind of consumer goods we seem to find irresistible, and to resent taxes and other efforts to direct our resources toward communal needs and the needs of the less advantaged rather than toward private gain. In some ways the ideas of psychoanalysis present an important challenge to these assumptions." Wachtel offers insights into the multiplicity of human desires and the highly varied ways they might be satisfactorily met, as well as into the power of self-deception often involved in the particular choices we do make. He adds that "psychoanalytic insights into our vulnerability to anxieties about our bodies and our social selves reveal starkly the manipulations employed in advertising messages."[18] As Leiss puts it, individuals are led by the imposed need for rising levels of consumption to misinterpret the nature of their needs and to misunderstand the ways these needs may be satisfied. While television programs extolling "lifestyles of modest sufficiency" (rather than those of the rich and famous) seem unlikely, such lives are eminently possible.

Most of these observers are uncomfortable with the dominance of contemporary social life by advertising and the values and attitudes on which it is—for the most part—based. Many, if not most, citizens are also generally irritated by the ever-increasing intrusiveness of advertising. Yet advertising expenditures continue to grow by some 6 percent per year, easily double the rate of growth of the GDP. There is little restraint on the quantity or the content of ads, save some limits to the blatant use of outright lying regarding products. Governments have taken an ever more hands-off role, in part because those in office are themselves highly dependent on both advertising and media. For the most part they choose to regulate neither—either in terms of content or quantity. There are obvious, sensible reasons to avoid governmental control of content, but there is no reason government could not, for example, open public airwaves to a greater presence for noncommercial voices. There is no longer even any restraint of the ever more centralized ownership of media outlets, an outcome that arguably poses as great a threat to liberal democratic values and practices as does governmental control.

Moving Toward a One-Channel World

Most daily, as well as so-called community weekly, newspapers are now part of large print media chains. In North America a large proportion of the largest radio stations are run by formulas repeated in almost identical fashion in dozens of cities. Virtually all owners of media have one thing in common: they are very wealthy individuals or (often tightly held) corporations, and are in any case beholden to large corporate advertisers. Electronic capitalism is, of course, characterized by an ever-increasing concentration of all industries on a world scale, and the media are no exception. In the 1970s some concerns were raised in some jurisdictions about the dangers for democracy and press freedom associated with media monopolies, but such concerns would appear to have faded.[19] Needless to say, they are not frequently expressed in the media.

In the United States by the end of the 1980s the control of almost all national media was in the hands of twenty-three corporations, down from fifty in the early part of the decade.[20] This trend toward consolidation, growing cross-media ownership, and ownership concentration has continued or intensified.[21] A few giant firms now control vast media empires that generally include within one firm most media forms: magazines, television, film, books, videos, and a significant Internet presence. The media "products" of these firms are also increasingly marketed globally. In recent decades, media firms have, through merger or purchase, become ever more global in organizational structure and scope. In both Canada and the United States, the rules regarding the ownership of multiple outlets in the same city and cross-media ownership have been relaxed and concentration has rapidly accelerated. There is at present little reason to think that such restrictions will not be further reduced.

More than 80 percent of U.S. newspaper circulation is in the hands of chains—especially Gannett and Knight-Ridder. From 1966 to 1990 the Gannett chain grew from twenty-six daily newspapers to eighty-eight (as well as twenty-three weeklies, thirteen radio stations, seventeen TV stations, and a significant presence in satellite and cable systems).[22] Only a few highly influential papers like the *New York Times* and *Washington Post* remain outside the control of major chains. In Canada at one point more than half of all newspaper circulation was in the hands of one person: Conrad Black, who still publishes major papers in Britain and Israel, and has only recently sold hundreds of smaller papers in the United States. Black's political views are on the extreme right (explicitly and openly to the right of Canada's Progressive Conservative Party). There are almost no independent papers remaining in Canada—only the largest paper in the country (the *Toronto Star*) and a few others are not openly on the far right in their editorial positions.

Other aspects of media are also highly concentrated, including magazine ownership (as a proportion of total circulation), book and magazine distribution, and increasingly in recent years, book publishing and book retailing. One of the few shifts toward voice and control multiplication is in cable television (reducing the audience share of the major national television networks) and the Internet (discussed separately below). Cable channels are, however, in many cases affiliated with each other or with major media organizations. University presses are one of the rare communications forms that have not (thus far) been prone to mergers and concentration.

The increase in the number of channels has frequently been used in Canada as an argument in favor of reducing public funding for public radio and television (CBC). In the United States, public television reaches a limited audience and, given stringent limitations on public funding, is generally sponsored by corporations as a public service (with discreet announcements rather than explicit advertisements). Public television in the United States is also frequently reduced to on-air solicitation of funds to the detriment of audience appeal, but despite all these constraints nonetheless makes a notable contribution to public discourse. Other than the public broadcasting networks, what the multiplicity of cable channels almost never present is current affairs programming that raises fundamental questions about the nature and quality of contemporary society. Only PBS, and occasionally programs like "60 Minutes," evidence what might be called investigative reporting. Most local television news emphasizes crime reporting, accidents, sports, and weather.

Business news is reported constantly on many stations simultaneously. An observation of Michael Parenti—a left media critic—in this regard is pertinent: "Every evening, network news shows faithfully report stock-exchange averages, but stories deemed important to organized labor are scarcely ever touched upon. Reporters seldom enlist labor's views on national questions. Unions are usually noticed only when they go on strike, but the issues behind the strike, such as occupational health and safety or loss of benefits, are rarely acknowledged."[23] From the perspective of media decision makers, however, the matter of ideological perspective in many cases may never have risen to the level of consciousness. Business news has a prosperous audience that commands a lineup of prospective advertisers for every available advertising time slot. At present, labor figures are almost never seen other than when there are labor problems, and environmentalists are only ever asked to comment (ever so briefly) on particular and suddenly visible environmental issues, narrowly defined. This selectivity is not unrelated to (that is, may contribute to) the effective demise of the labor movement in some wealthy nations. The selectivity is also an essential source of what this book has termed the operant "economism" of electronic capitalism.

In the end, many questions are only rarely asked and almost never answered in the media world. It is not so much that there are things that cannot be said on television, but that many important matters are rarely considered seriously in any forum, electronic or otherwise. All interests (other than "the economy," from which we are all presumed to benefit) are taken to be "particular" interests, more pejoratively "special" interests. Environmentalists do not expect to be asked to comment on taxation or annual governmental budgets (other than perhaps with regard to spending on parks or environmental protection). Both are, however, highly pertinent to overall environmental outcomes. Discussing the economy, especially on the airwaves, is seen by all to be the prerogative of economists, politicians, and businesspeople. Everyone involved in the discussion therefore agrees on virtually all the questions that matter. There are scripted disagreements, to be sure, but fundamental or value-based disagreements are almost never aired with regard to economic matters. There are occasional "don't forget about giving us our share" assertions, but no serious discussions about possible public priorities or governmental interventions that might or might not make sense.

Some questions that are almost never seriously engaged in media discussions include the following: Has the increase in global trade and investment provoked a race to the bottom in terms of wages (especially among poorer nations), social policy, taxation, and/or environmental protection? Is economic growth always beneficial or worth the cost? Are the remuneration levels of upper corporate management excessive? (Note, in comparison, that we are no longer shy about inquiring into the sex lives of political figures.) Are the oceans being fished clean and are forest corporations in the process of clearcutting the whole planet? Will there be enough wood thirty years from now without the elimination of thousands of existing species? Does climate warming carry any nontechnical implications with regard to the processes and patterns of production and consumption?[24] In what ways is the distribution of wealth in the world shifting, and what can be done about it? Do some societies get more (or less) social benefit from their level of wealth than others? Which societies distribute wealth most equitably?

Admittedly these questions are difficult and not readily dealt with in terms of sound bites. Moreover, many people do not have the time or inclination to think about such matters. That is the point. To the extent that our society is media driven and our culture is now defined by electronic media, such questions will not easily enter broad public discourse. There are, however, some possible solutions, which will be explored below: (1) restructuring the social sciences such that the discipline of economics is broadened in scope and other social scientific perspectives gain in relative credibility within policy discourse; (2) fostering the Internet as a multicentered media form open to diverse inputs; (3) creating government policy and shifting public moral-cultural sensibility that might lessen the extent to which advertising dominates public culture; (4) encouraging resistance to global cultural integration that is imaginative (artistically and politically) in more and more nations and cultures; and (5) establishing new media policies of governments (or new technologies) that increase opportunities to establish quality noncommercial local media.

The best hope of breaking the media-advertising cultural monolith, however, is the creative imagination as embodied in such publications as *Adbusters* and, to some extent, in the 'zines and hiphop subcultures.[25] *Adbusters,* like the foundation linked to it, is devoted to debunking advertisements—especially for tobacco, pesticides, automobiles, military weapons, and handguns. The pseudoads produced are as slick as, and harder hitting than, "real" ads. Some are brilliant. Many are not shy about appropriating and manipulating carefully cultivated brand images. Most are very visually oriented. This group has also produced "antiads" for television, but despite efforts to buy airtime, few if any ads have been broadcast. The best response to the slick smoothness of consumerist unidimensionality may be slickly smooth alternative and noncommercial rejoinders. Other efforts of interest here include awards nights for the least truthful corporate ad campaigns or public pronouncements of a sort that has come to be called "greenwashing."[26] Such events may not be reported extensively but could gain cult credibility precisely because they are not. Also potentially promising is self-consciously locally rooted theater. All these strategies have some potential to disrupt McWorld without initiating jihad.[27]

The Opportunity Costs of Media Dominance

A subtitle for this section might be "The Issue-Attention Cycle Meets the Age of Missing Information." It has been thirty years since Anthony Downs published his notable article outlining the concept of the issue-attention cycle. In brief, he argues that most political issues face a systematic "issue-attention cycle" wherein "each of these problems suddenly leaps into prominence, remains there for a short time, and then—though still largely unresolved—gradually fades from public attention."[28] The fading is in part the result of the third stage in the cycle—the gradual spreading of the realization of the cost of significant progress on the issue. At that point some members of the public become bored, some get discouraged, and still others feel threatened by thinking about a problem that is not easily resolved (without significant costs). Downs argues, however, that environmental issues "will be eclipsed at a much slower rate than other recent domestic issues."[29] This is because, in his view, environmental problems (especially air pollution) have "high visibility," because these problems directly affect a majority of citizens (almost everyone, in Downs's estimate), and because pollution can be attributed to a small group of villains (industrial polluters, whom he judges to be "scapegoats").

This, in my view, is a relatively benign, if insightful, view of the issue process and the role of media. Much is missing, not surprisingly since electronic capitalism was, in 1972, only in the early stages of its formation. To begin with, there is a good deal of difference between the glib and urbane press secretaries or attachés of the 1960s and 1970s and the usually masterful media-oriented spin doctors of today. In the private sector, relations with public, governmental, and media agencies or firms command ever-larger budgets and increased time on the part of management. Moreover, society as a whole is now even more thoroughly immersed in and saturated by media and those media are, for the most part, more centrally controlled. Those whose job it is to influence media interpretations of events have many more tools and skills at their disposal. Pollution is no longer visible to a majority without effective media coverage, in part because some of the most visible impacts have been partially ameliorated. Arguably as well, the media are increasingly cautious about granting attention to environmental concerns and environmental organizations.

Overall, the two largest differences in terms of policy outcomes between 1972 and now are the pervasiveness and sophistication of opinion polling, and the staggering sums of money now spent by corporations and political elites for political media management and advertising, including political campaigns. The issue-attention cycle is for the most part effectively managed. Those who speak or act in public deliver words and deeds crafted and scrutinized by specialists thoroughly versed in polling data and the subtleties of event timing. The media themselves are not unmindful of their central role in the contemporary global social order. As Gerald Levin, CEO of Time Warner, once boasted regarding his industry as a whole: "It is fast becoming the predominant business of the 21st century. . . . It's more important than government . . . a more efficient way to deal with society's problems than bureaucratic governments."[30] In his enthusiasm for the global media industry, Levin seems blithely unconcerned about the absence of elections and public input or about the influence of wealth decision makers or the profit motive on participation or outcomes.

Thus, one matter Downs misses is a continually improving capacity within the media, corporations, and government to exert increasing influence over, if not to control, the issue-attention cycle. This capacity is indeed a key to understanding the day-to-day functioning of electronic capitalism. The most important potential competing (alternative) values routinely fail to generate issues of political and policy significance, or to keep what issues they do generate in the public eye long enough to see through anything more than minor adjustments (or less—in the form of yet more studies or voluntary compliance programs). As I will detail in the next chapter, social equity and environmental sustainability are potential competing values to the central thrusts of electronic capitalism—unimpeded consumption and increasingly concentrated wealth. The pursuit of these latter objectives is so single-minded that it is rarely noted that they are themselves probably contradictory.

Reasons for such a lack of balance are advanced in McKibben's *The Age of Missing Information.* McKibben does not focus on the ownership structure of media barons, nor does he emphasize their ideological predispositions. He is generous with regard to the intentions of all who labor in that challenging setting. But he is not hesitant to suggest that the media, particularly television (far and away the dominant single media mode), have rendered humankind in some crucial ways less and less informed by the fact of their continued existence and operation. A media-saturated, highly educated, postagricultural, postindustrial humankind is, of all things, missing a great deal of fundamental information. We are, to begin with, hyperspecialized (as workers and as consumers). It took, for example, far more knowledge to own and ride a horse than it does to own and operate a car—the newer the car the truer that is. The greatest loss, however, comes from what we do not do either at work or while watching television three to four hours a day on average.

McKibben puts it this way:

> Even the dullest farmer quickly learns, for instance, a deep set of limits. You can't harvest crops successfully until you understand how much can be grown without exhausting the soil, how much rest the land requires, which fields can be safely plowed and which are so erosion-prone they're best left for some other purpose. This sense of limits of one particular place grants you some sense that the world as a whole has limits. Instead of learning about limits before they reach kindergarten, kids watch, say, *The Gobots,* a cartoon assemblage that turn from robots into late-model automobiles and back again. On this day [the day McKibben watched via tape all the programs shown on America's largest cable system], they unveiled a new invention: a "proton cultivator that will solve the problems of feeding the people of the earth. It will make barren land fertile"—indeed a single dose turned

cartoon desert to cartoon corn. Losing this sense of limits matters—one reason we're so blithe about doubling the present population of the world must be that we think some such device will double the amount of food we grow.[31]

The problem with television and other contemporary media is not, for McKibben, a matter of deliberate deception. The problem is oversimplification of a complex world. It is an inability to convey anything very interesting about the world's two most significant problems: climate warming, which moves at an excruciatingly slow and uneven pace and for the most part lacks visuals, and poverty, which simply is not news, since it is there, it has always been there, it seemingly always will be there. The failure here is rooted, in McKibben's brilliant phrase, in television's "relentless dailiness." Both climate warming and poverty, of course, are also problems that would tend to put viewers off television's central message: that they can and should go out and buy happiness right now. McKibben is most respectful and fearful of the power of television—it is, he says, and I would concur, the most important single development of the past forty years.[32] Surprisingly, he does not discuss at any length the ways television has altered the nature of contemporary politics. Putnam, as we will see, has perceived this, but even he, in my view, does not attribute the problem as expressly and fully as is warranted to the dominant presence of media in contemporary society.

McKibben's point here, however, is crucial and can only be fully conveyed in a small number of additional quotations. Television can cover most natural disasters, accidents, and arrests very effectively, but again not the two that matter most—climate change and worldwide poverty. In his words, "The worst disasters move much more slowly, and thereby sneak past the cameras." There is a glacial slowness about the evolution of climate change and a relentless daily sameness about poverty. As McKibben notes, those who produce news programs recognize the seriousness of these problems, but television fails to communicate their importance. He does not ask television to solve them, but he makes clear that it is utterly unable even to make them widely understood.[33]

McKibben also observes that these last forty years have been an exceptional period, unlike any prior period in human history. His observations on this point reinforce the notion that our dependence on electronic media is central to our seeming inability to come to grips with sustainability issues:

All the trends I discuss in this book—the retreat from nature, the rapid globalization, the loss of skills needed for self-sufficiency, and so on—all came to full blossom in this period. It is the most discontinuous, jarring, strange, out-of-the-ordinary stretch of time since we climbed down from the trees—a short bender in the more sober course of history. By some estimates, for example, human beings have used more natural resources since the end of World War II than in all the rest of human civilization. This needs to be seen for the binge that it is, and it probably needs to end—sooner rather than later, we need sustainable, steady-state societies that live off the planet's interest and not its capital. But if you marinate in the [television] images of the last forty years for hour upon hour and day after day, this binge seems utterly standard, and it's exceedingly hard to imagine other models, societies, ideas."[34]

The political implications of this reality are more fully understood in a brief return to one of the most important social scientific revelations of the last decade, declining social capital.[35] Putnam and others have established the crucial role of civic participation and social networks—in other words, of a strong and active civil society—in the functioning of democracy and in a variety of positive social and economic outcomes, from the control of crime to the sociology of economic development. Putnam demonstrates the extent to which civic interaction has declined through four decades since the 1960s. He cites U.S. voting figures (a 25% or greater decline over a thirty-year period at every level of governance), attendance at public meetings concerned with town and school affairs (a 35% decline from 1973 to 1993), and a sharp increase in distrust of (national) government (from 30% in 1966 to 75% in 1992). Importantly, he notes as well that involvement with organizations as diverse as women's clubs, civic organizations, churches and church-related organizations, labor unions, literary societies, and bowling leagues has also declined significantly. He observes that membership in some types of organizations has increased, but carefully demonstrates that these expanding organizations do not engage members in face-to-face interaction of a civic character.

The newer organizations (including environmental organizations), Putnam observes, typically involve membership ties to common symbols, common leaders, and perhaps common ideals, but not to one another.[36] That is, participation rarely involves more than writing an annual check and receiving a magazine. This parallels the fact that while bowling leagues have declined, bowling is actually more popular than it used to be. Recalling the work of Lipset discussed in chapter 1 (and to which one might add the view of William Kornhauser and others regarding the crucial societal importance of social organizations), one begins to understand one of the most important qualitative differences between electronic capitalism and mass industrial society.[37] One also begins to understand why the owners of media are arguably more significant to the functioning of society than is government. As noted, they themselves are not unmindful of this possibility.

The most important part of Putnam's article is perhaps his explanation of the reasons for the decline in civic life. He offers five contributory explanations: the shift of women into the labor force, residential instability, shifts in the character of contemporary families (more divorces, fewer children), a decline in community-based enterprises, and the increased role of electronic media (which Putnam describes as the technological transformation of leisure). Each of these is related in some way to our model of electronic capitalism, especially of course the last item on the list. In Putnam's words, "There is reason to believe that deep-seated technological trends are radically 'privatizing' or 'individualizing' our use of leisure time and thus disrupting many opportunities for social-capital formation. The most obvious and probably most powerful instrument of this revolution is television. Time-budget studies in the 1960s showed that the growth in time spent watching television dwarfed all other changes in the way Americans passed their days and nights."[38] This shift coincides both with the expansion of women in the workforce and with the decline of civic engagement. The three are interrelated on many levels.

Putnam goes on to observe that "television has made our communities (or, rather, what we experience as our communities) wider and shallower. In the language of economics, electronic technology enables individual tastes to be satisfied more fully, but at the cost of the positive social externalities associated with more primitive forms of entertainment. The same logic applies to the replacement of vaudeville by the movies and now of movies by the VCR."[39] It also, with one difference that may prove important, applies to the Internet. The Internet is perhaps the ultimate in wide communication, but given that it is interactive it is not necessarily shallow (but of course it will be if most "netizens" spend their time exchanging question-answer snippets with sports heroes and pop stars). This remains to be seen.

What is thoroughly obvious is that the technological transformation of leisure has all but undone effective civic and democratic involvement.

Meaningful civil engagement by, or even civic interaction among, the majority of citizens is in sharp decline. This reality is compounded by the overwhelming intersection of ever more spectacular political fundraising capabilities within politically engaged elites, ever more sophisticated opinion polling, ever-slicker spin doctoring, and the stunning political use of electronic media.

The Electronic Media, Party Finance, and Democracy

The 2000 presidential campaign in the United States saw for the first time in recent memory a real attempt at a serious discussion of the issues surrounding party and campaign finance in the quintessential media nation. The discussion, initiated primarily by Republican presidential hopeful John McCain, even touched on the central question of the scale of media and related costs as a distortion of democratic possibilities. Well-financed candidates for political office can lose, of course, just as multimillion-dollar new-product launches can fail utterly. But the heart of this issue lies with the now highly evolved capacity to sway opinion through electronic communications.

Opinion polling, focus-group research, spin doctoring, speech writing, event management, television ad campaigns, direct mail fundraising, and related activities have fundamentally transformed the nature of democracy. This process as a whole has arguably put off something approaching, at times even exceeding, a majority of the electorate. Cynicism predominates as regards all things political, a cynicism not unrelated to the scale of money that pervades (and is required by) media-dominated political processes. This is the very core of electronic capitalism's power structure. Nonmedia politics is in decline, but the media will not cover campaign finance issues with energy or commitment because indeed they are its principal beneficiaries.

The scale of electoral spending is dictated primarily by the cost of media access, polling, professional advertising, and public relations advice and is now truly staggering—especially in the United States. The 1997–98 House and Senate campaigns cost $740 million.[40] The total cost of federal political campaigns alone in a presidential year exceeded $2 billion in the Clinton-versus-Dole year (1996) and since. So-called (less regulated) soft money totaled in the tens of millions annually in the 1980s, but well into the hundreds of millions annually in the 1990s. Not inconsequential amounts of this money are linked to corporate concerns regarding, for example, environmental protection. Between 1989 and 1999 the member corporations in the Global Climate Coalition contributed $19,826, 657 in soft money to the Democratic Party and $43,644,061 in soft money to the Republican Party. Large oil and gas companies led the way with totals in the $3 to $6 million range; Ford and General Motors were in the $2 million range each. Common Cause also identified (in a shorter time period in the 1990s) $2.3 million of political contributions from members of the Crop Protection Coalition (not farmers) seeking a delay in the phasing out of methyl bromide use in agriculture and a similar scale of donations from mining firms seeking a delay in new rules regarding the use of cyanide in gold mining.

It is arguable that there is no way to raise the amounts of money seemingly necessary to contemporary electioneering that is compatible with democracy when democracy is understood as a system of rough equality of influence in the democratic polity. That is, if the money to successfully pursue public office is in the millions for single constituencies or hundreds of millions for national campaigns, the process is almost inevitably corrupted by the pursuit of economic self-interest. It is a contest of wealth and influence, or the attraction thereof, much more than it is a contest of ideas and genuine popular enthusiasm. Democracy dominated by contemporary high-cost electronic media is inherently problematic. Campaign finance reform could, of course, lessen the risks. All contributions, direct or indirect, could be identified and capped at some reasonable maximum. Small contributions could be encouraged and subsidized by the tax system. Total spending in each campaign could be regulated and limited. The province of Manitoba, having recently endured some highly dubious electoral behavior, has proposed a flat ban on all political contributions from corporations and unions.

But, arguably, such steps are not enough (nor would they be easily achieved in a firmly entrenched system of money-and-media political dominance). A complementary approach to democratic reform would seek as well to find ways to restrain centralized, monolithic media power and influence both in electoral campaigns and in society. In the electoral process, the media could be legislatively required to provide equitably distributed amounts of airtime without charge (or airtime could be purchased in whole or in part from the public treasury). Paid media advertising could then, in such a context, be curtailed, limited, or eliminated. However, the influence of media and money is patently so pervasive in politics that nothing less than a fundamental transformation of the process is essential to reestablish meaningful democracy. Arguably, media and money are to democracy what radar-equipped trawler fishing is to fish stocks and whole-tree clearcut logging is to the health of forest ecosystems. It is another case of human technological ingenuity and professional specialization overwhelming the processes of natural, and in this case human, communities.

What is, in effect, needed to recreate democracy in a media age is the creation of a series of firewalls between the exuberant and highly inequitable economic system and the fragile and, by definition ideal, roughly equitable democratic polity. This need exists now in ways that it did not prior to the rise of the electronic media. An effective media presence is now politically essential and requires money in vast quantities—from highly paid public relations and media advisors to paid advertising time to achieving some personal access to those at the top of the media hierarchy. At present, corporations, unions, and the wealthy are the overwhelmingly predominant sources of that money for political actors. Without a media presence all political actors lack both credibility and visibility. All politics is increasingly viewed through the decidedly unneutral eye of the media, and this reality determines the kind of candidates who can and will participate. Media-mediated democracy is currently not a democracy of peers, or any semblance thereof.

Spaces where ideas can be shared need to be recreated and nurtured both outside the pervasive eye of the media and within the media (other than in books and on the Internet). The former would require turning off the television and engaging one's coworkers, friends, and neighbors (see the discussion of Putnam above) and may be as important as the latter. The latter (see the final section of this chapter) will not be easily achieved, but is essential to virtually everything else discussed in the balance of this book.

Diverse Voices: the Internet as a Multichannel Medium

The Internet is of course a different kind of medium—it is highly multicentered, though not without significant attempts at the guidance of participants and use patterns. It is participatory because an input presence (website) can still be obtained at relatively low cost, with reasonable-quality production affordable to nonwealthy individuals and small groups. The Internet is far and away the cheapest way to communicate on a worldwide basis for those who have access to a computer. It also has had something of an antispamming ethos that may (or may not) help to avoid commercial domination. There remains, however, a considerable danger that the Internet will evolve from being principally a multicentered information source to being principally yet another means of commercial advertising and/or goods acquisition. One wonders sometimes whether e-mail will ultimately succumb to spam.

The Internet may even morph into something more akin to interactive digital television where much technically sophisticated (and expensively produced) programming proceeds on a commercial basis. In effect, it could become much like commercial television, but with a difference—the commercials will be integrated into the programs and there will be no need to venture out to a shopping mall. One will just click a box on the screen using the remote in one's hand. Order what you see while you see it, with no need to pick up the phone and no need to continuously enter and reenter a credit or debit card number. The clothes or jewelry that the personality on the screen is wearing or the furnishings in the room can be yours; just point and click and your set-top box will transfer the precleared access to your bank account. The item will be delivered, in large cities likely that same day, or in the case of the precooked meal on screen, perhaps any time of the day and almost instantly. There will no longer be sales lost between advertisement and action; there will be no pause to reconsider or forget and no need to act beyond firing a beam at a box in the corner of the screen. Given the time taken up by increased hours of work and twenty or more hours per week of media absorption, there might be precious little time to shop. "Zap and get" is the answer to a question no one has asked.

Orwellian consumerist visions aside, the Internet has the potential to be a significant and positive step away from media unidimensionality. Almost any such step is worth taking even if it comes with unavoidable risks and limits. The Internet as it yet might evolve is arguably the only communications medium, other than books and small magazines, where the centralization of power and wealth could be challenged in any significant and consistent way. The Internet is an island of hope within the smoothly mindless and commercial, ideologically unidimensional, monolith of modern media. It seems at times almost too good to be true in terms of the extent to which there may now be wide access to a medium not utterly dominated in terms of content by the smooth voice of infotainment and large-scale capital.

The Internet is already a significant weapon against explicit political and religious repression outside the liberal-democratic nations. It may prove to be a significant new means of getting information and opinion both into and out of repressive authoritarian regimes. (Arguably, the globalization of trade and tourism may have the effect of opening up these regimes as well.) The Chinese attempt at an Internet firewall may not succeed in the long run, and many less sophisticated repressive regimes do not have a hope, at least for now, of blocking access to information to minorities wealthy enough to gain Internet access. However, one must remember that in a poor nation like Afghanistan it was possible to block all manner of media, and there remains the risk that just having Internet access in some jurisdictions might render one suspect. There is also little prospect of preventing undetected electronic eavesdropping in the long run if that is the intent of governments.

Commercial intrusiveness is, of course, hardly unknown on the present Internet and could increase in the face of limited user responsiveness to less intrusive options. Indeed, the medium opens up a number of worrisome possibilities in terms of new forms of intrusiveness. The large Internet retailer and portal AltaVista.com offered free Internet access in exchange for the completion of an optional commercial-information questionnaire by users and the acceptance of a tailored on-screen advertising presence (individualized and made more salable by the information gleaned from the questionnaire). Other providers have sought permission from users to have their search patterns monitored, thus producing information with commercial value. Other smaller-scale e-businesses pay e-mail users to include tagalong commercial messages with every personal message. The anti-spamming ethos of e-mail is systematically violated without penalty by pornographers, boiler-room investment purveyors, and others.

Many portals and sites, of course, carry and depend on (or hope someday to depend on) ongoing advertising to fund their information-organizing services. This presence on a portion of the screen is, however, parallel to advertising in newspapers and magazines and is less intrusive than, for example, radio or television advertising. But it cannot be avoided by active channel surfing. It is also far from certain that this relatively low level of invasiveness will be maintained in the long run. Some bank machines now run advertisements prior to the conduct of transactions, and it is only a small step, technically, to imposing this logic on the Internet or, for that matter, tailoring such ads to Internet user interests, or to the size of the bank customers' accounts. The Internet has the technical potential to intrude in much more complex ways through the automated use of information gleaned through electronic use and purchase trails. Such trails open the possibility of delivering selective ads in the Internet medium, or transferring the knowledge into more intrusive media such as direct mail or even telephone sales.

The Internet could also become a new means by which to invade noncommercial privacy, including political privacy. An indirect glimmer of the possibilities here can be seen in the recent sale or donation of newspaper subscriber lists (of a conservative national paper in Canada) to a particular (extreme right) candidate for the leadership of a particular (extreme right) political party. The lists were used for a mass telephone solicitation of new party memberships sympathetic to the candidate. What assurance is there that one's meanderings and searches on the Internet will not one day result in unsolicited political attentions of various kinds? Given the risks of ever more virulent computer viruses, it is difficult to argue that the electronic trails that make this possible are unnecessary. The speed at which the obscure creators of viruses are traced to particular computers at obscure points on the globe shows how easy it is to follow these trails.

Thus the Internet does provide a potential means by which repressive regimes could identify and locate dissenters since both senders and receivers of information always leave an electronic trail. Automated search engines may be set to watch for and monitor keywords and word combinations among the endless babble of voices and messages, but this is not the greatest risk to the diversity-of-voice potential of the Internet. A greater risk is that effective participatory access will never be affordable for anything approaching a global majority. This has been widely discussed as the "digital-access deficit."

Another risk is that the Internet will be modified or evolve in some way so that corporate voices can gain a more dominant position. One means by which this might be partially accomplished is through the selling and/or licensing of interconnections. Popular portal sites might guide or restrain interconnective access to ensure that the bulk of websites are effectively marginalized. Access to small sites will not be hindered, but easy access to large sites might be promoted in any number of creative ways. Being fully visible in cyberspace might require advertising one's electronic existence in other media. Cyberspace visibility to a considerable extent would be determined primarily by ability to pay.

Maintaining and expanding ease of access to the Internet's intellectual diversity poses an ongoing challenge. The danger is that the medium will go the way of television, which seemed at the outset to hold such promise as an educational tool and as a means of delivering to a mass audience diverse forms of cultural experience. An additional danger is that the presence of diverse voices on the Internet, however infrequently accessed, might be taken as an excuse to allow ever-narrower control of other media forms. The greatest risk is that the Internet will take on a commercial/entertainment character that undermines its potential as a source of information and opinion and as a means of communication. At this point, however, cyberspace is unlike any other media form, and there is even a hope that its diversity of viewpoint will spread to other media forms.

Within the commercial realm, IBM's endlessly repeated television advertisements notwithstanding, the Internet is not necessarily a boon to all small businesses—allowing everyone to operate effectively on a global scale. Charlene Li of Forrester Research, a Cambridge, Massachusetts, consulting firm, has noted: "With the cost of building a full-featured commerce site running at well over $1-million, few local merchants can create a commerce-friendly on-line store. Likewise, without a recognizable brand, local merchants have difficulty driving site traffic through advertising and portal deals." The conclusion drawn by Li was that the share of online sales in the United States held by small, local firms would decline between 1999 and 2003 from 9 percent of the total to about 6 percent of the total. The proportion of all sales that are online sales is, of course, projected to continue to rise especially for books, music, health and beauty products, consumer electronics, admission tickets of all kinds, and perhaps brand-name toys. Large widely advertised retailers can best take advantage of the strength of online sales—massive selection and a lower sales price achieved through lower costs for rent (a very small number of low-cost locations) and relatively automated order fulfillment.[41]

Globally, the advantage of the Internet may be even more disproportionate. Those in large, rich, and well-established firms and nations have an overwhelming advantage, as Schiller makes clear.[42] The Internet, of course, began in the United States and is far and away most developed there. It will not be easy for firms in other locations to catch up in terms of technical sophistication and content development. Selling globally on the Internet requires global brand recognition and that is not easily achieved over the Internet alone—it is achieved primarily through the power of television, film, and paid endorsements and to a lesser extent through the print media and other, but also expensive, means. A website only brings that part of the world to your door that knows where that door is and is willing to trust the assertions and products available. This is not necessarily a bad thing, but it suggests that the Internet is unlikely to turn the corporate world upside down as thoroughly as some have anticipated. Other media forms may remain the most important forms.

Within the realm of ideas, the balance of forces is significantly different. The Internet remains the only electronic media form where ideas can have an autonomous presence and can compete outside the direct control of large-scale commercial interests. It is also the only electronic medium where ideas have a degree of autonomy from commercial objectives (with the possible exception of public broadcasting, which has been under continuous political attack since the beginnings of electronic capitalism). On the Internet, citizens and firms, in the words of conservative policy analysts Thomas Courchene and Colin Telmer, can "access, send, and otherwise manipulate information in ways and in quantities that were undreamed of a few short years ago and in ways that governments of all stripes are powerless to prevent."[43] This is undeniably true, but one must be mindful that governments are not the only—or even the primary—institutions that have an interest in and the capacity to promote selective, and thereby limited, information exchange.

Many questions regarding the impact of the Internet remain. How important will the noncommercial functions of the Internet be in people's everyday lives? What proportion of the population will acquire effective ongoing access? (At present it is less than 1 percent of the global population.) Will the Internet be truly significant in the realms of ideas and politics? It clearly has the potential to bypass corporate-dominated media gatekeepers. It opens a discrete and effective channel for the socially ostracized, including dangerous voices such as pornographers and racists. But the Internet is also a helpful channel for less dangerous voices, such as those of greens, labor, or the left, which are also relatively powerless and invisible in the wider world of electronic media. There is, however, little likelihood that the Internet alone can stand against the array of corporate-owned, commercial media and the power of party finance under present structures and habits.

A Lament for the Cold War

Thus, where the Internet has potential as a step away from unidimensionality, the end of the cold war has (in some ways) been, despite the spectacular gain in intellectual freedom for millions, a step toward it. The moment in history when the cold war ended was, of course, a great triumphant leap for free thought. When the Berlin Wall suddenly fell I remember pulling my car over to the side of a highway in New York State and having a joyful cry. Marxism in power was an utterly false betrayal of all who imagined it to be a hope, but it was the only real competition the capitalist socioeconomic order has ever faced. Ironically, it turns out that capitalism, a socioeconomic system defined by, and obsessed with, competition, fares less well when, as a system, it is faced with none. Electronic capitalism, unchecked by ideological and organizational competition, has delivered (thus far) a remarkable (if uneven) expansion of productive capacity, but it has also delivered a frightening and ever-increasing concentration of both wealth and power. It succeeds in this in part because it is no longer checked by a rival system that made claims, however false, about equality and socioeconomic justice.

During the cold war claims regarding relative system performance had to be attended to, even when they were more rumor than reality, more false claim than demonstrated certainty. Those trapped within lives in poor nations, or poor lives within rich nations, were often impressed by the rapid economic growth achieved by the Soviet Union from the 1920s through the 1970s. Others, without that spur, simply hoped that some of the positive social policy achievements in socialist societies would spur parallel actions in the West. Heilbroner, for example, envisioned (in 1962) a future for the United States in the year 2000 that has not come to pass, perhaps in part because capitalism, contrary to the Marxist historical script, up and buried socialism. As Heilbroner put it, "If the present trend of technological advance is maintained (and there is every reason to believe that it will accelerate), this compression of labor time is certain to continue and very likely to increase. If Russia succeeds, as she has announced, in reducing her basic work week to 35 hours by 1965, we can be sure that the United States will reduce her own. By 1980—or at least by the year 2000—a work week of 30 hours, even of 20 hours, is by no means unimaginable."[44]

The cold war competition between systems, it turned out, cut both ways. Russia did not achieve the anticipated thirty-five-hour week—it was far too caught up in an arms race and an economic growth race (which it was by then losing far more badly than almost anyone knew). Moreover, its leadership was perpetually too little inclined to actually believe (and apply in practice) its own often-stated ideology regarding improving the lot of industrial workers. However, while innumerable harms were committed on both sides of the iron curtain in the name of competition with the other, there was also a positive side to the competition that has now been lost. Affordable (if ugly) housing, education, and health care were delivered widely in the Soviet Union even if consumer goods were not. At the same time, spurred by unions and a viable left (as well as prosperity), the welfare state in the West expanded for decades. During the days of functioning communist states the demands of Western labor unions were taken seriously, even in the United States—certainly more seriously than they are now. Political and corporate leaders were concerned that labor militancy and politicization might increase should gains not be made. Many citizens believed that society as a whole should and would continue to move toward greater equity. Much of that "system-competitive perspective" has now disappeared with the demise of the cold war.

So too, though to a lesser extent, has the negative side of cold war competition and rhetoric. It is now just a little more difficult to successfully argue for excessive military spending and arms production. The difference is, however, surprisingly small given that the remaining enemies of Western military might are trivial compared to the Warsaw Pact in its heyday. However, there were other negatives associated with cold war competition. In those times, exploitation of ordinary citizens was sometimes accelerated and justified in the West (and in the Soviet Union in spades) by the intense intersystemic rivalry. The health and safety (and lives) of uranium miners, for example, were sacrificed to the arms race, especially in the 1950s and 1960s. Also, the manifold opportunity costs of the cold war were at times spectacular. Money that might have been spent on education, childcare, or health was more urgently needed by the military, the CIA, or the KGB. Military "cost-plus" contracts stripped many U.S. civilian consumer industries of the best engineers and designers, accelerating the decline and relocation of several industries (such as electronics and steel). The Soviet Union never did develop quality consumer goods, and Russia and many other Eastern nations are paying the price for that imbalance today.

But, irony of ironies, some of the social negatives created by cold war logic are today repeated almost verbatim, justified in the name of a need to remain globally competitive in economic, rather than strategic, terms. The rhetoric is shockingly parallel. Intense global competition, the "need to remain competitive," justifies everything from lower industrial wages to eliminated or reduced social programs, from the impossibility of "extreme" and "excessive" environmental or other regulations to spectacular CEO salaries. So too did the cold war in its day (though then the spectacular CEO salaries gained a cold war rationale primarily only within defense industries). It is as if globalization arrived only just in time. The hands of well-meaning elites are again tied by another convenient foe, this time not an evil empire as much as a hundred desperate ones, each more willing and determined than the next to see its citizens work for less and to sacrifice its land, air, and water more completely. Or so it is claimed and widely believed.

Capitalism unchallenged in its fundamentals would appear to be capitalism unfettered. Why is this seemingly the case? The alternative to capitalism that was imagined to actually exist during the cold war turns out to have been even more of a lie than most had understood it to be. But the lie was also a dream and the dream was often positive and even noble. The decidedly non-Hollywood film *Il Postino* captured that noble side of the Marxist dream beautifully, as did the actual lives of actor Paul Robeson and others. Electronic capitalism's tragedy is that no widely articulated political vision of a broadly shared better future remains. All is cynicism and greed-as-virtue. Most governments now deny it is within their power, or even their mandate, to actively reduce inequality. The economy is almost universally presumed to operate according to inexorable laws (and/or global trade rules), and it is not mere governments to seek to alter such realities. All intervention, it is now suddenly presumed, will always do more harm than good. It is thus not altogether coincidental that the end of socialism (and left-right ideological contestation), and the return to rapidly growing inequality, have been virtually simultaneous.

Without some widely shared competing vision of existing society, at once both different and seemingly possible, the power of the powerful is unchallenged in some essential way. Economic elites now know that their power is no longer contested save perhaps by those who seek a not-very-different "third way" to selectively defend some existing social protections (the health-care system in Canada, full employment in the United States, some social programs in Europe). The political cycle of Western democratic politics has, in effect, been fundamentally altered. Where once progressive steps toward greater equity alternated with conservative consolidation wherein "advances" slowed but new state activities were largely accepted, the political cycle typical of electronic capitalism is very different. We now see waves of neoliberal dismantling of social programs and state activities followed rapidly by tax cuts, especially for investors, alternating with slower movement in the same direction (directed perhaps at the defenseless poor rather than at all but the rich). The core of this shift lies in the new power relations in a globalized economy—an economy with an increasingly central place for monopolized electronic media in everyday life. But the shift has clearly been reinforced by the failures of state socialism and the end of the cold war.

The challenge is to rethink the meaning of the end of the cold war. It is not the end of history. It is rather one source of a decline, perhaps a dangerous decline, of countervailing power, part of a loss of balance among sociopolitical forces in nations. Without a contestation between capitalism and socialism, one motivation for moderation among the powerful is lost, as is one source of energy among the poor. False hopes are at least hopes. The ideologies of the powerful now prevail with little public question (outside the world of books and "letters"). Within this new world, all nonsexual moral assertiveness has become suspect. Claims of any kind on behalf of the poor are perceived as economically (or practically) naive. The consumption of an ever-increasing proportion of the world's goods by a single nation is seen as an act of socioeconomic heroism, without which the global economy might easily collapse. It is almost nostalgic to imagine that such a trend might once have been called an acceleration of imperialist exploitation. We have come a long way in terms of perceptions and perspectives in but a decade. The decline of ideologically grounded debate is a relief, but it has a price. How well will democratic institutions stand up in a world where there is no systematic and consistent challenge to the power of wealth, either intellectually or organizationally?

As social science (see below) and as political practice Marxism was a failure; as moral argument it was, and should remain, important to the way the world is understood. At present too few people understand that the cold war distorted *both* views of the appropriate relationship between market values and sociopolitical values. We understand now the dangers of attempting to overwhelm the former with the latter, but analysis does not fully escape cold war errors until it is understood more fully and widely that successfully functioning markets do not require the exclusion of humanistic values from socioeconomic decision making. On the contrary, long-term market success may depend on their imposition in defiance of the inclinations of short-term profit-takers. Nor will market forces alone ever rectify the moral shortfall, the unidimensionality of economism, or the abdication of democratic politics in the face of global economic competition.

A Slow Grinding of Hard Boards: Social Science and Unidimensionality

It is obvious enough now that within media-saturated electronic capitalism too few citizens can get "outside the box" to see the obvious: that a global race to the bottom cannot be won even in its own terms. Only within economism as an all-pervasive perspective is it not obvious that the everyday lives of many people are less positive than they might be. Any glimmer of multidimensionality in perspective would suggest that ever greater concentrations of wealth will lead to market excesses related to capital glut (overvalued corporate shares, investment bubbles, and the like) and to social failures of all kinds. Moreover, outside an economistic perspective, it is clear that ever-lower relative costs for raw materials will lead to sustainability failures and unnecessarily high levels of environmental damage. As improbable as it may seem, the path out of this dilemma lies in part in, of all places, academia and in particular in the social sciences.

This will likely seem an outrageous proposition. But there are encouraging signs that the social sciences are moving away from what C. Wright

Mills once termed the twin dangers of abstracted empiricism and grand theory.[45] Political economy, particularly international political economy (IPE) and some contemporary sociology, have largely escaped the narrower presuppositions of cold war–style Marxism without drifting into ahistorical, atheoretical empiricism. In addition, the rise of environmentalism as a social movement has encouraged new academic subdisciplines, from environmental ethics to environmental history, environmental sociology, environmental politics, and environmental economics. Findings in these subdisciplines suggest that economic growth should not be the sole, or even necessarily the highest, objective on the policy agenda. Also promising in this regard have been recent analyses of the social determinants of health and the importance and sources of social cohesion and community.

Many of these assessments have increasingly been drawn together into a three-dimensional model of societal performance encompassing measures of economic, social, and environmental well-being. This model, which will be presented in chapters 4 and 5, could pose a serious intellectual challenge to economism and thereby contribute to the resolution of democracy's dilemma. The need is to find ways to make these perspectives more visible within nonscholarly channels of communication, including the public school system as well as the media. However, this prospect may be frustrated by a growing intrusion of corporations into education and a growing emphasis on education as training rather than as the development of the capacity for intelligently critical citizenship. Schiller effectively documents this intrusion.

In the realm of higher education Schiller notes there were 1,200 "so-called *corporate universities* by 1998," with the largest, Motorola University, having taught some 100,000 students by that point including many who were not Motorola employees.[46] In Schiller's view corporate-based higher education in the United States approaches university-based higher education in scale. It is closely linked to the continual reengineering that is the norm in the new economy. More than this, Schiller documents a corporatization of the university system—from a radical increase in the hierarchical structure of salaries (including sharply increased part-time, low-paid instruction) to increased corporate domination of research funding. And most important perhaps, "At every level, from pre-school and remedial to doctoral and crafts-based education, and in an endless variety of genres and formats, both old and new, networked education provision furnished alluring prospective entry points for profit-making companies."[47]

Needless to say, most of the educational materials of corporate origin reflect corporate interests and a corporate viewpoint. Electrical utilities prepare materials regarding nuclear power and food companies present their view of nutrition. Underfunded schools are grateful to get math lessons that contain a bit of a corporate twist and a few product placements. But the greater concern is what is not presented as slickly, if at all—critical interpretations of history and patterns of governance, noncorporate environmental studies, or consumer education with a cutting edge that questions the need for a shopping-oriented, advertising-dominated existence. It is not clear that citizens will learn in large numbers to think three dimensionally and seek balanced governance unless we can first limit the intrusion of a corporate (privately self-interested) perspective into the public educational system and bring a greater presence of a critical and reflective intelligence into media.

Multiplying Media Voices and Creating Islands of Silence

Gaining a voice or a hearing for any complex and critical perspective in the commercially driven media is not, of course, an easy matter. Perhaps the only greater risk to effective democracy than the present structuring and entertainment-only posture of today's media would be direct governmental operation of an overwhelmingly dominant share of society's communications channels. The defense of democracy in the realm of media requires effective opportunities to hear many more voices, and especially to hear more distinctive (noncommercial, non-market-share maximizing) voices. Governments, as yet, have had little difficulty being heard. What are not often heard (or heard of)—especially on the electronic media—are the variety of voices that are neither commercial or governmental, nor professional media "personalities," nor somehow bizarre, tasteless, or violent. It might make an interesting First Amendment constitutional case in the United States to argue that freedom of the press may now imply some right to provide media input to *bona fide* citizen organizations.

Evolving technology (especially the Internet) may contribute to the opening of effective channels for diverse and reflective viewpoints, especially if a defense of Internet voice diversity is vigilantly maintained. The greater challenge is to diversify the voices heard in other media forms. Both Internet-oriented and non-Internet-oriented initiatives should be seen as necessary to achieving meaningful, effective, participatory democracy in electronic capitalism. These initiatives, along with efforts regarding campaign finance reform, are thus essential to the resolution of democracy's dilemma at both the national and global levels. They will be among the threads of resolution that will be drawn together in the concluding chapter.

Structural changes to diversify media participation could be initiated through government or other institutions (foundations, universities, environmental organizations, churches, social agencies, trade unions, or research institutes). In broad terms the changes needed might take two forms: the recognition of a regulated, but broad, right of access to public airwaves or to any and all other means of media-based information delivery, and the recognition of a limited human right to silence as well as to personal, noncommercial space. In brief, the right of participatory access should be more often open to noncommercial interests and individuals should have the right to establish some autonomy from commercial messages and images.

Such changes may sound innocent, but they are potentially far reaching and would be strongly resisted by those who have a virtual monopoly over the major means of communication in contemporary society. The right of access could, for example, include the right to purchase, at reasonable cost, rebuttal time to respond to commercial messages. But what of the prospect for a wider, noncorporate, noncommercial culture?[48] Cutting CDs, creating websites, and photocopying 'zines are now widely affordable, but reaching a sizable audience is endlessly challenging. For every *Blair Witch Project* overnight cultural success, there are thousands of 'zinesters and musicians working in fast food outlets. Pointedly, as well, those who get the chance to actually earn a living at culture production may curse frequently, love wild animals, or express hatred for the police, but only rarely do they openly doubt the culture of wealth concentration and boundless mass consumption. Silence on these points is not unrelated to the prospects for sudden media opportunities.

A right to silence, should it ever arise as a political/cultural demand, would obviously be a limited right. But even raising the possibility to the level of public discussion would be a step forward. In such a discussion it would become clear that such a right need not exist when, for example, as in print media, one has the option of virtually unconsciously ignoring all commercial communications (or equally easily choosing to look at or for them). One also has the option of avoiding most electronic media sources and that counts for something by way of an opportunity for silence, but this comes at a considerable cost in terms of access to information. Some are prepared to pay that cost, but why must that cost be paid? Why are all media commercial media?

One also has the option, given the mute button, the channel changer, the off switch, and now the personal video recorder (PVR), of selectively silencing commercials (that is, there are now easy options to actually avoid—as distinct from just mentally tuning out or pretending not to hear). But this is still harder to do, even with the technological aids, than it is to ignore advertising in print media. Nonetheless it is arguable that, on an immediate level, one still has a limited right to silence. The introduction of simulated (advertisement-carrying) audiences in televised sporting and other events may, however, violate the right—as may the wearing of logos by athletes and product placements in programs and films. There is perhaps sufficient hostility to commercial intrusions in our lives to provoke a debate on such issues, but presumably a majority would remain prepared to tolerate many intrusions of these kinds into their mental space.

However, what might not survive a wide public debate are at least four other, more intrusive, impositions. These are streetscape advertising clutter that puts driver and pedestrian safety at risk; the absence of an enforceable right to refuse junk mail; the requirement that essentially public facilities incorporate spaces that feature an absence of electronic media; and rendering illegal the use of telephones, fax machines, and the Internet (including e-mail) for unsolicited promotions.

The first is the most obvious and goes without saying, but it is here because a case could be made that this is not sufficiently enforced, for example, on many commercial strips. Regarding the second item, deliverers of advertising flyers could, for example, be licensed municipally with said licenses revoked should holders fail to heed homeowner requests to cease and desist delivery. Such deliveries are indeed generally both a waste of resources and an invitation to crime (they "advertise" that one is not home). The post office, as a publicly protected and authorized institution, should also comply. As well, removing one's name from mailing lists should be very easy and highly effective. Finally, airports, for example, should not allow televisions to dominate waiting areas, and telephones should flatly not be used for marketing of services. Telephones, public and private, are essential to public safety and convenience—for any number of reasons they often must be answered and the act of answering thereby lacks the voluntary character of turning on commercial radio or television.

These possibilities would be but minor impositions upon commercial interests. The larger questions are associated with redefining a reasonable right of access to participation in the content of communications media. That is, how might democratic societies more effectively diversify the range of voices heard on the airwaves? How can society deepen and render more reflexive the ideas and perspectives that are widely heard and discussed? Needless to say, to be of value voice-diversification initiatives—whatever the auspices—must involve something more than just taxpayer-funded (or even listener-funded) outlets for chronically and congenitally boring programming. There is no communication without an audience. That said, I hasten to add that the tradition of public broadcasting, as it exists virtually everywhere, is a crucial voice, essential within most societies to both the viability of democracy and the flourishing of the arts. But an effective democratic society in a global age requires additional noncommercial voices. In this regard there are a few potentially useful initiatives that might be fostered.

Low-capitalization, low-reach radio might be encouraged by existing regulatory agencies. These could allow for commercial-free community or neighborhood (predominantly voluntary) radio, especially perhaps in ethnically and culturally distinctive areas. Public-access blocks of time could also be made available on commercial stations as a condition of licensing. Or community-access channels provided by cable companies could be strengthened in several ways (it is not clear, for example, why more environmental and community organizations do not prepare high-production-value programming for such outlets).

More important, there could even in principle be a legal right to rebut commercial messages (on a paid basis and not necessarily at the same time that the paid messages are broadcast). Commercial channels might be required to allow an hour a week of rebuttal broadcasts (even if shown at 3:00 A.M.—if they are good enough they would be taped and replayed). Is there not a potential here for a wonderful new art form—just as commercials themselves are, at their best, also arguably an art form? Clearly there would be only limited funding available for rebuttal ads, but if any such opportunity did exist they would provide a great opportunity for retired media professionals to clear their consciences. This may all seem fanciful, but the most harmful products and practices could imaginably generate sufficient contributions to air rebuttals from, for example, health or environmental organizations. The absence of a right to respond or to be visible is at the root of both rampant graffiti and the culture-jamming practices of San Francisco's Billboard Liberation Front.

The particular initiatives noted here are merely suggestive. It is the overall change in perspective that they imply that is important. In a media-dominated age the quality of democracy itself depends on equitable access to the means of social communication and on the diversity of perspectives that find a place in the media. Also important is the extent to which everyday citizens can detach themselves from the hold of monolithic and systematically self-interested media. Democracy's dilemma must, as will be argued below, be resolved at all political levels from the local to the global. It will not be resolved, then, without a wide capacity to understand local (community) histories, to apprehend long-term global sociopolitical and environmental trends, and to see beyond a world infused by commercialism and economism. Today's electronic media offer little on any of these counts, and thus media reform and greater media and communications diversity will be essential to the resolution of democracy's dilemma.

4

Toward a Three-Bottom-Line Perspective

The economic bottom line is measured and communicated second by second to the penny or peso. In the media-saturated locations of electronic capitalism it would be a challenge to avoid learning in timely fashion how world markets are performing. Citizens in Iowa see the changes in the Hang Seng index and, with any effort, citizens in Hong Kong could learn of each ongoing alteration in corn and soybean futures. Moreover, if the national GDP has risen by 3 or more percent, most citizens have a sense that the economy is doing well even if they themselves are less well off. People on the other side of the planet are quickly aware that things are not going well economically in Russia or Indonesia, even though they may know little else about life in these nations. Economic and financial performance is measured systematically and comprehensively and is communicated instantaneously and almost universally. It is an unquestioned commonplace that the "bottom line" for business is somehow important to all despite the fact that the overwhelming majority of the world's citizens own no part of the global economy and probably never will.

Little wonder, then, that it is widely assumed that market performance and economic output are the most important measures of societal wellbeing. Indeed they may be the only measures with which most people are familiar—save perhaps for unemployment, inflation, and crime rates. Few think about other measures of societal performance and few would seriously entertain the notion that any society could be sufficiently wealthy that it might reasonably be content to remain that wealthy in the future. A conscious political decision to accept restrained economic growth in the wealthiest nations in order to create more rapid growth in poorer nations would be seen as outrageous, as well as impossible. The environmentalists of the 1970s and since who have argued for "steady-state economies" have been seen as naive, pernicious neo-Malthusians by most labor and business leaders, political figures, economists, and everyday citizens. Moreover, for most people, even most policy analysts, there is no real "connect" between environmental problems and either economic or social policy. Further, few link environmental problems and personal consumption habits, and even environmentally conscious citizens rarely go beyond driving a fuel-efficient car in this regard. In brief, the economic bottom line tends to overwhelm other possible priorities.

Our knowledge of economic factors is almost always superior to our knowledge of social and environmental factors whether we are thinking about public policy or about everyday life. Things economic are, on a basic level, seemingly more understandable—not the world of finance, arbitrage, inflation, deflation, commodity markets, and interest-rate setting, but whether prices are up or down, whether they seem fair compared to what they are elsewhere, and whether the economy is generally doing badly or well. Knowing what labor conditions prevail where one's shirt or blouse was made or what relative environmental impacts are embedded in alternative everyday decisions (such as which apartment to rent or foods to eat) is another matter. Such interrelated matters can be extremely complicated, and even if there is an organization that claims to know, the producers of the goods will disagree vehemently with such assessments. Moreover, the media report only rarely the most urgent and oversimplified troubling issues regarding products. The net result of all of these factors is economism—a view of the world in which the economic dimensions of both public policy and personal decision making systematically prevail over social and environmental considerations.

Radio and television clearly cannot deal with all of the complexities of most issues. They could not even if they were willing to do so, and they are not. Sponsors and potential sponsors would (and do) object to such coverage in all but the most extreme circumstances (such as the recent concern regarding tire safety). Moreover, almost no one would watch programming oriented to social and environmental analysis even if it were broadcast; it would not be entertaining. Nonetheless, there is a growing capacity within the social sciences to evaluate policies, outcomes, industries, and products three-dimensionally. It is my view that the further development and wider exposure of such a perspective could significantly alter the present trajectory of electronic capitalism. There is a growing literature written from within this perspective; the question is, can a three-dimensional view of society gain currency as an alternative to economism? If so, the application of such a perspective within public policy research and actual public policy could make global electronic capitalism better than it might have been—socially, environmentally, and perhaps even economically—especially in the longer term.

Delinking and Dematerialization

Economism narrows our understanding of a world that is better understood in terms of three bottom lines: economic, social, and environmental.[1] Central to understanding the three bottom lines is an appreciation that there is more than one kind of efficiency and more than one kind of productivity. When one's perspective shifts in this way, interesting questions arise. How much economic output is produced by any particular product, firm, economic sector, or political jurisdiction per unit of pollution? Or, how much environmental damage arises with various product mixes and how much, for example, per ton of steel? In the broadest terms, how much GDP is achieved per unit of energy and material throughput (knowing that rising throughput usually results in some increment of pollution and some diminution of nonhuman habitat)? In terms of social equity, how much human health is "produced" per unit of GDP by various societies (or even how much health per dollar of health care expenditure)? Or, what level of societal quality is possible, and by what means can it be obtained (as measured by some index that combines literacy, health, equity, the relative absence of crime, a low incidence of homelessness, and other factors) both absolutely and per dollar of GDP per capita? Are, in fact, wealthier societies better societies? When are they, and when are they not?

Perhaps the clearest exposition of this way of thinking appears in "Reconciling Ecological, Economic and Social Imperatives: A New Conceptual Framework" by John Robinson and Jon Tinker who state: "there is little consensus among experts in each discipline on how the ecological, economic and social systems are related to one another."[2] There is, however, a growing agreement that ways should be found to assess societal outcomes simultaneously in terms of all three dimensions. Sustainable-development advocates speak of the integration of economy and environment (but also consistently include social well-being in their assessments). Where Elkington speaks of three bottom lines, Robinson and Tinker consider environment, economy, and society to be best thought of as three parallel "prime" systems: "We suggest that it is more fruitful to think in terms of three interacting, interconnected and overlapping 'prime systems': *the biosphere* or ecological system; *the economy,* the market or economic system; and *human society,* the human social system. This third prime system includes the political system (governance), the social system (family, communities, and so on), and cultures."[3]

Each "system" is understood to have its own value-laden imperative, and sustainable development is seen as an attempt to reconcile the three distinct imperatives. Again in the words of Robinson and Tinker, "*The ecological imperative* is to remain within planetary biophysical carrying capacity. *The economic imperative* is to ensure and maintain adequate material standards of living for all people. *The social imperative* is to provide social structures, including systems of governance, that effectively propagate and sustain the values that people wish to live by."[4] My hesitation regarding this division is that the economic system as it actually functions has no such imperative; the imperative ascribed is in fact part and parcel of a sociopolitical imperative that might (or might not) gain wide public support when and where such support actually affects economic outcomes. The economic imperative in a capitalist system is clearly the maximization of total economic output and the maximization of yield to the owners of capital (goals sometimes compatible with each other, but less often compatible with, and possibly contrary to, the goal ascribed by Robinson and Tinker).

Robinson and Tinker then argue, rightly, that the three imperatives are interconnected though each is independently important. Ignoring any of the imperatives is unacceptable; each of the three "societal bottom lines" is essential to human well-being. However, the attainment of "adequate material standards of living for all people" implies a significant political conflict with the owner-managers of the global economic system and, given the possibility of ecological and resource limits, there may even be three-way bottom-line conflicts. It is perhaps better to have these complex tensions out in the open than to simply assume, as so many do, the existence of a beneficent economic system. Many neoliberals will argue that only what seems to be greed begets dynamic growth and only dynamic growth will lead, eventually, to adequate minimum standards. Whether or not that is the case is a matter that is sufficiently empirical in character: the interrelationship among the ecological, economic (in terms of growth), and social (in terms of broad human well-being) should be demonstrable. Moreover, there is no reason to think that a balanced outcome could not be achieved were it to be consciously and collectively attempted.

Thus Robinson and Tinker's principal policy objectives are what is most important here. They advocate "uncoupling economic growth from environmental impact." That is, they seek ways societies can achieve more economy per unit of environmental damage, or per unit of energy and virgin raw materials used. In their words, "Industrialized countries need to 'dematerialize' the economy by uncoupling human well-being from the throughput of matter and energy in our society." Such a process could be called ecoefficiency. They also note that "de-materialization of the economy is the basic premise of 'industrial ecology.'"[5] In this development of a conceptual framework Robinson and Tinker cite the work of Friedrich Schmidt-Bleek and others, which is discussed below and in the following chapter. They call for the development of a "policy wedge" to accelerate, through time, the separation of goods and services consumption from energy and materials throughputs. Such a wedge might involve, for example, additional increments of energy taxation (and presumably corresponding decreases in the taxation of, for instance, income or property).

One definition of dematerialization is implicit in a "simple test" of dematerialization developed by Carley and Spapens, who suggest that analysts ask this question regarding economic activities: "Can this product or service be acquired and used by seven to ten billion people without causing environmental damage to the planet or social damage to its people?" This approach may, however, confound social and environmental values when a clearer understanding is likely to result by keeping the three realms analytically separate. Only in this way can we anticipate and appreciate the many and complex trade-offs involved. Carley and Spapens do appreciate this as regards the economic realm in relation to their concept of environmental space (discussed below) and observe that "in terms of dematerialized growth, it is important to note that the term growth refers not to levels of production or consumption, but only to growth in monetary flows. This reinforces an underlying premise of environmental space: if materials consumption can be brought within sustainable limits, this imposes no particular limitation to economic growth per se. In this tightly defined, ecologically sound concept, economic growth can be sustainable."[6]

This is a crucial distinction. Without this clarification there would be little prospect for the timely achievement of even an approximation of sustainability in electronic capitalism. In addition, given the likely array of resource constraints in the future (including especially total energy throughput and total biomass production), without the increased uncoupling of economic output from materials and energy use, the prospects of the less advantaged of the world would surely be hopelessly bleak. Without radical decoupling and continuing growth, only the most optimistic would foresee the poor holding their own economically, especially in relative terms. Not only are they more likely to gain relative ground within an expanding economy, but even if they do not they might slowly gain ground in absolute terms. It is even possible, though not likely, as we will see, that the poor will gain slowly in the literally material aspects of economic life (more calories of food per day for example)—while, in contrast, the wealthy will learn to "dematerialize" their wealth. The most hopeful aspect of this is, however, that there would appear to be an inherent drive within industrialization in general and electronic capitalism in particular toward a less material- and energy-intensive economy—a drive that could be accelerated without necessarily provoking a significant overall economic growth penalty.

Robinson and Tinker also envision a second policy wedge that they somewhat ominously call "resocialization." *Resocialization* is a term that may conjure visions of a domineering, if not totalitarian, ethos. Robinson and Tinker's resocialization does indeed seek ways human well-being might be uncoupled from the consumption of goods and services. This, needless to say, is the more controversial of the two policy wedges—despite the fact that it is in keeping with the moral teaching of most of the world's religions, as noted above. It is seemingly thus far well outside the moral and political bounds of electronic capitalism. In stark contrast, some environmentalists (though not Robinson and Tinker) have indeed been explicit and altogether humorless, in expressing their doubts regarding any number of everyday choices and preferences—from too many children to too many cars, from too much junk food to too many golf courses (which might better be used, one conjectures, to grow organic oats). The seemingly irreconcilable nature of this clash notwithstanding, there is more potential for common ground than meets the eye (as we will see in the later chapters of this book).

Robinson and Tinker, and many others in recent years, prefer to come at this "second decoupling" from a more positive direction, emphasizing work-time reductions. They speak of "a shift to an economy characterized by lower participation in the formal economy (for example, a shorter average work week) and greater leisure and participation in the informal economy (community service of various kinds, childcare, coaching and managing recreational sports, and so on). This would represent a decision on the part of individuals to take part of their 'income' in the form of increased leisure and unpaid activities."[7] This is one basis for partial resolution of the tension between environmentalism and electronic capitalism. Carley and Spapens's notion of "sufficiency" is another. It is not impossible that many of us might indeed be happier with less by way of material comforts—walking to activities more often, eating less, having a somewhat smaller residence to maintain—and, in general, working less and playing more.

In much the same spirit, John Gray observed that GDP growth has been separated from growth in well-being by globalization and laissez-faire. By this he meant that growth in GDP was proceeding apace while well-being advanced not at all. The objective of Robinson and Tinker's second policy wedge is to reverse such a drift. Delinking growth and well-being aims to advance community and individual well-being without necessarily requiring (nor rejecting out of hand) rapid economic growth. In other words, the objective is to get more social well-being and less environmental damage per dollar of GDP.

In effect, the economy is asked to serve people more efficiently and productively—delivering more comfort to more people per unit of GDP, getting us more well-being per unit of GDP. Electronic capitalism already does this in many ways—automation and the race to the bottom do deliver goods at lower cost to those still earning enough money to buy them. But are goods equal to well-being? Clearly there is not a one-to-one relationship—lower environmental standards can mean higher cancer rates and cancer treatment is part of GDP growth, as are the calories consumed in excess of what is good for our health and as are books purchased that might have been borrowed from the public library had its funding not been cut.

Make no mistake; this is tricky moral territory. Are not individuals, one can hear an intelligent neoliberal voice asking, always the best judges of what they wish to do with *their* money? Before confronting that concern directly, there are two indirect approaches worth considering: one can point to situations where such choices are precluded by public policy or corporate decisions, and one can reflect on the notion of "their money." Regarding the first approach, at the most obvious level public transit simply does not exist between many suburban communities in North America—one's choices are to drive a car, to traverse an extra distance by traveling into and back out of a big city, or to stay home. Or, as another example, in many North American locations, one cannot buy beverages in refillable containers regardless of what one is willing to pay. To take still another example, for those who want to just slow down, it is the case that many employers will not look favorably on a résumé containing gaps. Even auto insurance rates are usually sharply increased for anyone who might opt for a year or two without a car.

Regarding the current view that "our" income is always and wholly "our" money that government "takes" from us (as if government were some alien entity that hoarded or consumed in some personal way whatever it took in), there are many possible replies. One is a radical approach whereby income taxes are replaced with energy and materials-extraction taxes. The future (replacement and other) costs that energy use as well as materials use implicitly and explicitly impose on society at the same time that they supply benefits are thereby recognized within the tax. Income is not taxed. Another way to see this matter, currently out of fashion, is a wider recognition that "we" humans would only rarely, if ever, survive as autonomous entities. Viable communities and societies are accordingly almost always well worth the cost. Most of the money is thereby rightly society's money, and we are fortunate to personally decide how to expend some small share and to collectively participate in decisions regarding the proportion that is in public hands.

Habit is also a significant determinant of consumer choice. Adopting more socially and environmentally efficient habits requires inducement. People live in sprawling suburbs in part because they grew up in them. We work too much because we get restless when we do not. Thus Robinson and Tinker's notion of resocialization, while seemingly reminiscent of Marxist "false consciousness," could also involve mild-mannered approaches, more akin to "just try one bite of spinach and then you can have your dessert" than to Maoist-style reeducation. Resocialization is really the seeking of a middle ground between "economic growth at all costs" and "ecological protection though asceticism." In this one is reminded that some of our environmentally most doubtful practices are still heavily subsidized by tax dollars. Moreover, we are painfully lacking in what might be called "opportunity structures"—socially created opportunities to easily opt, now and then, for what is good for us. The goal is to imagine and articulate policies that, while continuing to exclude environmentally dangerous behaviors, concentrate especially on pricing doubtful behaviors fully and avoiding the preclusion of socially and environmentally better options.

One particularly interesting aspect of this exercise is the extent to which it is difficult to examine each of the three realms independently. This challenge holds even when one sees and accepts that each of the three bottom lines is crucial to human well-being, that economic life is not somehow of a higher order of importance. This economistic presumption, interestingly, is as prominent in the writings of Karl Marx and other socialists as in today's media-saturated world. The most interesting questions arise, however, only when we keep the realms analytically distinct and direct inquiries to the interconnections between any two realms, or all three. Only then do we begin to fully appreciate the several possible meanings of efficiency and productivity. Only then do we expand, recalibrate, and enrich the qualitative and quantitative understanding of global society. A three-bottom-line perspective is essential to the democratic development of global-scale policies that in turn allow electronic capitalism to become the positive development in human history it has the potential to be.

Thus, before we can simultaneously balance the three bottom lines in this spirit, we much consider each separately and then together, two at a time, within each of the three possible pairs. Otherwise we are trying to juggle before we can catch.

The Economic Bottom Line in Electronic Capitalism

Many contemporary critics have concluded on various grounds that global-scale capitalism is highly unstable economically. Rifkin concluded that employment levels (in the United States) could not be sustained in an economy that was simultaneously automating and globalizing. He was wrong. Wage cuts, tax decreases, adaptability, and downsizing thrust the United States back into a "global leader" role, and near to full employment has been the result. While new employment opportunities worldwide may not keep pace with labor-efficiency gains through automation and delayering, many wealthy nations can probably have low unemployment simultaneously. The greater economic risks may arise from outside a narrowly defined economic realm—for example, within an excessive concentration of wealth that undermines global purchasing power, or within a series of resource failures brought on by a follower-nation race to the bottom in terms of environmental protection. But let us look at strictly economic factors first.

Martin and Schumann saw capital flight, currency speculation, and tax avoidance as potentially destabilizing of the developing global economic order. The verdict is not in on that, though clearly currency speculation was not irrelevant to the havoc wreaked in several Southeast Asian and Latin American countries in the late 1990s, and capital flight has often been a significant element in Latin America's and Russia's economic troubles. Tax avoidance and capital flight have also significantly undermined social programs and basic governmental services in many other nations. It must be noted, however, that the worst excesses could, in each of these cases, be checked in any number of ways. The problems are not inherent in trade and economic interconnectivity or even rapid financial flows so much as in the excessive political power of capital and the declining authority and autonomy of government.

The governments of poorer nations frequently lack both the political will and the capacity to check capital flight. In wealthy nations media-based power lessens (by a silence associated with a corporate preference for deregulation and reduced taxation) the political will to deal with tax avoidance and currency speculation. It is presumed in corporate and financial circles that such speculation and offshore tax avoidance are not sufficient in and of themselves to destabilize the system as a whole, and that judgment may be correct. There have, however, been a number of incidents that give one pause—most notably Enron, Worldcom, Barings Bank, the government of Orange County, California, the doings in several Japanese financial firms, and the massive hedge-fund bailout by the U.S. Federal Reserve following the Asian currency crises of 1998.

Reducing the vulnerability of the global financial system would require a will to firmly enforce corporate governance and tax rules on a global scale and perhaps as well some form of speculation-restraining tax such as the Tobin tax on currency exchange. The problem lies initially with the massive benefits that redound to those (often-small) nations that exist on their willingness to aid in the avoidance of such enforcement, but more importantly with the present unwillingness of other key nations to simply exclude the possibility of financial flows through such portals.[8]

As noted in chapter 1, Greider's fears center on an economic crisis rooted in excess productive capacity. He documents a global-scale crisis of excess capacity in the production of steel, automobiles, aircraft, and chemicals. He identifies many of the ways supply capabilities tend to outstrip demand capabilities. He opines that "citizens are expected to get smarter, work harder, and cheer for the home team. The trouble is, the more everyone behaves in this virtuous manner, the more likely the underlying supply problem will be compounded for the system as a whole."[9] The United States in his view cannot forever be the ultimate consumer of the world's goods; he argues that the nation's economic resilience is weakening as its debt obligations accumulate and that sooner or later, like any other kind of debtor, the United States will be unable to afford its role as buyer of last resort. He also spoke (in 1997) of an ongoing decline of the U.S. dollar relative to other currencies. He too was, thus far, generally wrong with regard to the performance of globalized capitalism in the economic realm.

While the 1998 economic crisis in Asia appears to have resulted in part from concerns like capital flight, currency speculation, and perhaps, once it had occurred, excess capacity (insufficient global buying power), it must be remembered that every capital outflow from one nation is a capital inflow to another. Speculative capital that shifted out of many countries shifted into the United States and Europe. Moreover, the price of goods coming into North America fell (as did the price of commodities flowing from North America to Asia and elsewhere), resulting in damage to the economies of British Columbia and Iowa, for example. But massive stock market gains in the United States led, in combination with lower prices, to an even greater capacity to import goods. Desperation returned as a social norm in Indonesia, but the U.S. balance-of-trade payments were offset by capital inflows from a more nervous world. The result was that the economic instabilities of electronic capitalism have not thus far been global, as had been so widely feared. The outcome has been grossly inequitable, but rising global economic integration has not led to global-scale economic instability. On the contrary, integration appears to help curb inflation, and the coordination of central bank responses appears to stabilize the economies of wealthier nations and the global system as a whole.

Gray (writing in 1998) saw the Southeast Asian crisis as perhaps the beginning of the demise of a global free market that, in his view, was destined to fail in any case. On the final page of his otherwise fine book he asserted: "History does not support the hope that global *laissez-faire* can easily be reformed. It took the disaster of the Great Depression and the experience of the Second World War to shake the hold of an earlier version of free market orthodoxies on western governments. We cannot expect feasible alternatives to global *laissez-faire* to emerge until there has been an economic crisis more far-reaching than we have experienced thus far. In all probability the Asian depression will spread throughout much of the world before the economic philosophy that supports the global free market is finally abandoned."[10] The worst fear of a thoughtful critic has again apparently turned out to be, at least for now, wrong. It is extremely important in this case to understand why the global economy as a whole has been so resilient. That is, did we just get lucky and the real economic collapse is just around the corner?

Economic interconnectivity operates much like an expanded electrical grid. The larger system is less frequently vulnerable to long-term local failures because one or more subsystems can lean on others in the short term to restabilize, and the temporary losses of smaller components are easily absorbed or compensated for within the larger integrated network. However, a larger vulnerability is introduced through the very fact of system integration—the whole system, which previously did not exist as a system, can be brought down by the simultaneous failure of several subsystems (or perhaps by the failure of a single very large subsystem, e.g., the United States or Europe). Just as the noted blackout of the power grid of much of the East Coast of North America in the 1960s was triggered by a series of simultaneous coincidences and weaknesses, such an outcome in economic terms is possible on a global scale. But enduring economic difficulties of strictly economic origin are arguably made less, rather than more, likely by the fact of interconnectedness.

It must also be noted, however, that the laissez-faire character of early industrial society, Heilbroner's apologia for nineteenth-century Britain's poverty levels notwithstanding, imposed an undue share of costs on, and delivered an insufficient share of benefits to, poor individuals, communities, families, and classes. Over the longer span of history distributional failures have regularly triggered and accelerated economic (and then social and political) disruptions. Global laissez-faire probably imposes net costs on both poorer nations and poorer groups in rich nations. Clearly the process of selecting economic winners and losers is increasingly skewed and unfair. But the short-term result may not be greater economic instability on a global scale. Perhaps the greater danger is economic growth that imposes tragic environmental burdens without delivering either economic or social well-being to more than a minority of the human population. When only the economic bottom line is valued, social critics feel compelled to envision significant failures in those terms. Gray, and others, both hope for and fear the outcomes they anticipate. Electronic capitalism seems so immune to noneconomic considerations that critics are forced to find a basis for plausible short-term failures within the economic realm.

An "Asian depression" did not ensue as Gray had expected, nor has the globalized economy succumbed to several other potential fault lines. One is left with a sense that electronic capitalism is more economically resilient than its critics would have it. But is electronic capitalism more prone to economic crises in the long term than it need be? It is impossible, of course, to answer that question with certainty, but it is difficult to imagine why the global system could not, for example, do more by way of debt forgiveness and more by way of actively encouraging states to restrain the ease of currency flight. One can also say that the horrors attendant on failure within a highly integrated global system certainly justify significant sacrifices in the name of prudence.

The reminder by Gray of the parallels between the 1930s and 1940s and today's laissez-faire "restoration" is highly pertinent. The almost uninterrupted horrors of that period flowed in large measure from the absence of the very social programs that are everywhere today being trimmed back rather than broadened, and from the absence of effective financial regulations. It seems as if history cannot be held at the front of the collective mind for more than a few decades. Even if a globally integrated economy does reduce somewhat the overall vulnerability to economic crisis, every indication of history is that, aside from brutal repression, only an ongoing balance between social well-being and private opportunities can maintain either social or economic stability, or economic growth, over the long term.

The Social Bottom Line in Electronic Capitalism

Where the economic bottom line is dominant in our culture and modes of communication, the notion of a social bottom line requires explanation. Though its nature is politically contested on an ongoing basis, much of what should be included in a measure of the social bottom line would seem clear enough. One might begin with measures of societal performance with respect to health, education, and welfare. Indicators of social-bottom-line performance might then include infant mortality rates, longevity, literacy, proportion of population graduating from high school or obtaining university degrees, homelessness and housing-quality measures, participation in community and social organizations, rate of family formation and family breakdown, crime rates and other measures of social dysfunction, and even suicide rates or survey data regarding a sense of happiness, security, and well-being.

More controversial measures would be the proportion of the population above the poverty line and the ratio between the highest and the lowest quintiles or deciles in income. Some measure of employment levels and employment quality should also be included. Quantitative measures of the social bottom line, as used by the United Nations and other agencies, will be discussed in greater detail in chapter 5. Less readily measurable factors are, however, also important; these might include social cohesion, community and political stability, political participation, and even perhaps democratic effectiveness.

Such factors are more than just "nice goals" primarily of concern to educators, social workers, and health professionals. These are measures of societal performance easily as important as the GDP and should be integral and central considerations in all the social sciences.[11] They should also be significantly elevated in public awareness through effective media reporting and be systematically reported both comparatively and through time. Improvements and setbacks should be treated as news, much as are changes in economic growth and inflation statistics. The reporting of school performance figures on a county-by-county or school-by-school basis, which has become more common, is a small step in this spirit, although this effort is often used to deflect criticism from higher levels of governance. A much broader array of social measures, for whole nations, might, however, help to offset the strong bias toward economism within electronic capitalism. More citizens might more carefully consider how much quality of life they are or are not getting per unit of national wealth. Richer might, on average, still be deemed better, but the results (depending on the measures chosen) are far more mixed than many would assume, and that is an important thing to know.

Continuous downsizing, plant closures and reengineering of firms and public institutions as a normal practice and expectation, as well as the accelerating gap between rich and poor, have doubtless had a range of negative social impacts. The impacts of such occurrences are, of course, less severe in leading economic regions and nations. There overall unemployment rates are low, lessening downward pressures on wages, and the downsized soon find other opportunities. The disruption takes a toll, but not nearly so severe a toll as did the prolonged periods of unemployment and the delayed starts in life that were the norm a decade ago in North America and that remain common in much of Europe. Social existence in the leading nations of electronic capitalism may be insecure, but is thus usually manageably so. Leading-nation status is, of course, itself subject to rapid change. Outside the leading nations the economic dynamism and perpetual adjustment typical of electronic capitalism may result in lowered social cohesion, increased personal stress, additional mental illness, high levels of family disintegration, increased addiction and crime, and increments of domestic abuse and family violence. Globalization's general downward pressures on public spending often compound such problems.

The late 1990s witnessed, for example, both a rapid rise in unemployment and a sharp increase in domestic violence and suicide in Japanese society. The early 1990s in North America, which were characterized by intense downsizing and high youth unemployment, also were characterized by rising teen suicides, particularly among males. In addition, a highly visible increase in the appeal and activities of extreme right-wing militias. By the same token the low unemployment rates of the middle and later 1990s correlated with rapidly falling crime rates. High levels of economic dislocation in Europe correlated with increased voting for the extreme right in, for example, France and the former East Germany. Merely a threat of further economic integration seems to have produced such a result in Austria. The social disruptions and general decline in Mexico, Indonesia, Russia, and much of the Middle East, despite its oil wealth, have been severe. Other poor nations have, on the other hand, fared better. The question is, can we begin to sort out why some societies gain ground in social terms under electronic capitalism, while others have deteriorated?

There are also enormously uneven impacts at the community level, especially in small and medium-sized communities, where a single large industry closure or combination of smaller closures can overwhelm social services and severely undermine everything from family functioning to the housing market. The stability and balance in community life can be lost as ambitious and able young people move away and only the elderly remain. Such localized outcomes can take place in prosperous times in wealthy societies. Indeed, it is arguable that such situations, albeit often temporary, are a hallmark of electronic capitalism. Profitable industries and factories with experienced, able, and hard-working labor forces are suddenly closed owing to a global rationalization of a particular firm.

Technological change or transportation cost shifts encourage the servicing of more markets from a smaller number of more economically productive sites. Or the resources on which an extractive industry depends may be nearing exhaustion. For whatever reason, the outcome is the same: communities, individuals, and families are frequently devastated. Even short of such fundamental disruptions there is a constant and increasing pressure on every firm and every plant to compete with the lowest-cost producers throughout the world. Thus there is an ongoing downward pressure on wages and benefits, workforce size, and taxation and an upward pressure on work time and work-related stress.

Such intense competition provides economic benefits at a considerable social cost. There is rarely a calculation as to whether the social costs might not offset the economic gains. Some less dramatic social costs are taken to be minor matters and are often difficult to measure in monetary equivalents. The more frequently downsizing and plant closures occur the more often family and community life and intergenerational contact are undermined. This can be particularly problematic when both parents are working. If one partner suffers job loss, most often few of the choices facing the family are good ones. If the choice is to move, assuming that both partners can find new employment in the new location, as recent arrivals both are vulnerable to future workplace adjustments. If one partner undertakes a long commute to new employment, family life inevitably suffers, often severely. If one partner remains unemployed other tensions arise (especially in a society where the expectation is that both partners will have lifelong work histories). The social costs of the ongoing turbulence of electronic capitalism are very real and, in general, simply not taken into account by those in business and government who make the relevant decisions.

What is even less often noted are the many ways community life is continually undermined. For example, when families must move frequently, personal and organizational contacts and community roles (including local politics) may be slow to re-form. Such associations only develop effectively on the basis of person-to-person contact over long periods of time (even generations). Community and local organizational effectiveness in small and medium-sized communities, it might be hypothesized, is enhanced by, and may even require, a considerable measure of residential stability. Putnam calls this the "repotting hypothesis" (humans, like plants too often repotted, may not thrive).[12] While communities can arguably be too static as well, it is little wonder that many individuals are reluctant to be as involved as they might have been in the past. If one is new to town, one does not know how things work and, further, if one's employment position is insecure, one does not prioritize community involvement when that community may soon also be left behind. Moreover, community leadership takes much more time to evolve than community involvement, and may thus suffer more.

The important question regarding the social bottom line, however, is not answered by a detailed documentation of the unintended social costs associated with globalization and electronic capitalism. The question is, how can we maximize improvements in the social bottom line? Or, perhaps, how can we improve the social bottom line within electronic capitalism as it evolves? There is no avoiding, in my view, a broad conclusion that maximizing overall social gains requires achieving faster economic growth rates in poor nations and poor communities than in rich. It might also require a rising, rather than a falling, proportion of GDP passing through public rather than private hands, though this is a far less certain and more complex matter. The latter assertion depends very much on how effectively public monies are spent. For example, high-paying public-sector jobs may contribute little to the overall social bottom line, at least directly. The first assertion, however, is the more important one and is both influenced and complicated by the realities imposed by the third bottom line: environment.

The Environmental Bottom Line in Electronic Capitalism

The environmental bottom line, perhaps even more than the economic and social bottom lines, must be evaluated in both the long and the short terms. The hard truth is that the long-term environmental bottom line may carry a limit to energy and material throughput growth. At the least it is prudent to assume that there are real limits to how much energy we humans can extract from nature and how much physical material we can process. Obviously, these limits are not rigid. It matters a great deal which materials and energy sources are utilized and how the materials and energy are processed and used. I will detail some of the signs that we are pressing toward this overall long-term limit shortly. Short-term limits are also important. These are often both local and cumulative in character. A river can only be warmed by industrial use and urban runoff by so much before coldwater fish species can no longer live there. Some of the usually toxic leachate from most (if not all) landfills will eventually reach ground and/or surface waters unless heavily engineered and operated indefinitely. There soon will be few old-growth or virgin forests to harvest, and even now every additional hectare of such forests harvested is likely to bring closer the time when additional animal and plant species are lost.

Robert Goodland of the World Bank has made an explicit attempt to document the full range of important environmental limits, with some emphasis on long-run limits. He writes: "We have reached the limits to throughput growth and . . . it is futile to insist that such growth can still alleviate poverty in the world today. We thus need to devise other strategies, such as qualitative development. Many local thresholds have been broached because of population pressures and poverty; global thresholds are being broached by industrial countries' overconsumption."[13] Goodland identifies five major pieces of evidence that humankind is threatening throughput limits: excessive human biomass appropriation rates, disruptive climate change, rupture of the ozone shield, land degradation, and diminishing biodiversity.

Goodland and others have argued that the best evidence that human activities are approaching an absolute limit is that "the human economy—directly or indirectly—uses about 40 percent of the net primary production of photosynthesis."[14] This is astonishing if one thinks about it, and frightening when considered with human-population-growth projections in mind. One hundred percent appropriation is obviously impossible, and the more land we urbanize and pave the less is available to grow anything. At less than 100 percent the living world would literally be consumed on an ongoing basis by one species. Projections of recent expansion of human land consumption suggest that this outcome could occur within a century. Arguably at even 50 or 60 percent total appropriation, little that is wild would remain save protected islands and the near-to-inaccessible reaches of mountain ranges. It simply has not pierced the consciousness of many humans that our species will soon in effect have domesticated, harvested (on an ongoing basis), or simply overwhelmed most of wild nature. We have already overfished all of the oceans of the world.[15] In many nations trees are removed considerably faster than they can grow back. Indeed, in not emphasizing fish and forests, Goodland perhaps understates our nearness to overall environmental-bottom-line limits.

The problem of climate change, Goodland's second sign that we are approaching overall throughput limits, is now on all such lists. Only a few oil companies and research renegades still deny the scientific evidence. There is no doubt that the climate is warming; at issue are only how fast it will warm in the future, with what exact implications, and the precise proportion of the change that is anthropocentric in origin. The future effects of climate warming are not predictable in detail, but they are almost certain to be sharply negative in net terms in terms of ecosystem health and human well-being. For example, as Goodland notes, "The prodigious North American breadbasket's climate may indeed shift north, but this does not mean that the breadbasket will follow, because the rich prairie soils will stay put, and the Canadian boreal soils and muskeg are very infertile."[16] This patterned outcome is likely to be repeated elsewhere both in terms of agriculture and in terms of the diversity within, and ecological health of, wild nature. Regarding those same Northern reaches of Canada (and elsewhere), Gorham has suggested that climate warming could possibly itself lead to net additions of greenhouse gases (either from methane resulting from decay, or carbon dioxide resulting from the drying and difficult-to-extinguish subterranean burning of muskeg).[17]

In broad terms, human-induced climate warming will at some point take nature outside the normal range of climatological flux and thereby significantly affect many plant and animal species. From an ecological perspective, it is not just that weather patterns will be altered. Quality soils have formed over millenniums in locations where rainfall and temperature patterns were suitable to promote the continuous production of plant life. They do not exist where temperate climates may "relocate." Most human agriculture depends on those same temperature and rainfall patterns. The patterns and the quality soils must exist in the same places for agricultural productivity to remain as high as it is at present. Human settlement has usually also developed in relation to agricultural capabilities. While we humans can fertilize and irrigate and move food from one place to another, those activities would themselves likely contribute additional increments of greenhouse gases, and all have other very real limits. There is an enormous water-quality and ecological price attendant on ever-more-intensive agricultural practices, and even those practices are relatively ineffective in the face of drought or flood.

Goodland's remaining three pieces of evidence regarding limits are also compelling and comprehensive. Effective action has only been taken with regard to one of them. The rupture of the ozone shield—predicted in 1974 and detected in 1985—did result in the Montreal Protocol within less than a decade from the date of detection. That action was impressively timely given the range of political actors involved—but only perhaps possible because the economic cost of the (partial) remedy was minimal. In contrast, conditions have deteriorated with regard to land degradation and biodiversity losses in many locations.

Land degradation was, of course, thoroughly documented by G. P. Marsh well over a century ago. Goodland notes that soil erosion is heavier whenever more marginal lands are cultivated, as they frequently are whenever either human populations or national debts rise (or would be were climate warming to advance). He reports that soil loss presently exceeds soil formation by tenfold or more. Biodiversity losses are clearly accelerating, and the two richest forms of ecosystems—tropical rainforests and coral reefs—have been subject to extreme and increasing pressures in recent decades.[18] The recent economic dislocations in Southeast Asia and

Brazil have occurred in the nations and regions that have been most severe in the assault on their forest ecosystems, and new economic difficulties will only accelerate that process.

A similar survey of the array of ecological and sustainability challenges that might be said to comprise an environmental bottom line has been presented by Gorham.[19] Gorham's list differs somewhat from Goodland's and is if anything more extensive. In particular, Gorham notes the long list of elements for which anthropogenically induced flux is approaching (or has exceeded) natural rates of flux. These would include nitrogen, sulfur, cadmium, lead, nickel, zinc, selenium, and mercury. Humankind, in other words, induces change in the chemical environment of the planet that rivals the flows and cycles associated with all of nature's activities. Each of these chemicals affects the functioning of living systems that have previously adapted to nature's flux rates and patterns and will not necessarily adapt well to our now nearly equal alterations. Many of the elements on this list are toxic to humans and other animals when ingested at rates above minimal amounts. Gorham also stresses topsoil loss owing primarily to agriculture and to forest cutting that amounts to some twenty-three billion tons per year, approximately 0.7 percent of the total available. Most of this topsoil finds its way to the bottom of streams and larger bodies of water.

For Gorham, many of these problems can be connected to the level of human population. In prehistory, he notes, human populations were roughly equal to the populations of other large mammals. Settled agriculture and the industrial revolution have radically altered that ratio. The human population is now about 1,000 times that of that of all other large mammals living in the wild. In addition to our own population we also extract from nature sufficient food and space to sustain billions of domesticated mammals and an even larger number of domesticated fowl. Our hunting prowess and forestry practices, combined with the sheer space that our numbers take up, has severely restricted the space available to all other wild species save those that are at least in part parasitic on humans (e.g., rats) or that thrive in spaces we have radically altered (e.g., pigeons). Where the bottom line lies here is not always obvious and varies enormously with the values and ethical principles we humans bring to the judgment.

In the end we humans will get the planet we (re)make. That is the import of a new reality wherein we and our pets and our domesticated future meals overwhelmingly outnumber self-supporting and free large mammals, and our elemental flux contributions approach those of all of nature's staggering array and scale of activities. "Nature" will not tell us how many species there ought to be; the species will simply be diminished in number, or disappear one by one. We humans determine the outcome, consciously or unconsciously.

We must face the moral consequences. Is it enough that a species exists only in a cage in a zoo (or only in a frozen gene bank)? Is the number of extant species the real bottom line? How much wild nature should there be? Is it enough nature for humans to visit when bored with our self-created, managed spaces, or might the world get by with only enough in which to produce nature films? Do we, on the other hand, have any right at all to even alter something so magnificent and ecologically rich as a coastal salt marsh or freshwater wetland or coral reef or a tropical rainforest? Will the first century of electronic capitalism be cursed by all the succeeding generations of humankind? Or will some future government just erase the electronic records of biological nature when they are found to provoke depression in the young? Or, for that matter, will the children of the future be as fascinated with tigers, parrots, and elephants as today's are with dinosaurs and, not having participated in the destruction themselves, feel no pangs at all regarding the demise of these species in the wild?

My own sense of an environmental bottom line regarding wild nature is at least as much focused on ecosystems as on particular species. In this matter we can no longer avoid the simultaneous consideration of three bottom lines. There is a real and significant economic and social cost to setting "aside" even examples of each variety of wild natural system. Many of those systems must be large enough to provide adequate habitat to species that require very large territories for healthy survival (large predators, for example). This effort would include the restoration of some habitats already all but lost, such as North American tall-grass prairies. Especially rich habitats arguably should be preserved in especially large tracts. Without a full range of such efforts on a massive scale, species losses will continue and many species numbers will continue to decline. Declines and losses will include virtually all large mammals, as well as species as diverse as migratory songbirds, redwoods, reptiles, fish, butterflies, amphibians, and bats.

But the environmental bottom line is larger than "just" the loss of biodiversity and wild habitat. The environmental bottom line is perhaps best understood as being three dimensional, with the preservation of nature being one dimension, pollution a second, and the sustainability of economically important resources a third. I will not elaborate on pollution issues here; they are well documented elsewhere. Suffice it to say here that environmental factors contribute to a significant proportion of reproductive problems, cancer, and asthma, as well as many other diseases in humans. Resource depletion is also very much a part of the environmental bottom line. The immediacy and severity of resource depletion is tied very closely to the other two dimensions. Forest resources are limited to the extent that we choose to protect habitat for human recreation, for watershed protection, for habitat, and for the sake of ecological integrity. Mineral resources are limited by energy availability and price, by air- and water-pollution tolerance, and by land-use competition. Overall energy availability, particularly fossil fuel as a limiting factor, is considered below.

A caution should also be noted. Many environmentalists of the 1970s, and at other times, were too prone to predicting imminent apocalyptic outcomes. The problems they saw—pollution, resource depletion, excessive growth in human population—were all (and remain) real. The demise of industrial civilization so often foreseen, however, has in some cases been not so much a probable result as a vengeful wish. The real outcome is more likely to be less dramatic and final. It may include, however, declining habitat for many species, some—likely accelerating—extinctions, additional cases of human cancer and asthma, the loss of most remaining wild-ocean fisheries, and many, many other undesirable outcomes. But societal and/or economic "collapse" has not been and is not likely to be in the near future the result of "our" ecological errors and crimes against nature. Even climate warming may take decades to have a dramatic effect on agricultural productivity and planetary habitability. The combination of human population and economic expansion, and the peaking of fossil-fuel supplies, could soon pose a severe challenge to further expansion, but the prior question is less a matter of nature's "decisions" regarding the bottom line than one of what kind of world we humans would prefer.

Balancing Economy and Society

Most of the political history of mass industrial society was based on the tension between economic values and equity, or social, values. This tension was blatant in the nineteenth-century poverty described by Heilbroner as providing the capital accumulation necessary for industrialization. It was also at the heart of Galbraith's noted late-twentieth-century private luxury and public poverty, wherein we today must reflect on the curious unevenness of (our) blessings.[20] Politically, economy-equity tension was manifest in everything from the creation of industrial unions to the rise of the activist democratic states that abolished child labor, created the first pensions, expanded public schools, regulated hours of work, and established minimum wages, workplace safety, and basic forms of consumer protection. It also resulted in socialism, communism, and the cold war. It has never been entirely clear, however, whether economic values were not, on balance, advanced more effectively in "losing" the struggle with equity values than in "winning." That is, the higher wages generally resisted tooth and nail by holders of capital provided customers for mass industrial society. The social protections established by the activist democratic state of mass industrial society provided sociopolitical stability and softened the perturbations of the business cycle.

For more than a century there was, in most wealthy societies, an uneven but real movement toward equity and toward a social balance within which the situation of the majority of citizens and society as a whole advanced. Mass consumer societies, some tending toward a balance of power between the public and private sectors, were the result. Electronic capitalism altered this rough balance by adding two new dimensions to the ongoing contestation—a multilayered global economic competition and an increasingly centralized and more ideologically active mass media. Global economic competition has altered the relative power of capital and labor and changed the left-right political landscape. Political discourse has evolved into a contest between those who would gradually (or not so gradually) eliminate many, if not most, public activities and the "third way," which accepts privatization, ongoing tax reduction, and restrained public expenditures, but looks to preserve middle-class-oriented state services such as health and education through economic growth. The "third way" typically achieves media time by putting forward irresistibly telegenic leaders, creating an increment of global credibility for the nation as a whole.

How has global economic competition resulted in a shift in the political balance of power? The formula is simple: capital is increasingly mobile, labor and citizens are less so. Even where labor is relatively mobile (as within the European Union) it, of necessity, follows capital and employment, not quality social programs that are (in Europe) largely harmonized in any case. Investment and reinvestment takes place where conditions are best. Assuming a minimum of social stability (no riots in the streets or any inclination to "labor unrest"), investment seeks low taxes, moderate wages, minimal regulations, large market access (to the extent that this is any longer a variable), concessions and subsidies, infrastructure, and the availability of an appropriate mix of workplace skills. Suddenly business decisions, more than public decisions, determine social outcomes for most citizens-as-employees. Elections are thereby contests between teams who can create the most favorable climate for mobile capital and, thanks to the media, all citizens understand this new reality.

It is too simple, however, to say that the result is a straightforward race to the bottom in terms of social policy. Pressures in that direction are surely created, but what if the result of social policy reductions were more rapid economic growth than might otherwise have occurred? Would not such gains be, to some extent, delivered socially in the form of lower unemployment and some market-based upward pressures on wages? Would not additional public revenues also allow simultaneous reductions in tax rates and the preservation of social programs that might otherwise be unsustainable? It is perhaps too soon to answer these questions with certainty regarding overall long-term patterns, and such patterns may not ever be either consistent or definitive, but some basic facts can be noted. Lower unemployment in the United States in the late 1990s clearly softened some aspects of the gap between rich and poor. However, many nations did not experience lower unemployment to anything like the same extent, if at all, and overall the gap between rich and poor even in the United States (where growth and employment have been solid in the last decade) has by many accounts and measures widened.[21] On a global scale, the gap has grown even more rapidly.[22] In addition, social expenditures, as a percentage of GDP, have declined in many nations.

One also must ask several additional questions, which admittedly are not easily answered. First, other than the matter of attracting investment capital, does rapid economic growth actually *require* public expenditure reductions (and/or ever-declining corporate tax rates)? That is, assuming for the moment that capital could be generated internally, must public expenditures be trimmed and the poor lose relative ground in order to achieve a reasonable rate of economic growth? What is the evidence for this? Second, even if economic growth were slower (regardless of the matter of the origin and mobility of capital), is the loss in GDP not worth the potential gain (or forgone loss) in quality of life? For whom is it worthwhile and for whom is it not? Would investment no longer be inhibited were governments to coordinate and harmonize social policy rather than competing on this basis (at a cost always borne by their least fortunate citizens)? Do investors and international corporations actually care about tax restraint and social-program reductions as much as some governments seem to believe they do?

Clearly a great deal of mythology operates in the contemporary debate regarding social equity and the preferences of economic elites. Regarding the last question in the preceding paragraph, McQuaig argues that there has been a fundamental shift dating from the mid-1970s, when the postwar boom had faded and oil-price increases were accelerating both inflation and governmental deficits. In her words (regarding this period), "With deteriorating economic conditions, there was a struggle between the general public and the financial elite over who would get what portion of the dwindling pie. The financial elite has proved more effective at asserting its claim, and has largely succeeded in restoring the kind of privileged economic position it enjoyed before the First World War. This has been no small feat, because a major change had occurred since those earlier times: the rise of democracy. . . . The task has been made easier, however, by the emergence of the widespread belief that governments are powerless—because of technology and globalization—to do anything other than what financial markets dictate."[23] In our terms, this explains why democracy's dilemma cannot be resolved without undermining the subtle ideology of economism and without the development of some form of multidimensional global governance.

McQuaig argues that there is really no conspiracy here, of bankers and officials, or anyone else. Pressures have perhaps increased, virtually all governments have in fact retreated on a number of fronts, and commentators on both the left and right as well as the media have concluded that forces beyond the control of government are now operating in the world. McQuaig seeks to bolster the courage of her government—Canada—to act to preserve its long history of middle-of-the-road and moderate-left social and economic policies. She may overestimate the power of a single government to act autonomously in favoring financial regulation and/or social equity over providing ever-greater advantages, and an ever-greater share of the pie, to international corporations and investors, large and small. But is there not some possibility that governments could be pushed to collectively and selectively avoid some forms of racing to the bottom, or at least to agree on where that bottom should be? At present those in power in most nations prefer to promote the view that they are doing the only thing possible: helping their own particular nations to compete more effectively with all other nations.

One other dimension of what might be called contemporary economy-society mythology requires further comment—the view that economic growth will eventually make up for a variety of sins. One variation on this theme takes us toward the environmental realm—here in terms of health (perhaps the most significant social variable). This view as applied to health has been best articulated by Wildavsky, namely, that positive health outcomes will be maximized by putting aside "excessive" concerns regarding risk avoidance and pushing ahead with economic growth, which in turn will all but ensure overall health improvements.[24] Wildavsky offers an analogy with a jogger who must incur a greater short-term risk of a heart attack while running in order to achieve a lower long-term risk of heart disease.[25] That is, if nuclear power (an example Wildavsky uses) adds a small increment of health risk in exchange for a considerable boost to economic growth, that growth can in turn "buy" a large gain in health. Wildavsky offers as evidence statistics that show a strong overall correlation between national wealth and national health. That is, richer countries are, on average, healthier countries.

The same sort of argument might be made regarding other social costs incurred in the name of economic growth, including rising inequity in the distribution of income—in common parlance this is known as "trickle down" or "a rising tide raises all ships" (it just raises some more than others). There are, however, several problems with Wildavsky's argument. Greater wealth does not always, by any means, lead to better health. Life expectancy in Kerala, India, is far higher than in any number of wealthier jurisdictions around the world.[26] By any number of health measures the United States, for example, does not deliver an increment of health to its population anywhere near to its wealth ranking. There are a number of reasons for this, including a high incidence of extreme poverty (Third

World living conditions for many amid the general luxury) and the absence of public provision of universal health care. In reply to Wildavsky, there is also no guarantee that increments of wealth (presumably) gained through the use of possibly risky technologies will lead to increases in health-care spending. And more surprisingly, additional health-care spending does not ensure additional health. On the contrary, the United States, with the highest level of per-capita health expenditures by far, also has a relatively high level of total years of life lost to sickness and accidents per 100,000 population.[27]

Other factors may also be more complex than Wildavsky's model would lead one to believe. It may be the case that additional societal wealth produces net increments of health up to a certain level of wealth and thereafter one finds either a threshold or diminishing marginal returns. As a concrete example of this possibility, the introduction of modern transportation would clearly save lives in any number of ways, but "excessive" automobile use might cost lives in additional accidents, air-pollution increases, and even traffic snarls that slow emergency vehicles. Wildavsky's case is not proven by the overall pattern shown. Many other questions exist. What if the same increment of wealth in question were achieved by other, less risky means? That, surely, is more to the point than a gross general association. Moreover, does any particular risky technology actually add more economic gain than a less risky alternative might have added? In effect we must understand both the economic and the social effects of the full array of such alternatives. This latter question is particularly important because there is considerable evidence that distribution of income, distribution of quality health care, and even the richness and stability of community life all contribute significantly to health outcomes.[28]

This important fact is true for all the obvious reasons and some that are not so obvious. The obvious reasons would include the fact that many of the ways health is negatively affected by poverty exist whether that poverty is amid poverty or amid wealth—poor nutrition, lack of education, substandard housing, and the like. The relative weakness of public, universal-access health, education, and social welfare programs also contributes to the health shortfalls in obvious ways. More surprising, however, are several studies suggesting that human health may be adversely affected by hierarchies of authority and rank within workplaces.[29] That is, human health (itself but one component of overall human well-being) is likely affected by people's sense of self-esteem, self-worth, and efficacy. Additional societal wealth might have less of a positive effect on overall societal health if a disproportionate share of that wealth accrued to a small proportion of individuals, families, groups, and communities.

Overall, the main point here is this: the relationship between economy and society is enormously complex and we are a long way from understanding it fully. More important, well-being is a social variable that can and should be distinguished from prosperity. To create better societies we need to not presume that prosperity somehow automatically begets the best possible outcomes, or is in itself the best possible outcome.

Balancing Economy and Environment

Thus social outcomes are affected by the economic bottom line (and vice versa) in complex rather than simple ways. The same is true regarding the interaction between environmental and economic variables. On the very broadest level almost every additional human economic activity carries some incremental environmental cost. The price is often small and if the additional activity were to replace an activity with a higher environmental cost, the net environmental effect would be positive. A presumption that such positive shifts can be common lies behind some versions of sustainable development advocacy.

This presumption is, however, commonly misinterpreted. Sustainable development as practiced has been less concerned with the substitution of relatively benign technologies for risky technologies than with including some proportion of relatively benign technologies within new increments of economic growth. Growth lurches forward, at best adding less damage per unit of incremental GDP than the levels per unit of prior output. For example, in the name of sustainable development ecologically crucial forests are logged with some care regarding streambeds and steep slopes, rather than left in place while paper is produced from recycled sources and/or agricultural crops grown for fiber content.

One key to effectively integrating economy and environment is the recognition that the environmental bottom line is rooted in a fundamentally different sense of time than is the economic bottom line. Environmental thinking is glacial by comparison—ecological, biophysical, and geological time are multigenerational, while the media mind of electronic capitalism is, as we have seen, ahistorical and dominated by the frenetic immediacy of bulletins, headlines, quarterly profits, momentary shifts in the stock market, fashion and style, buzzwords and model years. Many environmental problems only emerge over decades or longer. More critically, many environmental solutions require decades to see through once the decades prior to visibility have passed. Ever-changing electronic capitalism, however, may have already moved on for other reasons, leaving it unclear who is responsible for the bills owing to nature (or to the unfortunate humans living downstream or downwind from, or within the midst of, the mess). Sometimes, as well, environmental effects are so diffuse that it is impossible to know with certainty who has lost what, as might be the case with multicausally induced environmental disease.

This is all well known in environmental circles, but despite decades of environmental education, it remains largely beyond the grasp of, or a matter of indifference to, many political and economic decision makers—persons otherwise the reigning masters of quick studies and rapid-fire decisiveness. Those in positions of economic power who reflect and worry, who spend time thinking beyond the next institutional reckoning that they must face, will not likely survive the next board meeting or election. They have arrived where they are because they live in the economically measured moment better than anyone else. They know what needs to be done to make things (one dimensionally) better now, or maybe next week or next year. They are not expected to reflect on the long term or to think multidimensionally. They are held responsible, often with a considerable vengeance, for the here and now. They may well be inclined to disdain all who have never met a payroll (or fought off a hostile takeover). They, and their lawyers, are very clear about what is and is not their personal responsibility. They just presume that there is enough nature somewhere else and that all the "maybes" will take care of themselves. They only rarely have the time, or the inclination, to consider what the world may be like thirty or fifty years from now.

Thus the economic and environmental realms are not easily integrated. A cynic might observe that sustainable development thus far has been about humoring environmentalists, about saying the right things during those cycles of public opinion where everyone must appear to care.[30] Environmental sensitivity, in this view, is shown by economic and political elites only when the development game would otherwise be lost, when the alternative to environmentally sensitive development is no development at all. That game is, however, rarely lost; the economy-environment balance point is highly skewed. The time frame of electronic capitalism, and democracy as practiced within its confines, cannot consistently incorporate the needs of nature—not without an alteration of some of electronic capitalism's basic rules of operation. This is part and parcel of democracy's complex dilemma and is best seen with specific examples that focus on aspects of the time disjuncture between the economic and the environmental bottom lines.

Many of the difficulties that have arisen with regard to toxic chemicals have arisen because their effects on nature and human health are considerably delayed within a decades-long progression from chemical discovery and mass production through exposures resulting from unexpected and undetected pathways, then to suspected effects, to firm scientific evidence, to an understanding of the significance of that evidence, and, finally, to (strongly resisted) action. Throughout this passage of time decision makers will assert, and the media will duly report, that "there is not sufficient evidence" or "no scientific consensus" (that is, virtual unanimity), or that regulation is not warranted on a (short term) cost-benefit basis, or—more recently (and usually without media coverage)—that if action is taken a plant will close or investment halted. Any number of such cases have been documented, including DDT, lead, asbestos, tobacco, and PCBs.[31] There is little evidence that the level of prudence that these past problems would warrant is even now effectively practiced, in the case of so-called endocrine disruptors, for example.

Many types of ecological loss and damage also involve time-frame mismatches. Neither firms nor governments think in the time span of a forest, especially an ancient forest. Vast tracts of forest have been removed in locations throughout the world with little understanding of what is lost in terms of ecological services, microgenetic variability, biodiversity, climate, limitations on successive forest "crops," ecological restoration, soil loss, or many other factors. Some of these things cannot be fully known in less than the time it takes to pass through two or three forest "crops" (up to perhaps two centuries). The overwhelming bulk of forest extractions have come since 1950, and at present extraction rates many types of forests will be long gone (other than as remnants) before we have any understanding of what is missing. Above and beyond these considerations, present overall global rates of forest extraction are not sustainable. The long history of human interactions with forests suggests that humans have yet to devise institutions that think in centuries (or often last for centuries). The culture and habits evolving under electronic capitalism would seem the antithesis of such a perspective.

Expanded global trade imposes another significant ecological risk: an increase in problems associated with exotic species.[32] Increases in global commerce all but guarantee the increased transfer of plant, insect, and other animal species (as well as microorganisms and pathogens) between habitats. The list of such ecological errors is already almost endless: rabbits in Australia, zebra mussels in the Great Lakes and surrounding waters, the gypsy moth, purple loosestrife, buckthorn, and hundreds of others moved in the ballast of ships, within the packaging of exported products, and in ill-advised deliberate transfers for home gardeners or pet owners. Plant and animal species arrive in new settings where natural enemies, predators, and diseases are absent—their populations explode and they exclude any number of domestic species, including those of enormous economic, aesthetic, and ecological value. The changes that result are utterly outside of human control in most cases—we humans cannot control living nature, however able we are to disrupt it. The unpredictability of these outcomes should also suggest great caution regarding the introduction of genetically modified plant and animal species.

The biggest time-scale mismatches between economy and environment, however, exist in the realm of sustainability—particularly with regard to long-term energy supply. Market analysts speak of "soft landings" regarding the deliberate restraint of economic growth in the face of excessive "market exuberance," but they are thinking here of adjustments in terms of weeks, months, or perhaps several quarters. There remains on the sustainability horizon a not-so-soft landing issue that has been building since the beginnings of mass industrial society—the peaking and coming decline of conventional oil supplies and output. There are recent credible estimates that this prospect may be only one or two decades ahead.[33] Neither markets nor governments are paying the matter much heed at this point, even in the face of recent rises in oil prices. In North America the memories of the 1970s and early 1980s have been run over, as it were, by sports utility vehicles (SUVs)—each new brand larger and less fuel efficient than the one before. All they lack as a 1950s retro design are tail fins.

But this is the more visible part of the energy-inefficiency iceberg. Climate warming, demand-side management initiatives in electrical utilities, and the 1970s energy crisis have all spurred advances in energy efficiency. But what has changed very little is the extent of our reliance on automobiles and the dispersed urban forms that exist as a direct result. Urban form is a primary example of the economy-environment time-frame mismatch. Buildings last for centuries, and given the embedded energy and ecological costs they embody, they should last that long. Urban form also all but locks a society into a level of energy use within the transportation sector. So too do global economic integration and an emphasis on comparative advantage-based national and regional specialization. As the world learned so painfully in the 1970s and 1980s, the prices of many goods and services—including food and commodity prices—are radically dependent on energy prices. We should be especially mindful that the cities, transportation modes (emphasizing trucks and air), and global economic integration presume low energy prices. Yet the 1990s economic and political decision makers seemingly could not remember as far back as 1979 and behaved as if low energy prices were guaranteed for the indefinite future. The good news from the 1970s/early 1980s energy crisis is that modern economies can adjust to higher energy prices, albeit painfully.

However, adjustments to rapid rises in energy prices cannot be made quickly within a globally integrated economy—and the adjustments that will probably ensue will therefore likely be highly inhumane. That is, the SUVs may continue to roll around sprawling suburbs while poorer families the world over are suddenly colder and more often hungry. The peaking of fossil fuels—both local and global—will be enormously expensive in terms of all three bottom lines because the market does not incorporate the costs of future energy-price adjustments into present energy prices. In effect, the low energy prices of the 1990s and the behaviors and habits they engendered will contribute to raising the costs of future adjustments.

Moreover, so too does uncertainty regarding future price increases—even today very little hedging in terms of efficiency improvements is done against the risk of future rises in energy prices. Given the pricing patterns for energy and commodities between 1985 and 2000, few assumptions are yet made for ongoing future energy-price increases (in effect the assumption is that there will be no consistent pattern of price increase) when builders or building buyers, for example, choose insulation levels in new construction. Nor, other than the not-very-deeply-felt pressures associated with climate warming, do many consider such matters in relation to their personal consumer choices—a rather sharp contrast to the near-obsession of only fifteen years ago. Overall, this may prove to be the most important single case of market failure in all of human history. In this sense the price increases of recent years are a great mercy rather than a misfortune or a plot.

All this is not to say that additional economic growth is not needed—the world does not produce enough to provide even a modestly comfortable life for all humans. Moreover, many nations still remain in the condition Heilbroner described regarding the beginnings of mass industrial society—and unable to generate savings sufficient for industrialization. It is to say, however, that many present forms of economic growth and existing production borrow from the future. Goodland and Daly put it this way: "The world is hurtling away from environmental sustainability at present. Global society is being maintained only through the exhaustion and dispersion of a one-time inheritance of natural capital, such as topsoil, groundwater, tropical forest, fisheries, and biodiversity."[34] This list should also include, of course, fossil fuels. In addition, the forms and patterns of economic growth typical of electronic capitalism deliver little or nothing to the poor. Thus this rationale for continued economic growth is at present an excuse; there is no evidence that further overall growth will provide a remedy for the central problem at hand. This consideration brings us directly to the third set of paired bottom lines: society and environment.

Balancing Society and Environment

Balancing the needs of society and environment is truly sitting between the proverbial rock and hard place. There are a myriad of ways in which these two sets of needs confront one another. When an endangered tiger attacks village children, what is to be done? When an overfished fishery is one's principal source of food, what does one do? When oil is found beneath ecologically rich mangroves of a desperately poor country, what options exist? As Goodland and Daly note, "Short-term behavior by the poor, such as by rapid slash-and-burn agriculture, even shorter rotations, harvests exceeding regeneration rates, depleting topsoil, cultivating steep slopes and marginal land ('consuming seed corn') is understandable because it permits survival in the present."[35] It might be added that the relative lack of economic dynamism in many poor nations also promotes high birth rates out of despair, indifference, and lack of hope as well as from inadequate funding of health care and the absence of work and educational opportunities, particularly for women.

Clearly poverty undermines the prospects for, and likelihood of, environmental protection. So too do high rates of unemployment. Unemployment generates political pressures that most of the time easily offset the political pressures that can be generated on behalf of environmental protection. Electronic capitalism, of course, generates ongoing pressures on work opportunities and existing sources of employment through simultaneous automation and downward pressures on public revenues and thereby public-sector employment. High unemployment in turn can add to policing and social welfare costs, leaving environmental protection expenditures even more vulnerable. But the effects of unemployment on environmental protection are often more direct and take these five forms, among others: (1) in broad terms, the level of public concern with environmental protection may vary inversely with the level of economic insecurity; (2) resource decisions made in times and places of duress are more likely to be shortsighted; (3) the enforcement, and indeed the existence, of environmental regulations can be undermined by high unemployment rates; (4) local governments may be more vulnerable to pressures in support of unsuitable development when and where unemployment rates are high; and (5) the willingness of employees and managers to whistle-blow about violations of environmental regulation declines with rising unemployment rates.

Not all of these forms require further comment, but the first two may be particularly significant. Several analysts have written about "waves" or "cycles" of pro-environmental public opinion during which legislative initiatives are particularly strong (and corresponding troughs when cutbacks are easily accomplished).[36] In North America the recent surges have taken place just before and after the first Earth Day in 1970 and again in the late 1980s and early 1990s. Sometimes the momentum gained lasts into the onset of economic instability, but not long beyond. The late 1990s and since seem different thus far in that prosperity has not so far yielded a sharp surge in pro-environmental opinion (nor, as is normal, in a strong upward surge in industrial wage pressures). One possibility is that the downsizing of the early 1990s was especially severe, and to some extent has been ongoing. Another possibility, and this is even more worrisome, is that it is now widely assumed that environmental protection initiatives are outside the power of domestic governments and are typically "resolved" (dismissed) by all-powerful global trade panels. Or, governments behave as McQuaig described, and convince citizens that they (governments) are powerless to act even when they are not. Or, as some in the media have learned, pushing frightening environmental stories can cost sponsors money, and so they have turned their sensationalist inclinations and attentions to crime, accidents, "reality" TV, and natural disasters.

Even without these cyclical linkages between the social and environmental bottom lines, there are great regional differences between and within nations. On a case-by-case basis one can isolate examples where terrible resource decisions were made in locales where persistently high unemployment has existed. Severe health and environmental problems associated with uranium mining on First Peoples' lands have occurred in the United States, Australia, and Canada. Robert Bullard and many others have identified any number of cases where environmentally doubtful activities were sited amidst minority populations in the United States (where unemployment rates are higher).[37] To the extent that such siting possibilities exist, there is far less pressure on firms to develop technologies to handle these problems cleanly or that would avoid them altogether. Perhaps the worst single case of overfishing in human history (the loss of the cod fishery off Newfoundland) can be traced to the high rates of unemployment in that Canadian province (20% to 25% unemployment is not uncommon). Government regulators delayed the closure of the fishery owing to political pressures to avoid exacerbating an already-difficult socioeconomic reality.

Social-environmental tensions have become a significant political fault line in many jurisdictions. They can turn ugly whenever unemployment rates are already high. In the early 1990s endangered spotted owls (on whose behalf U.S. courts closed some ancient forests to clearcut logging) were hunted in the Pacific Northwest so that they could be nailed to signs along public highways as a warning to environmentalists. The political and personal tensions between primary producers (including ranchers, forest workers, and mining interests) and environmentalists in the North American West became increasingly common in this period and persist today.

Many of these tensions in British Columbia have been played out within the New Democratic Party, traditional political home to both greens and woodworkers.[38] Within poorer nations such tensions are often between multinational resource firms as well as their employees and supporters on the one hand, and tribal peoples and/or subsistence hunters, fishers, and gatherers on the other. The outcome has on more than one occasion been fatal for the latter.[39]

Some 1970s environmentalists were insensitive to the political implications of such tensions; fewer are today. It is now generally argued by environmental advocates that poverty alleviation and environmentally prudent development are less environmentally costly (and more economically sound) than is a status quo that simply presumes and waits for trickle down from rich to poor. Moreover, it is also argued by today's environmentalists that many pro-environmental activities have a positive employment impact. For example, sustainable low-impact logging is more, not less, labor intensive. In the 1970s an end to economic growth was taken by some to be a necessary part of environmental protection. Now it is widely assumed that poverty can also exacerbate environmental damage, though it is still often noted that excessive wealth can do great harm as well. The issue is now an empirical one: Do electronic capitalism, trade, and economic growth deliver gains, both absolute and relative, to the poor or not? If there is an environmental cost, is there a real social gain? Only then can anyone consider if the gain is worth the cost.

In overall terms, most environmentalists would now agree with Goodland and Daly when they conclude: "Can development without throughput growth (sustainable development) cure existing poverty? Our belief is that it cannot. Qualitative improvement in the efficiency with which resources are used will greatly help, but will not be sufficient to cure poverty. The reduction of throughput intensity per dollar of GNP in some rich countries is all to the good, but means little to poor countries still striving for adequate food, clothing, and shelter. Basic necessities have a large and irreducible physical dimension, unlike say information processing."[40] My only hesitation regarding this view is a need to add that food, clothing, building materials, and so on flow increasingly from poor countries to rich. Some restraint on this net flow is part and parcel of the other changes Goodland and Daly advocate, including net North-to-South wealth transfers, reduction or elimination of resource-extraction subsidies, and reduced tax evasion, particularly within the "Southern plutocracy" where it is widespread.[41]

Goodland and Daly observe that it is very difficult politically in wealthy nations to face up to the need for income redistribution and population stability. They are to be commended for having the courage to emphasize matters not widely supported in contemporary governmental and economic circles. Environmentalists may also need to face up to another politically challenging possibility of an "opposite" sort: the downward pressure on wages, and even in some cases on public-sector spending, that globalization imposes in wealthy nations may be, on balance, a positive step in terms of the dual dilemmas of the social and environmental bottom lines. The principal problem is that the downward pressure is greatest on those least able to bear it, and the programs that are cut are typically most necessary to those in greatest need. Another problem is that people whose wages are restrained are getting nothing in return for their losses except longer hours at work. They do not even gain the satisfaction they might get if the restraints imposed on them resulted in actual gains in poorer regions or nations, as Goodland and Daly would wish too see. Many people might accept personal losses if they did not believe that foreign aid was essentially a transfer of money from the poor in rich nations to the rich in poor nations.

The political challenges in all this are enormous. The energy-price increases of the 1970s were, in part, both a "green tax" and a net transfer from wealthy nations to some poor nations (some of which are now no longer poor). The result, recalling McQuaig, was a political turn to the right in some wealthy nations as inflation and rising unemployment occurred simultaneously. That shift, in turn, undermined for a time both environmental protection and social equity. The challenge is to simultaneously redress social inequity and enhance environmental sustainability without provoking the neoliberal political tendencies that seem to be associated with even the mildest economic downturns or threats of any sort to the prosperous. It is difficult to avoid the conclusion that only an additional increment of economic growth, distributed more evenhandedly, can avoid highly negative political outcomes.

All things considered, the very best prospects for resolving, or at least ameliorating, these three-dimensional tensions lie in a redirected, environmentally and socially more benign, globalization. Is this possible? Anyone who answers that question, one way or the other, with great confidence is probably untrustworthy. A positive answer requires at least four assumptions (at this point essentially guesses): (1) the processes of globalization and technological advance can continue to produce significant overall economic growth; (2) through energy, materials, and land-use efficiency gains this growth can be developed without a proportional increase in overall energy and materials use; (3) those efficiency gains will be sufficient to avoid intolerable levels of ecological damage or the collapse of crucial resource stocks and options; and (4) it is politically possible that, given that there is some (unknown) upper limit to both those stocks and efficiency gains, the proceeds of the economic growth achieved through globalization will at the very least redound proportionately to those most in need. These are enormous assumptions, but without them it is hard to avoid great pessimism regarding the future. The best prospect for such outcomes may well lie in a more balanced and democratic process of global economic integration than we have seen to date.

Global Governance as a Blind Juggling Act on a Moving Stage

In general, neither economic stability nor economic growth is, of course, easily achieved—even with questions of ecology and social cohesion aside. Self-consciously steady and moderate growth is particularly difficult. Moreover, given that the detailed management of the economy by government has failed for the most part, other means of guidance must be found. Sustainable growth (assumption 1) is likely impossible, and in any case largely pointless, if none of the other assumptions hold true. The outcomes implicit in assumptions 2, 3, and 4 require careful monitoring (discussed in chapter 5) as well as some new, thus far essentially untried, global-scale means of guiding, or at least nudging, the integrated global economy toward the actual achievement of that which these assumptions hold to be possible (a task addressed in chapters 6 and 8).

How could anyone, most readers will want to ask, even consider the possibility that a disparate multiplicity of governments, organizations, and interests could somehow collectively guide a complex global economy on any basis, let alone one that is three rather than one dimensional? All one can say is that electronic capitalism will not, on its own, attend to either the social or environmental bottom lines. It is not even certain that present global trade and investment arrangements, patterns, and rules are sufficient to optimize economic stability. There is, however, a hope regarding the global rule making that might emerge from the increasingly visible shortcomings of unguided electronic capitalism (global economic integration without democratic and multidimensional rule making). The hope is that perhaps we can collectively learn one lesson from history: that neither the detailed central management of markets, nor one-bottom-line thinking, will produce (or even permit) anything like the best world that could be achieved.

The key recognition here is that the market is a wondrous tool, equally capable of effective self-management within diverse sets of rules. It even has its own default rules. The social default rule is that those with an advantaged market position win more often than not. The only *economic* limit on their margin of victory is their employees' survival and continued willingness to work as well as a capacity for continuing purchases by their customers. The default rule on environment is comparable—the parts of the natural world that are economically essential need to exist. Or, failing such continued existence, what is needed is a technological capacity to stay ahead (by substitution and innovation) of whatever resource shortfalls might arise. A forest in economic terms, for example, consists only of trees (plus perhaps some limited recreational value). All of living nature in strictly economic terms is essentially equated with the parts of nature that can be eaten by humans (or hunted for amusement value). The default rules alone, of course, create realities uglier than almost any organized society would tolerate. Thus the need to continually redirect the market from its tendency to lapse into default rules is increasingly apparent.

Mercifully, the market will (or would) also follow other rules. The global market does not even need a session at obedience school, as much as it needs global environmental rules and established global social minima. What is necessary are new tools to guide the market (or to empower the market to guide us) increasingly away from the default mode. Some of these rules, tools, and minima are already visible to thoughtful observers. Their precise parameters would be made more apparent by the evolution and increasing public visibility of a three-dimensional social science. This perspective must replace, or at least more effectively compete with, the present dominance of an economy-only, one-dimensional view of both public policy and everyday life. The next chapter sketches the outlines of this emerging social science. Chapter 6 identifies some of the possible global rules, tools, and minima.

Suffice it to say here that an exceedingly curious perspective guides contemporary society and policy. This perspective is open to altering the genetic structures of plants and animals that comprise the planet, to tapping nuclear energy, and to altering any and all of nature's cycles, including the climate, but imagines that we cannot collectively and consciously guide the economies that we ourselves have created for our own benefit.

This chapter's two broad points would seem apparent. The first is that energy and material extractions and throughputs of many kinds may be nearing the limits of environmental desirability, if not sustainable possibility, and may increasingly restrain future economic growth. Therefore, it would seem only prudent to actively encourage economic activity that is ever more efficient in energy and material terms. The second point is that some significant proportion of present and future growth (at the very least a proportional share) should go to the nations and individuals most in need. Achieving these objectives does not require global government or managed economies. It does not warrant intractable resistance to globalization, as much as it requires the establishment of new terms and conditions of a more benign, and more effectively monitored, evolution of global economic integration.

5

Measuring the Three Bottom Lines

One of the ways economistic thinking, as captured in McKibben's lovely phrase "the assumption that economic expansion will fill our lives with sunshine," has attained iconic status is through the perpetual, up-to-the-second one-dimensional media presentation of economic statistics. This is not, of course, intentional indoctrination. Even for those who do not participate in the economy in terms of ownership, the rate of economic growth in a given quarter or the current unemployment rate has a bearing on day-to-day decisions—say, whether to buy a new car or appliances, renew a mortgage, or increase savings. Economic data are continuously useful in everyday life. It is thus not their omnipresence that is problematic as much as the absence of a widely shared alternative, multidimensional model of society and a wide familiarity with multidimensional quantitative information as a counterbalance.

The everyday dissemination of quantitative information regarding society is always rooted within widely shared models, assumptions, and understandings. These need not be complex. Today's implicit "model" is a long way from reflecting the complexities of the world—rapid economic growth is assumed to be good, moderate economic growth tolerable, and anything less is communicated as either highly problematic or frightening. As we have seen, this perspective is shortsighted in a number of ways. It is one dimensional when the effective functioning of human societies is only understandable in three (or more) dimensions, each measured in their own terms.

What is essential is a model of, and perspective on, society that conveys multidimensionality and demonstrates in both quantitative and qualitative terms the problems associated with an overwhelming predominance of economistic values. Only then might it become clear that prosperity is better seen as a means to an end (well-being) achieved with greater or lesser efficiency in terms of the carrying capacities of nature (sustainability). This perspective will not be widely accepted without measures and indices of social well-being and environmental sustainability that become nearly as much a part of everyday discourse as are GDP growth and the Dow Jones Industrial Average and its equivalents in the other markets of the world.

One widely reported attempt to measure social well-being is the UNDP Human Development Index. This index contains much useful information, and the very fact that it is widely reported suggests that there is at least a potential interest in multidimensional perspectives. The index itself might be improved in ways suggested below. There are also several candidates for leading environmental indicators, including societal metabolism, total material requirement (TMR) (also sometimes called energy and material throughputs), or TMR per capita. A great deal of work is underway on combined indices. This chapter will hopefully encourage, and help to develop the rationale for, further work in this area. It is difficult to imagine any more worthwhile or fruitful area for research in statistical analysis or the social sciences. Moreover, the development of reliable and valid environmental indicators is an ideal meeting ground for the natural and social sciences.

Independent measures of each of the three dimensions (economic, social, and environmental) have a clear place within the overarching model contained in figure 5.1, adapted from work by Marina Fischer-Kowalski and Helmut Haberl.[1]

The key to understanding this model and its importance lies in seeing its basic components as a "positive feedback-loop between three measurable aspects of society: 'quality of life', 'prosperity' and 'metabolism'."[2] These factors, of course, parallel the "economic," "social," "environmental" values discussed extensively above, but with a subtle difference—"metabolism" is not a direct measure of environmental impacts, but can serve as a more readily measurable and unified indicator. Arguably, metabolism—the physical extraction from, use of, and return to nature of all energy and materials—is overwhelmingly the source of environmental impacts. As Fischer-Kowalski and Haberl comment on their figure (presented here in modified form as figure 5.1), "The problem [faced by industrial societies] consists in delinking 'metabolism' from both 'prosperity' and from 'qual-

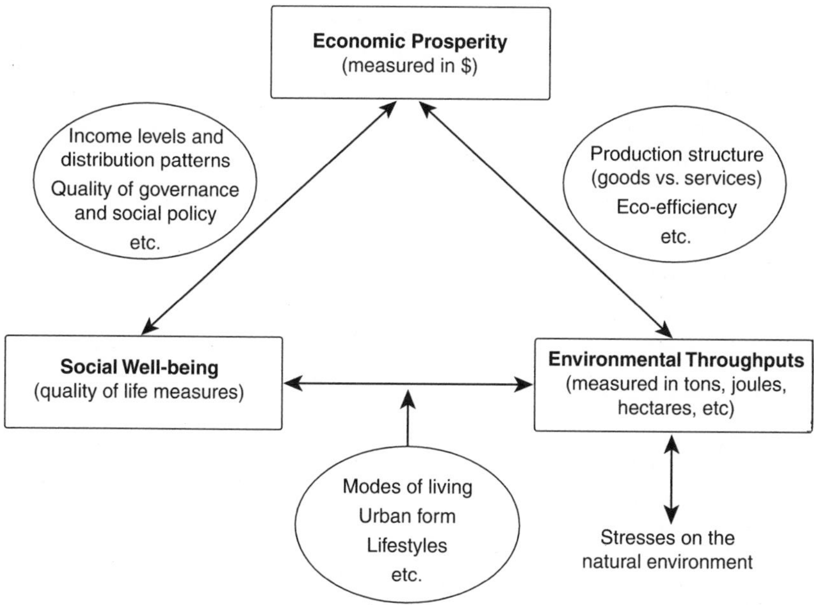

Figure 5.1
A systems model of economy, society, and environment. Source: Adapted from Marina Fischer-Kowalski and Helmut Haberl, "Sustainable Development: Socioeconomic Metabolism and Colonization of Nature," *International Social Science Journal* 158 (1998), 583. © IFF-Social Ecology, 1995.

ity of life'. This bears some similarity to the way Meadows et al. (1972) put the problem. There it was argued that continued economic growth ('prosperity') invariably meant environmental degradation and, therefore, should come to a halt. On the other hand it was argued that you could delink improvements in the quality of life from economic growth, or that further economic growth was not needed to improve quality of life. This 'zero growth formula' met harsh political rejection. We explicitly triangulate the argument: It is not economic growth that puts pressure upon the natural environment, but it is the growth in physical amounts of energy and materials a society processes."[3]

Fischer-Kowalski and Haberl go on to say that "economic growth typically leads to a growth in physical terms, but this does not necessarily have to be so. Even under given circumstances the two dimensions do not grow proportionately."[4] This is, of course, similar to the argument of Robinson and Tinker, but it is presented within a more elaborate multidimensional model of society with a fuller array of visible opportunities for efficiency, productivity, and delinking. There can be widely varying degrees of well-being (happiness, social cohesion, health, education, and security, for example) per unit of prosperity and, as noted, varying amounts of prosperity per unit of physical throughput (as well, of course, as varying amounts of environmental damage per unit of physical throughput). The model also implicitly acknowledges that greater prosperity and higher metabolism can lead to increments of well-being. This model is, in effect, an open invitation to multidimensional quantification and analysis.

Greater prosperity only leads to widespread improvements in well-being if that prosperity is somehow widely shared. At the same time, well-being can be improved without advancing prosperity, but there are clear limits to this, both in terms of political possibility and in terms of the form that most of the assets of the rich take, specifically industrial capital. Were the proceeds of such capital redistributed directly it is highly probable that investments in private productive capacity (as well as the sales of Mercedes and yachts) would decline and demand for food and building materials (for new or larger living spaces) and basic appliances (and the energy to run them) would rise. The sharing could, alternatively or in part, take the form of improved education, public transportation, and health-care access—all relatively benign in terms of energy and material throughputs per dollar of expenditure and (if effectively and efficiently delivered) per unit of well-being. Well-being, in effect, results from prosperity but is produced in less than a one-to-one ratio. Prosperity depends on metabolism, but can even—in principle—be increased at the same time that throughputs are decreased, though this would not be easy. The whole equation is complicated by the fact that both prosperity and well-being can be compromised directly by environmental stress resulting from pollution or from unsustainable rates of extraction.

Conventional economic analysis simply assumes away, or at least gives insufficient attention to, the more interesting questions suggested by this alternative model. Which nations or policy patterns produce the highest levels of health, or some multivariate measure of well-being, per "dollar" of prosperity? Why? What public policy initiatives might produce significant adjustments in metabolism with little or no loss in prosperity over the short or long term? Are there public policy initiatives that might simultaneously reduce metabolism and increase well-being? Are there options, in terms of technologies or policies, that will do that and also increase prosperity? Can (will) electronic capitalism accelerate reductions in energetic and materials waste (dematerialization) relative to industrial society? Does prosperity differ in the extent to which it can advance and promote well-being depending on the mix of different measures of well-being? Can we isolate factors other than prosperity that promote well-being (variously measured)? To what extent do various well-being factors advance other well-being factors (e.g., to what extent do equitable income distribution and workplace efficacy promote health?)? One might even be able to get at Carley and Spapens's concerns regarding the possibility of a threshold effect regarding the relationship between societal wealth and happiness (as discussed in chapter 4).

In their book *Factor Four,* von Weizsäcker, Lovins, and Lovins pursue with great care the relationship between resource use (metabolism) and wealth (prosperity).[5] They conclude, optimistically perhaps, that a shift by a factor of four is possible—that is, there could be twice the present prosperity on half the present level of resource use (or four times the prosperity, and presumably well-being, at present levels of throughput—measured in this case in terms of TMR). I suspect that this could be near to the medium-term upper limit of material and energy-use efficiency short of a radical transformation in the way North Americans and Europeans lead our everyday lives, or in the distribution of human populations on the planet. It is important to note that the expected doubling of the human population would see per-capita wealth remain constant within any successful halving of resource use (or no reduction in resource use were average prosperity per capita to double).

Others believe that there is even more flexibility than this in the materials and energy efficiency of the socioeconomic system (for example, Schmidt-Bleek advances the possibility of a "factor 10" scenario), but many have doubts about such a, perhaps extreme, possibility. As Fischer-Kowalski and Haberl observe, "In no way can we see a material and/or energetic reduction by Schmidt-Bleek's (1994) 'factor 10' or Meadows et al.'s (1992) 'factor 8' to be achieved by such means. As we showed above, the overall per capita energy consumption (including food) of a farming village in the last century was just by a factor of 5 smaller than that of contemporary Austria."[6] The means referred to here are sweeping tax shifts from income to energy and materials. The farming village in question resembles the agricultural-craft societal model of chapter 2. Fischer-Kowalski and Haberl's caution is well taken, but it must be remembered that earlier housing was often poorly insulated and that such supermodern amenities as multimedia Internet access and laptops are not extremely materials and energy intensive (compared to the transportation systems they might in part replace in time, for example). Thus, factor 2 or 3 or even 4 need not be a straightforward return to the past. It might also be noted that life in a nineteenth-century Austrian village was typically both reasonably comfortable and within reach of cultural riches arguably unsurpassed in history.

Thus, the per-capita use of energy and materials in wealthy economies (and, as we will see, especially in North America) could be (gradually) reduced, perhaps by a factor of two or more with minimal loss in prosperity and perhaps even some improvement in well-being. Highly technologized, and fundamentally prosperous, urban lives could be significantly less throughput-intensive than they are now, and probably less intensive than typical rural lives (a modest caution regarding the caution of Fischer-Kowalski and Haberl). Everyday intraurban travel could more often be by public transit or as a pleasant bicycle trip or walk (and travel to work could be less frequent). Warm homes in modest-scale, energy-and materials-efficient dwellings could indeed be less energy intensive than the typical dwellings of a nineteenth-century Austrian village. Computers, electric lights, appliances, and so forth are, of course, net additions to the norm in the Austrian village, but need not in themselves radically alter total energy and materials requirements, which are more affected by the size of spaces, the total mass of disposable products, the durability of nondisposable products, and the mode and amounts of travel. Transportation, manufacturing, and low-grade heat remain the most significant sources of energy demand, and construction is perhaps the greatest single source of materials demand (and is in turn highly responsive to the durability of what is constructed).

Many North Americans and Europeans would, of course, ask themselves why one would even think in such terms. Why would one think about making prosperity any harder to achieve than it already is? Why imagine getting any less prosperity than the absolute maximum attainable? Future resource shortfalls, in effect, are almost always assumed to be someone else's problem. Even higher gasoline prices are typically seen as a problem imposed on the comfort and convenience of one's family by government or OPEC, or both. The widespread outrage regarding the rise in gasoline prices throughout North America and Europe in the summer of 2000 certainly suggests that such a politics of denial and scapegoating is almost automatic even in prosperous times. Some of the causes of such a politics are discussed below under the heading "Communicating Sustainability." But in the end the problem is rooted in a lack of information and especially in a lack of a context within which to understand it. It is rooted, in a word, in economism, a perspective that simply ignores sustainability and fails to understand that human well-being could also be advanced within fixed prosperity levels and, more important, that prosperity is not necessarily dependent on increasing (or even constant) metabolism.

Such considerations highlight the need to independently measure each of the three bottom lines and to consider the efficiency by which we achieve each of them in terms of the other two. New, widely accepted (but not necessarily single-standard) comprehensive indices of each dimension are urgently needed. How much economic benefit is achieved per measure of energy and/or materials extracted from nature? The variation among and between societies is considerable. How much human health or education or overall societal well-being is achieved per dollar of GDP? The variation here is even greater. Such measures of efficiency can be applied comparatively to different societies, communities, and varying policy initiatives and options.

High-quality analysis will require a variety of effective measures, but these do not necessarily require official sanction to be highly useful (though adjustments must be made in the kinds of "economic" statistics gathered by appropriate national agencies). Robert Prescott-Allen, for example, has combined thirty-nine indicators—including health, wealth, freedom, peace, crime, and equity measures—into a Human Wellbeing Index and thirty-nine other indicators into an Ecosystem Wellbeing Index.[7] The Ecosystem Wellbeing Index incorporates air- and water-quality measures, species diversity, water supply, contribution to climate change, and resource pressures. This is precisely the type of analysis that is necessary as a means of building the will to create policy incentives that are three dimensional rather than just one dimensional.

Also among the most important measures of environmental impact are TMR, space (land use), and fugacity (an integrated measure of toxicity), all of which are subsumed under the broader notion of "societal metabolism." Other promising comprehensive environmental indices include "environmental space" and "ecological footprints." Social indices include the United Nations Development Programme (UNDP) Human Development Index, to which we now turn.

The UNDP Human Development Index

The UNDP Human Development Index (HDI) is thus far the most widely reported single measure of either of the "noneconomic" corners of the figure 5.1 triangle. The HDI has been calculated annually since 1990. It combines in equal proportions three measures: health (as measured by life expectancy at birth), education (two-thirds adult literacy and one-third combined gross primary, secondary, and tertiary school enrolment ratio), and GDP per capita. One objective of the HDI is to establish and inform an understanding of development that is broader than what would be obtained from purely economic measures, such as GDP per capita. That is, wide acceptance and use of the HDI could (or should) provide a partial counterweight to an economistic understanding of society and human affairs. The richest nation is not necessarily the most developed nation (by this measure) and, in fact, the richest nation (Luxembourg) ranks seventeenth on the HDI, the third richest nation (United States) ranks third, and the fifth richest nation (Kuwait) ranks thirty-sixth. The first ranked nation (Canada) is the seventh richest and the second ranked nation (Norway) is the fourth richest.[8]

The annual Human Development Report contains a wealth of other information, including additional measures of health and education (specifying the level of public expenditures on each), as well as other (newer) indices such as the Gender-related Development Index (GDI), the Gender Empowerment Measure (GEM), and the Human Poverty Index (HPI). The report also contains "yes-no" data on conformity to international human rights agreements (such as those regarding racial discrimination and political and cultural rights) and the status of fundamental labor rights conventions (such as the collective bargaining rights and child labor). In addition, the Human Development Report makes several attempts to identify development performance successes and failures relative to a nation's level of prosperity. For example, the report identifies pairs of nations with nearly identical HDI scores and significantly different levels of GDP per capita—Thailand's HDI score is essentially the same as Saudi Arabia's, but Saudi Arabia has twice Thailand's GDP per capita.[9]

The report also carries a highly revealing column of figures for all nations titled "GDP Per Capita Rank Minus HDI Rank." A negative figure in this column suggests an HDI performance below (wealth-predictive) expectations; a positive figure suggests a better-than-expected performance. Kuwait had a –31 and many other oil-rich Arab nations had negative figures—after September 11 not a fact to be ignored as a contributing factor in regional and global political instability. South Africa had a score of –54 and Gabon a score of –60. Such scores may in part reflect, for example, gender discrimination in education or lower-than-average health and education expenditures or extreme gaps in wealth distribution. In contrast, Tajikistan had a +43 and Cuba a +40, suggesting strong health and education expenditures and/or healthy lifestyles and widespread and consistent food availability. Costa Rica is also notable at +18 and Sweden at +15 because high positive numbers are perhaps less easily obtained at high levels of prosperity (indeed, even if Sweden were to finish first in HDI, it could only score a +20).[10]

Also informative is the use of the HDI data in time series, especially when sorted for "fastest progress" and "slowest progress" over time. For example, among nations starting with a high HDI Ireland and Luxembourg, while still relatively low in terms of performance relative to GDP per capita, gained the most ground between 1975 and 1998. Also, Jamaica and the Republic of Korea were at the same starting HDI point in 1975, but Korea's gains have been much more rapid (reflecting a faster rate of economic growth in this period as well as other factors). Generally HDI has improved over time. However, seven countries in sub-Saharan Africa (which all saw substantial gains between 1975 and 1985) lost HDI ground between 1985 and 1998 (primarily because of declining life expectancy resulting from AIDS). The late 1980s and 1990s have also witnessed widespread (but not universal) declines in Eastern Europe and the nations of the former Soviet Union, including Russia.[11]

The HPI is highly revealing with regard to both rich and poor nations. Though there is an association, there is no necessary link between HDI and HPI in developing countries (HPI-1). Uruguay, Costa Rica, and Cuba are all high performers in terms of HPI-1. The HPI for industrialized nations (HPI-2) incorporates a number of factors: "For industrialized countries the HPI-2 measures human poverty. Deprivation in a long and healthy life is measured by the percentage of people born today not expected to live to age 60, deprivation in knowledge by the adult functional illiteracy rate, deprivation in economic provisioning by the incidence of income poverty (since private income is the larger source of economic provisioning in industrialized countries) and deprivation in social inclusion by long-term unemployment."[12] This indicator is particularly revealing. The four Scandinavian nations and the Netherlands are more equitable as measured by HPI-1. Canada, HDI's number 1, ranks eleventh of eighteen for whom the calculation was made and the United States (HDI's number 3) ranks last.[13]

Canada has had relatively high unemployment (a component of HPI-2), in part softened by relatively strong educational, social, and health spending (on which it has lost some ground in recent years). The United States has the highest poverty rate (15.8%) and one of the highest rates of functional adult illiteracy of all the eighteen industrialized nations for whom the HPI-2 index was calculated. Of the thirty highest HDI nations only Denmark, Slovenia (number 29), and Portugal (number 28) have a higher proportion of people (than the United States) not expected to survive to age sixty.[14] In terms of this latter measure of equity (and health-care quality), the United States is outperformed by nations such as Malta and Costa Rica. North American underperformance in terms of some measures of equity, health standards, and other social variables is likely even more dramatic when the level of performance is predicted by prosperity (GDP per capita) rather than by HDI (which in effect compounds social and economic variables).

This is a crucial point and requires that we reflect briefly on the model in figure 5.1 and on the meaning of economism. Is wealth an end in itself, or a means to improved human well-being? To be most useful in terms of our model the HDI might be better if constructed "purely" in terms of social performance indicators, leaving economic indicators to stand on their own for analytic purposes. The same suggestion would apply to Prescott-Allen's Human Wellbeing Index, though in both cases one must acknowledge, of course, that wealth contributes to well-being. HPI-2 might be called social development (or other factors might be added, including crime levels and/or social capital). In any case, the key is to allow the comparison nations (or regions, as the UNDP admirably attempts using HDI and its other indices) or economic and social policy time-series patterns in terms of well-being yield per increment of GDP per capita. In effect, the UNDP—in revealing HDI performance relative to GDP per capita—is softening the differentials because GDP per capita is counted twice, on each side of the equation. This effect is further softened (for the most developed nations) by an assumption of 99.0 percent literacy for nineteen of the twenty top HDI nations.[15]

The objective in such changes is not so much to make particular nations look better or worse, but to advance social and policy learning. As has been suggested above, prosperity per capita may not advance rapidly and forever, especially if human populations continue to rise. We do not and probably cannot know in advance what those limits are, but we do know that there are limits to economic dematerialization and that the limits to fossil-fuel supplies will almost certainly increase the challenges associated with economic growth. Given these realities, continually maximizing human well-being per increment of GDP per capita is a crucial undertaking at every level of economic development. Particularly important is the identification and understanding of "higher-than-predicted" national and subnational performance in this regard. Where, when, and why is more health, education, security, equity, and comfort obtained? Where, when, and why are these aspects of well-being maximized per unit of wealth? To answer these questions one must measure social well-being independently and *per unit of economic development* (and economic output per unit of environmental "cost"), thereby assessing the effectiveness—social productivity, if you will—of economic achievements from the point of view of both society as a whole and of nature.

The essential point is that the globalization, increased trade liberalization, and even perhaps the accelerated economic growth that may characterize electronic capitalism may or may not prove to be a net positive development in human history. Unless one is to answer this question (either "for" or "against") without reflection, one needs sound noneconomic measures of human well-being. Increased prosperity may be an essential ingredient in achieving increased well-being, but it is not so much a direct measure as a possible means to that complex end. Using the HDI, for example, as one indicator one suspects that, given the general advance of HDI between 1975 and 1998, there may be some correlation between electronic capitalism and social well-being. But we need other and better measures to be sure that the well-being improvements come because of economic advance rather than in spite of it. More important, we need to understand the ways performance is not as good as it might have been—because in a challenging future with higher human populations and fewer "easy" energy options it will need to be better. It may also need to be more, not less, equitable.

Learning from Measures of Social Equity

There are numerous measures of social equity, each revealing another dimension of the problem and pointing toward solutions. One such study, carried out for the United Nations Children's Fund by the Innocenti Research Centre, was particularly revealing.[16] This study compared the relative poverty rate of families with children in twenty-nine industrialized countries. Relative poverty was defined as having an income below 50 percent of median household income. Relative poverty defined this way correlates with early school leaving, learning difficulties, drug use, crime, joblessness, and early pregnancy. The highest proportion of children living in relative poverty (in the twenty-nine countries) was in Mexico (26.2%); the next highest rate was in the United States (22.4%), followed by Italy (20.5%), Great Britain (19.8%), Turkey (19.7%), and Ireland (16.8%). The lowest rates were in the Scandinavian countries: Sweden (2.6%), Norway (3.9%), and Finland (4.3%). In the middle range were the other European nations, Japan, and Canada.

What is particularly interesting about this finding is that the poorest equity performance exists in the poorest and the richest nations in the list. Surprisingly, there appears to be no significant correlation with the unemployment rate (at least among relatively prosperous nations). Italy had the highest unemployment rate among G7 nations and the United States the lowest. Mexico has an extremely high unemployment rate; Britain has a low rate. Spain, with an unemployment rate in excess of 15 percent, and Japan, with a rate below 5 percent, each have roughly 12 percent of their children in relative poverty. Also particularly striking is the fact that Sweden, with the lowest rate of children in poverty, has the highest share of children living with one parent: 20 percent. Thus, both single-parent families and high unemployment tend to contribute to child poverty, but either or both can be overcome by a concerted national policy effort. Moreover, national prosperity neither ensures the diminution of relative poverty (note U.S. performance)—nor does the policy-driven diminution of poverty tend to so strain the public treasury as to prevent overall national prosperity (note Scandinavian and European GDP per capita).

Nor does prosperity necessarily lead to the alleviation of the worst ills of poverty or provide all citizens with what are its presumed benefits. As noted in chapter 4, national prosperity does not guarantee high levels of health, Wildavsky's sweeping overall correlations notwithstanding. This has been well known since Amartya Sen established that GDP and many measures of welfare (well-being) do not correlate very well.[17] It is also borne out by the data available in the annual UNDP reports. Following the work of Sen, and using UNDP data, Carley and Spapens produced a striking table regarding life expectancy (at birth) and GDP per capita (in 1993 dollars). Costa Rica (at $5,680 and 76.4 years) and Greece (at $8,950 and 77.7 years) placed ahead of the United States (at $24,680 and 76.1 years).[18] This result is not, however, a function of inadequate expenditures on health. U.S. health spending is far and away the highest on a per-capita basis. It is much more a function of income distribution, including (but not limited to) the equitability in the distribution of quality health care.

Again, what is crucial about this data is the almost complete absence of a correlation. Carley and Spapens's data in the preceding paragraph demonstrate that excellent national performance in terms of life expectancy can be achieved independently of very high GDP per capita. Health, measured in terms of life expectancy, can be (and has been) achieved by quite poor nations and can also be notably less than might be predicted by GDP per capita alone. An overall correlation does exist, but it is rather weak. The same generalization also applies to a broad range of other social equity and quality-of life-measures: infant mortality, literacy, and violent crime rates, for example. Sen's overall conclusion, as noted by Carley and Spapens, is to the point: the differences in performance are accounted for as much or more by well-coordinated governmental policies in health, education, and income security as by overall levels of wealth as measured by GDP per capita. This simply cannot be understood unless prosperity and well-being are measured separately and relative performance is continuously compared.

The Innocenti findings would seem to corroborate this conclusion. In terms of the ability of society as a whole to bear the costs of social, educational, and health performance, generally the wealthier the nation, the less the per capita burden such programs would impose. But, the willingness of the wealthier members of society to pay is not consistent, nor is their political capacity to resist public spending on social programs. Whatever the explanation, possible improvements are, to say the least, not the norm within electronic capitalism, progressive social policies have been in retreat within many nations, both wealthy and poor. With globalization, national moral and political failings become a trade advantage.

As Deacon puts it: "Economic competition between countries may lead to the economic costs of social protection being shed in order to be more competitive ('social dumping') unless there are supranational or global regulations in place that discourage this."[19] Thus, throughout the process of global scale economic integration, there have been wide tendencies for economic inequalities to increase. The explanation may be that at some level of overall inequality a wealthy segment of society (unwilling to share) can simply overwhelm the political system through disproportionately effective activism, direct political contributions, and centralized corporate ownership and control of the media.

If this is the case, today's patterns and practices will not be easily reversed. Indeed, the share of wealth owned by the poorest tenth of the global citizenry decreased from 2.3 percent to 1.4 percent from 1980 until the late 1990s, while the holdings of the wealthiest fifth grew from 70 percent to 83 percent.[20] Within the United States and Britain in particular inequality shifted dramatically. Between 1979 and 1995, the "index of inequality" increased by 1.17 in the United States (roughly a 25% increase) and by 0.86 (roughly a 20% increase) in Britain. In contrast, in this same period Germany improved its inequality index, and negative changes in France, Sweden, and Japan were very small, averaging less than 10 percent of the proportional shift in the United States.[21] This explains the pressures on European nations to roll back social welfare policies and to improve their competitiveness.

However, while there is much truth in this picture, there are at least two offsetting complications. First, the United States, the most liberalized of wealthy nations, has in some ways improved the situation of the poorest segments of society (since 1995) primarily because very low levels of unemployment were achieved. That is, not only do minimum wage jobs (even where the minimum wage is low) produce a higher income than does welfare (especially where welfare rates are also low), but full employment itself pressures employers to improve benefits and conditions of work in order to attract and retain employees. That effect appears to have taken hold in the United States in the late 1990s, though it has waned somewhat since.

The danger of course is that the effect will disappear instantly with any return of recession with the result that conditions will be especially problematic for the poor given the ongoing erosion of social programs. Nonetheless, given the effects of low unemployment, the race between nations may not be straightforwardly to the bottom. Leading nations in the race may well face their own internal pressures even if those pressures do not manifest themselves politically in terms of social policy restoration elsewhere. It is thus arguable that it is too soon to come to a firm conclusion regarding the complexities of income distribution in electronic capitalism, even though there is a clear overall trend toward declining equity.

Frances Stewart and Albert Berry have studied this question with considerable care and conclude that the 1970s and 1980s, at least, saw declining equity levels (measured by comparing the top 20% of incomes to the bottom 20%) throughout the OECD nations, with the exception of France and New Zealand, where there were small improvements. The ratio in the United States went from 7 to 1 in 1967 to 10 to 1 in 1989. In Britain and Sweden it went from about 4 to 1 to about 6 to 1.[22] The leading causes of the shift were the increased regressivity of taxation, increasing gaps in wage levels, rising unemployment (in most nations studied during that period as a whole), an increasing proportion of retired persons in the population, and a sharply increasing proportion of incomes deriving from profits relative to incomes deriving from wages and salaries. High (Germany, France) or rising (Japan) unemployment has remained in some nations, and all the other conditions noted in explanation here appear to be holding as electronic capitalism widens and deepens.

Stewart and Berry, however, note a second dimension of possible declining income inequality for the period from the 1970s through into the early 1990s. There may be some overall decline in inter-national income inequality (that is, some nations—most notably China—have gained ground on the wealthy nations). This shift contrasts sharply with the deteriorating equity of distribution *within* most poor nations, most dramatically in the "countries in transition" (from communism to market economies).[23] Regression on the within-nation front was the norm as well throughout

Latin America, with Costa Rica again being a notable exception. In this regard, Stewart and Berry comment: "Costa Rica appears to be the only Latin American country to have undertaken significant market-friendly reforms without suffering a large widening of income differentials. . . . It is possible that when changes are made more gradually, as in Costa Rica, they do not produce as great a negative effect on distribution as when the same degree of policy change takes place more quickly."[24] Change in within-nation distribution in Asia and Africa was more mixed, but generally moved toward greater inequality as well.

But, and this is the second offsetting complication regarding globalization and equity, the inequity of between-nation distribution of income has in some cases narrowed. The gains shown by China and a few other countries (and slow growth in the United States) in the 1970s and 1980s have partially offset rising overall within-country inequality when one compares the poorest quintile to the richest on a global scale. As Stewart and Berry put it, "Had there been no intra-country variation of distribution the world distribution would have improved considerably over the decade."[25] The importance of this change is considerable. Poor nations able to "take advantage of international markets to expand labour-intensive manufactured exports, showed some tendency to improve income distribution."[26] Middle-income and wealthy nations, however, have consistently experienced deteriorating distribution (as a result of deliberate governmental policies or as low-skill manufacturing jobs are replaced with low-skill service jobs, for example).

Stewart and Berry conclude: "On balance, the swing away from government intervention and towards the market has tended to increase inequality *within countries*. However, the acceleration in growth of large poor countries—notably China—has worked in the opposite direction, so that world income distribution appears to have improved. This acceleration of growth is partly due to the opportunities offered by liberalization and globalization."[27] Liberalization in this context refers especially to the liberalization of trade rules and the replacement of raw materials and agricultural production exclusivity with the export-led expansion of manufacturing. This suggests that globalization and trade per se are not the problem. It also suggests that the leap from trade liberalization to all forms of neoliberalism is wrongheaded. There is little if any evidence that rising GDP improves either income distribution or well-being (a much broader concept) in prosperous nations. This outcome might be possible were low unemployment to be generalized and sustained throughout the wealthy nations over an extended period, but this has certainly not happened thus far. Rising inequality persists throughout wealthy and middle-income nations, and in most poor nations desperation remains the norm.

It is nonetheless frequently argued that inequality is part of the price that must be paid in order to accelerate economic growth, and that all in the end will benefit. This is the "rising tide raises all boats" view of the world. In this view there is a need for ever-accelerating rewards for the most successful members of society, so that they will invest more to the ultimate benefit of all, and poverty is an incentive to work harder. There is little evidence to support either claim. China began with high levels of income equity but has gained ground; most poor nations have not. Moreover, the poor of nearly every nation have lost ground for no obvious reason other than to add to the relative share of the rich in those same nations.

Perhaps more important, as a World Bank study in 1996 suggested, "For any given level of GDP per person, a country with an unequal distribution of income or wealth will have a higher proportion of poor people who cannot borrow to finance . . . education, or business start up(s), and the economy will grow more slowly."[28] Carley and Spapens's array selected wealthy nations on a table that suggests that increasing income equality (not inequality) correlated quite systematically with growth in labor productivity in the 1980s. The desperate are not often forced to produce, nor should they be; rather they simply never get the opportunity to do so. What is needed is education, access to markets, and the increased availability of small-scale capital, not richer rich people and deteriorating social programs.

What do these data regarding equity suggest regarding globalization and electronic capitalism? They suggest, as was asserted above, that trade liberalization and the new economy are neither the one almost automatic way to the salvation of humankind, nor the work of the devil. They suggest that increased global trade and the other changes comprising what has been called electronic capitalism here may promote rising social inequity in many or most nations, but they may also promote both absolute and relative economic advance in some poor nations. It is not clear, however, that the current general rise in inequality contributes in any (positive) way to the transformation. Rather, it is an unintended consequence that might in time be partially offset—but only in wealthy nations that attain economic leadership status sufficient to create and maintain full employment. It is far from certain that low rates of unemployment can be generalized in wealthy nations on a sustained basis given ongoing exports of work to low-wage economies and ever more effective forms of automation.

It is, however, possible that through social policy minima pegged to the level of economic development, rising inequity could be reversed. Poverty in the wealthy nations in the era of electronic capitalism is a function of deliberate public policy. These policies result from a conflation of trade liberalization and the variety of other initiatives identified with neoliberalism: reductions in health and education spending and other social programs and tax reductions systematically favoring the wealthy. Political competition in wealthy nations is typically now between a party that openly and enthusiastically advocates policies tilted to the advantage of the wealthy and a party that adopts such policies because this is the only way the country can "remain competitive" with nations that already have such tax rates and policies in place. The United States, in particular, can adopt lower tax rates because it has been in an economic leadership position. This presses other nations to keep up as if it were the low rates and reduced social spending alone that created the economic advantage.

Every nation cannot hold a comparative advantage simultaneously. Continuously improving domestic equity could be achieved if national governments were to collectively resolve that this was a shared policy objective. Rising inequity is not a result of economic integration so much as the result of an absence of social policy coordination and of a common commitment to at least maintain social equity. The outcome is not accidental, but it is a matter of omission, not commission (and in that sense is an unintended consequence). Reversing the trend requires active and collective policy initiatives and an end to disingenuousness among political leaders regarding what is now a more-than-obvious, but altogether unnecessary, pattern. If the pattern were widely acknowledged as something other than an inevitable aspect of globalization, it could be reversed through taxation policy or through complementary agreements regarding minimum well-being performance (perhaps per unit of GDP per capita) among trading partners by a certain date.

The broad principle here is one that links social (and environmental) performance to economic integration and that pegs well-being performance to levels of economic success. Economically leading nations, and the desperately poor, would thereby be expected to do better and would not simply drive down the social policy standards of all. Poorer nations could continue to gain some advantage through lower wages, but the gap among those at any given level of development would be limited and the gap between those at the low end and those at the high end would be restrained somewhat and would be slowly closed over time. The objective is to gain some semblance of global *governance* without global *government*. Some other possibilities will be discussed in chapters 6 through 8. First, however, we must briefly look more closely at environmental and sustainability indicators.

Metabolism and TMR as Nonmonetary Economics

While measures of social equity and the HDI are well established, measures of sustainability are generally less visible. Nonetheless, exciting work is well underway.[29] The challenge is to bring such work to the point where it is more central to both social scientific and public discourse. Understanding metabolism is akin to understanding the functioning of human economies without considering the use of money. What quantities of physical material are extracted from nature to serve human purposes and what by-products, and what amount of by-product, are returned to nature (particularly by-products that are ecologically problematic)? It might be said that early industrialization was about learning how to expand human extractive and processing capabilities and that one goal of electronic capitalism must be to learn how to become more efficient in metabolic terms—how to maximize well-being per unit of GDP and to maximize GDP per unit of resources extracted from nature. That is, we must now learn how to minimize TMR through increasing the materials and energy efficiency of both economic output and societal well-being.

All three corners of the triangle must be measured with great care, and the relationships among the three must be thoroughly and widely understood. This is no small feat, especially with regard to the environmental corner of the triangle. Perhaps the best efforts thus far are those of the

Wuppertal Institute, an organization that has pioneered work in measuring the TMR of economies. TMR is a broader measure than the total of natural resource inputs (called direct material inputs or DMI) to an economy. It also includes "hidden flows" of materials, such as the erosion associated with agricultural outputs, the removal of overburden in open-pit mining, and the movement of materials associated with construction. Only the "use" of air and water is excluded. All of these material flows involve considerable environmental impacts. Indeed, these flows and the direct material inputs of raw natural resources into an economy could serve as a reasonable proxy for the environmental impacts within economic sectors or whole economies, especially if releases of toxic pollutants were excluded. Impacts per ton of TMR do, of course, vary—but they are never zero. Moreover, almost all material extractions (or throughputs) come at some cost in terms of habitat loss and greenhouse gas emissions, as well as nonrenewable energy inputs and thus resource sustainability.[30]

TMR data allow us to better understand how economies work in relation to the environment and in comparison with each other and over time. A study of TMR in four industrial economies (the United States, Japan, Germany, and the Netherlands) is very informative in that regard. The data show that these economies currently utilize from forty-five to eighty-five metric tons of natural resources per person per year.[31] This amount is, on average, rising slowly over time (between 1975 and 1995) even as these economies are gradually transforming from industrial employment to service employment. Improved TMR efficiencies are, however, being achieved per dollar of GDP, currently standing at about 300 kilograms of resources per $100 of GDP income.[32]

The Japanese economy is considerably more efficient in these terms, though some of that difference may be accounted for by currency equivalency factors. The important finding in this study is, however, that through time over this period all four countries showed considerable improvement in GDP/TMR ratios measured in terms of a constant currency value (the U.S. dollar in this case). In other words, all four economies are dematerializing, but are doing so more slowly than they are growing in absolute (rather than per-capita) terms. Damage to nature is thus likely increasing, and sustainability thereby declining, even though those costs may be slowly declining per unit of economic activity.

This striking finding is indirectly confirmed in a notable short article in *Science*. This article refutes the claims that economic development results at first in rising pollution and environmental damage, but at some point along the development path in sharp improvement (overall following an inverted U-shaped curve).[33] This pattern, they argue, applies to pollution only and even then to a limited set of pollutants. It does not apply to resource sustainability. It does not necessarily apply to deforestation or soil loss. It does not apply to the release of greenhouse gases and it does not apply to habitat loss. Moreover, the evidence regarding the limited list of pollutants only applies to one country and not to the economic system as a whole. That is, pollution may not be reduced so much as it is transferred from wealthier to poorer nations. Clearly, both possibilities are typically occurring simultaneously—pollution-abatement equipment is installed as nations gain in wealth, but dirty industries (mining, smelting, steel production, and others) tend to migrate from high- to low-wage countries (along with high-labor-content industries such as the production of clothing and electronic devices).

Some findings of the four-nation TMR study, in addition to the pattern of improving relative sustainability (TMR efficiency) and absolute decline described above, are also striking. First, the two European nations do not appear to be significantly more efficient than the United States in terms of TMR per capita or GDP/TMR despite having well-known advantages in terms of energy-use efficiency. The Dutch are not less TMR intensive, primarily because of twenty-nine tons per capita of soil erosion associated with massive imports of livestock feed incorporated within eighty tons of overall TMR per capita. Similarly, Germany's figures are altered upward by the mass of materials removed in coal extraction, on which German industry is highly dependent. Second, only the economy of the United States is near to being self-sufficient in terms of cross-border net material flows. Germany produces a larger share of such flows domestically, but both Japan and the Netherlands are importing materials (and could be said to be thereby exporting the larger share of "their" environmental troubles). Arguably, this is to be expected given that both are densely populated, small, and wealthy nations with a limited range of domestic resources. Third, strikingly, the improvement in materials-use efficiency (in terms of DMI) has flattened in all four nations in the period after 1985.

This latter finding may be the most important, though the study itself does not make much of it. Regarding the recent flattening of DMI/GDP, the authors of the four-nation comparative study comment: "The resulting pattern shows a modest decline in intensity, followed by a leveling off over the past decade, which implies that direct inputs of natural resources are now growing in parallel with economic growth. Improvements in technology and industrial practice or structural shifts to a more service-intensive economy, which might be expected to reduce this measure of material intensity, do not seem to be continuous."[34] Another explanation may be that global energy prices dropped in 1985, then remained constant for the balance of the decade (and declined relative to the price of all goods and services).

Moreover, no sooner had prices dropped than governments dropped most energy conservation incentives and promotions that they had pursued with uncharacteristic vigor while the mood of "energy crisis" prevailed.[35] More study is needed, but the best way to accelerate change in GDP/TMR (to dematerialize the economy) may be to impose a slow but assured rate of price increases for energy and materials, especially the former. Knowing with some assurance that energy prices will rise steadily through time would have considerable effect on urban form, on choice of transportation mode, on recycling, on industrial energy and materials efficiency, and on product design and consumer choices.

The brief oil-price surge of the year 2000 might eventually have restored the pattern that the TMR study showed for the period of the early 1980s. If oil prices return to that level soon, flattening could come to be the medium-term norm for electronic capitalism (along with rising demand in poorer nations). From the perspective of individual consumers in wealthy nations, what is saved in banking and researching online instead of driving to the bank or library will be "reclaimed" on a quick cheap annual holiday flight, or on the loss of a potential municipal recycling or public transit initiative that "just cannot pay its way."

The notion of "factor ten," discussed above, developed out of the TMR research of the Wuppertal Institute. The logic of a need for a "factor ten" level of improvement in GDP/TMR within the wealthy economies combined assumes that present levels of environmental damage, combined with limits to world resource supplies, especially fossil fuels, require a radical reduction in GDP/TMR ratios over the next thirty to fifty years. Gains at this level are a matter of prudence, in this view, especially if economic growth is to continue at a reasonable pace. If the reasonable needs of developing nations were to be met, then rich-nation GDP/TMR might need to be reduced by a factor that approaches ten. As noted, it is far from obvious that this is possible. Nonetheless, considerable reductions are possible and likely essential.

In 1996 the OECD Environmental Policy Committee endorsed a dematerialization target level of factor ten for the wealthy nations as a long-term goal. Thus the present average of 300 metric tons per $100 of GDP (in the four nations of the study discussed here) would need to be reduced to 30 tons.[36] An undertaking anywhere nearly that ambitious would obviously require massive technological innovations, policy interventions (incentives and pricing), and behavioral changes. One measurement concept needed to begin any move in such a direction is the "ecological rucksack" or material intensity per service (MIPS) developed by Schmidt-Bleek.[37] A "service" is what is delivered to a consumer, from a gold coin to a meal to comfortable travel over a given distance. MIPS indicates the cradle-to-grave materials use (including hidden resource extraction) associated with delivery of the desired service (the need that a product or service in the usual sense fulfills). MIPS can vary enormously and can be altered by redesign (as with energy-efficient lightbulbs), by a changed consumer understanding of what a need really entails (must furnishings or clothing always be new and ever-changing or might an open window be as good as an air-conditioner?), or by changes brought about by simply knowing the size of the ecological rucksack various materials, products, and services carry.

What this comes down to is learning to measure things that we are not in the habit of measuring. To build an economy that is truly sensitive to ecological and sustainability concerns, we must measure that economy's efficiency in more than dollars. We need an economics that measures and deals with materials (including energy) directly. We do not just need to maximize monetary flows, but also to continually and rapidly reduce the material flows per dollar of economic activity. We need new measurements, and a will to attend to those measurements with the enthusiasm we devote to things monetary, in order to achieve new forms of efficiency.

MIPS and TMR are perhaps not enough by way of such new measures, but they are at least a good ready indicator of progress or a lack thereof.

The four-nation study itself suggests that "raw" TMR data should be weighted according to the level of ecological impacts. The book *Factor Four* takes the same view and argues that while MIPS can serve as a generalized yardstick, more refined yardsticks are available for some ecological effects. In the authors' words, "There is toxicity, there is land use, there are greenhouse gas emissions. But in some way or other, all relate to the intensity of material turnover. And it is extremely valuable to have something simple for 'quick and dirty' assessments of ecological impacts."[38]

Thus, while these rough measures can indicate whether an economy as a whole is moving toward sustainability, the measures can and should be refined. There is, for example, a big difference between a ton of silt dredged from a harbor (a hidden movement) and a ton of coal burned without scrubbers. There can be an equally big difference between one ton of forest extraction and another ton depending on such factors as slope, climate, rainfall, ecological factors, and removal practices. We should, then, weight the material components in an ever more refined way, perhaps in the first instance assigning average ecological impact weights to the materials, or categories of materials, that comprise more than 1 percent of TMR in any given jurisdiction. With or without weighting, TMR measures (or even just consumed and "embedded" energy) would suggest the relative environmental importance of such jurisdictional differences as the size of service and technology sectors, urban form, recycling effectiveness, choice of transportation mode, building renovation versus demolition and reconstruction, modification of agricultural and forest practices, mining practices, packaging and waste-disposal policies, and dietary patterns. All of these findings are potentially relevant to future public policy decisions, as well as to matters of personal choice.

Measuring sustainability and ecological impacts is a complicated undertaking, but one that becomes more and more necessary as human population and total economic output rise. To the extent that global economic integration advances the growth of GDP, and likely thereby TMR, it becomes even more important to develop and refine, and to respond to, sustainability measures. High TMR is, of course, a function of low and declining commodity prices, an outcome not unrelated to globalization and electronic capitalism. Moreover, in a globalized world many of the most severe impacts of industrial activity are pushed to distant reaches of the planet. Concern with long-term sustainability (and for other species) is less easily prioritized in poorer nations and regions. Thus globalization geographically separates relatively high levels of environmental concern from some of the most severe environmental impacts. Only effectively measuring and communicating sustainability and ecological effects can help to overcome these tendencies. This communication must be rooted in a new, broader and more integrated social and natural science understanding—a three-dimensional perspective rather than one-dimensional economism.

In the end, we still-modern humans count what we value and perhaps can learn to value whatever we resolve to count. Money is easily and habitually counted with great precision and speed—economic values are, to say the least, well attended to in public policy deliberations and everyday behavior. The achievement of sustainability and well-being requires, but is of course not guaranteed by, new assessments of the "efficiency" with which prosperity produces shared well-being and minimizes impositions on nature. Electronic capitalism has the capacity to make great strides in both aspects of this new "double efficiency." As noted earlier, many of today's fastest-growing economic sectors are "dematerializing" in character—be they pharmaceuticals, software, films, cell phones, or gambling opportunities. The question that remains is, can three-dimensional thinking effectively compete within the one-dimensional economism of the media world? Will electronic capitalism realize the potential that is there for enhancing both equity and sustainability?

Communicating Sustainability

Perhaps the greatest irony of the age of communications and information is that the crucial equity and environmental realities of our age are communicated, at best, anecdotally. A toxic release from a chemical plant or an oil tanker grounding or a collapsed mine-tailings pond are reported as incidents, but environmental trends are far less clearly communicated. Effective state-of-the-environment reporting has been resisted by many governments and largely ignored by media. Comparisons and trends are important to understanding and to achieving effective environmental and social policy initiatives. Within the social realm, rising inequity may be acceptable to a democratic majority only if it is presented as seemingly inevitable. It is clearly not inevitable, however, if it is not universal. It is not justifiable as the basis for GDP gains if it is not in fact systematically and statistically associated with such gains. Moreover, those GDP gains matter little if virtually none of it reaches the majority. If nothing at all reaches the poorest minority, and this is widely known, then at least questions of fairness can be raised. As it is, none of these things are presently seen as "news."

Communicating the environmental and social dimensions of sustainability poses great challenges. Whatever the data presented regarding the environment, it can always be presumed that a technological fix for areas of particular concern lies somewhere down the road. Science and industry may discover clean, new energy sources. They may learn how to more effectively sequester carbon. Genetically modified plant species may provide abundant food and fiber with costs regarding which we need not overly concern ourselves. Some such things may, of course, actually come to pass. However, these are not small assumptions. We are, in all probability, unwittingly betting millions if not billions of future human lives on the first of these alone. If a clean and reliable new energy source does not emerge sometime in this new century, technologies will probably be put in place regardless of their environmental implications.

The freedom of future generations to opt for or against such possibilities rests with us and with our ability to quickly come to understand, communicate, and enhance environmental sustainability. So does the possibility of future generations living in modest comfort as fossil-fuel supplies peak and wind down. These possibilities alone should suffice as a motive for new thinking, as should the risks to ecological diversity or to other dimensions of environmental quality. The first and urgent challenge, again, is to develop integrated indicators of materials and energy efficiency. The second challenge is to develop concepts and techniques that will communicate this understanding widely. The third challenge is to develop and adopt public policies (including trade rules), and new lifestyles and everyday personal behaviors, that enhance sustainability. There is no avoiding the fact that this latter step will cost some industries and economies some economic growth opportunities. This involves an enormous political challenge within the present political context.

Effective and comprehensive sustainability indicators, the first challenge, should invite and promote comparison—and even competition—among jurisdictions. Most important, they should allow us to see trends through periodic (probably annualized) reporting of new data. In this spirit, the Institute for Systems, Information and Safety in Italy, with others, has developed a sixty-indicator array to compare the environmental performance of 100 Italian cities.[39] The sixty indicators are combined into ten indices for public reporting purposes, but the underlying data is always available to all who are interested. That is, for example, if one wishes to know why Milan consistently fares badly compared to other Italian cities on the water-quality index, one can learn easily that it makes little effort to treat its wastewater. The art in this important work is in the aggregation and reporting. Aggregated indicators, if they are to meet the second challenge, must be understandable, of concern to the public, widely available, and visibly and regularly reported and debated.

Annual, comparative multidimensional environmental and social data allow citizens to see past the day-to-day-ness of environmental and social policy decision making. This approach might even offset in part the skillful buck-passing of industry and public officials. It renders visible both overall successes and failures, one category at a time. The Commission for Environmental Cooperation (CEC, created by the NAFTA side agreement) has reported on toxic pollution from each of sixty state and provincial jurisdictions in the United States and Canada. The CEC has consistently found Texas and Ontario near or at the "top" of the list. The CEC annual listings, like the comparative urban reporting in Italy, provide information in a form that attracts media attention because it creates a competition, winners and losers, and the potential for regular news events around changing trends and patterns. Without such solid data, the public is left with little more than anecdotal information, initiatives created primarily to produce photo ops, and contrived celebrations of modest expenditure initiatives. The public has no way to really know if or when far more might be warranted given the problem at hand, when compared to efforts and outcomes in other jurisdictions.

The overall challenge is to develop and communicate arrays of data regarding equity/society and sustainability/environment that are as compelling and clear as, and approach the visibility of, economic data. No small challenge, of course, but even partial success would be a considerable advance from today's economistic norms. One difficulty will be getting governments to consistently facilitate the collection and release of information that might cast their policies in a negative light. In the United

States, the President's Council on Sustainable Development during the Clinton administration did not even lead to ongoing governmental reporting regarding materials flows. The Canadian government no longer engages in periodic State of the Environment Reporting. The CEC, as will be discussed further in chapter 6, was politically unable to publish a North American State of the Environment Report. Given that these outcomes arose during the tenure of relatively open governments (though Europe is far in advance regarding sustainability and environmental indicator research), it is arguable that these data should be developed, assessed, and publicized at arm's length from government data services—taking what help can be gleaned, but not relying on it.[40]

At present, sustainability information in particular only rarely reaches the level of public discourse. Indeed, of the social sciences, only economics and opinion polling have a significant and consistent media and public presence. This is not simply a matter of the political predilections of media owners and advertisers. A significant proportion of the media audience is concerned about, and understands, basic economic indicators: unemployment, GDP, inflation, and stock market indices. As noted in chapter 3, these data are generated and reportable minute by minute, or at least weekly or monthly. They are straightforward and have resonance for broad segments of the public; the measures that enter public discourse are few in number, standardized in terms of data-gathering methods, and accurately convey what they intend to convey. Developing a comparable set of measures for well-being and sustainability (albeit not calculated on a minute-by-minute basis) is not a task beyond the social and natural sciences and is well underway. Moreover, new media forms may be particularly well suited to widely conveying these new data.

For example, the concept of ecological footprints has received considerable attention in environmental social science circles, and even now, through the website of the Mountain Equipment Co-op, one can calculate one's personal footprint. To determine a "footprint" for a city, industry, or nation, Wackernagel and Rees, the developers of the concept, have calculated resource-extraction demands and environmental impacts in terms of the land area needed to sustain them.[41] That is, land devoted to mining, to waste disposal, to energy extraction, to forest removals, to human settlement, and so forth is calculated as the ecological footprint. Obviously, a densely populated city requires a vastly larger area to sustain it than it actually occupies. Geographically small but wealthy nations that import many raw materials also have a footprint larger than the land they occupy. Footprint analysis has determined that if the world as a whole were to use resources at the present North American rate, three earths would be necessary to supply the resources and dispose of the wastes (including excess carbon) on a sustainable basis. The notion of ecological footprints resonates and can be readily communicated because it is a visual image.

The concept of environmental space is less literally represented in visual, land-based terms, but is very useful nonetheless. Environmental space, as articulated by Carley and Spapens, in effect incorporates a moral dimension. The concept is defined as "the total amount of energy, non-renewable resources, land, water, wood and other resources which can be used globally or regionally: without environmental damage; without impinging on the rights of future generations; and within the context of equal rights to resource consumption and concern for the quality of life of all peoples of the world."[42] There is, of course, some lack of specificity embedded in this concept that will challenge those who do the actual calculations. Virtually all resource extraction damages the environment, and all nonrenewable resource extraction imposes to some extent on future generations even if other (lower-grade or more distant) resources remain available. Nonetheless, the concept will render starkly visible dramatic excesses and shortfalls in resource-utilization shares. The concept might be particularly useful in the debate regarding appropriate national levels of greenhouse gas emissions.

Integrative measures such as ecological footprints and environmental space make a useful contribution, but even more promising possibilities are being developed. Particularly important are integrated presentations of combined indices for each of the three corners of the triangle in figure 5.1: quality of life, prosperity, and environment (metabolism). Each index can incorporate multiple combined measures such as health or education or water quality that in turn would incorporate others. An environmental performance indicator might include an energy-use measure, a renewable resource–use measure, a water-pollution measure, a solid-waste-disposal measure, and so forth. The renewable resource–use measure might include soil loss, forest extraction, fisheries data, and other items. The pollution index might combine heavy-metals releases in all media, nitrogen oxide levels in urban ambient air, and so on. All of this data could overwhelm most people's tolerance for complexity and quantitative data, but there is an elegant, new-media solution to this problem: hypertext.

Broadcast media need only report the combined index findings comparatively with comparable jurisdictions and in terms of trends and then provide a website for further information. A website might present three speedometer-like dials indicating changes over time in the three societal dimensions—whereby it might be communicated that prosperity was up 3 percent, but well-being/quality of life down 2 percent and overall environmental quality improving (or not).[43] Alerts to the most significant rises and falls can be highlighted in on-screen bulletins (e.g., "new waste-treatment initiatives improve water quality" or "well-being improvements offset by rising crime rate or deteriorating medical services availability"). Clicking on a dial or a bulletin results in a display of underlying information complete with subbulletins. Subindices can yield a deeper layer of data down to the specific multiple measures that comprise the index, with links at all levels to comparative data from other jurisdictions. Needless to say, a high proportion of citizens need not probe all layers on a daily basis for such information to have a real long-term effect. It may be politically sufficient that the data is there and attended to by segments of the informed public with regard to areas of particular concern.

Such developments, if widely reported by the conventional media, might go a considerable way toward communicating the information necessary to meeting the third challenge above—the adoption of more balanced public policies that simultaneously maintain or enhance social well-being, environmental sustainability, and economic prosperity. This obviously is ultimately a political matter, but social science can contribute to public discourse regarding such matters without necessarily attempting to resolve them or determining for citizens and governments what is—nation by nation—the appropriate balance among the three. Only natural and social scientists can, however, measure and determine some of the relationships among the three dimensions in a more balanced way than we have in the past. This effort is vital to democratic decision making. How is a community or nation (or the global economy as a whole) performing in terms of the efficiency with which it uses materials and energy? What is, for example, its relative level of GDP/TMR? Is a community or nation performing as might be expected, given its level of prosperity, in terms of widely accepted indicators of well-being? Where is it performing well? Where and why is it performing badly?

The leap from better and more balanced information (even assuming that the electronic media attend to the scientific effort with intelligence, enthusiasm, and imagination) to policy initiatives will, of course, be challenging. Poverty (and the absence of well-being) has always been with us and it is easy to assume that therefore it must always be. Sustainability is by definition long term, and the future is unknowable. Again, it will remain painfully easy to just assume that technology will resolve the worst problems when they arise. Few are prepared to consider what is involved in resolving the sustainability problems that technology may prove unable to resolve. Moreover, we simply cannot know which are likely to prove beyond our technological capabilities. Acting in ways that will be perceived by some as deliberate restraints on economic growth when it is not yet certain that such restraint is imperative is, at best, politically challenging even with all the data in the world in front of everyone. Nor can anyone demonstrate conclusively which particular sustainability initiatives are most important at any point in time.

Fortunately, there is another way to view this central dilemma. Many of the more dynamic sectors of advanced economies would not be hindered by sustainability initiatives. Moreover, the necessary adjustments need not be planned in detail by governments but could be seen through at a publicly influenced and adjustable pace by market forces guided by a pattern of tax and other policies and price agreements. Many of the adjustments that would occur would likely be necessary in any case to slow or stop climate warming. Finally, sustainability problems are rooted in a power imbalance in the trading system, the correction of which should aid many poorer nations, especially those not positioned to jump rapidly into manufacturing exports. (Recall that these include many of the poorest nations: those that have not gained some relative ground in recent decades).

One root cause of sustainability problems is, of course, commodity prices (relative to the price of services and of manufactured goods). In this matter, one must be mindful that in environmentalism's early days Paul Ehrlich lost an important bet to Julian Simon. Ehrlich's bet was that resources would be less plentiful and more expensive in the (then) near-term future. He was wrong. Declining commodity prices within the time frame of the bet were in part due to improved sustainability behaviors associated with (temporary) energy-price increases, improved extraction technologies, and an ongoing imbalance in the terms of trade between commodity suppliers and exporters of manufactured goods. There are doubtless many

Table 5.1
Commodity Price Index (1990 = 100)

Year	1960	1970	1980	1990	1996	2002
Petroleum	34	21	224	100	78	84
Agriculture	209	181	191	100	110	79
Timber	129	127	110	100	122	86
Metals and minerals	139	162	132	100	78	72

Source: World Resources Institute, United Nations Environmental Programme, United Nations Development Programme, and The World Bank, *World Resources: A Guide to the Global Environment, 1998–99* (New York: Oxford University Press, 1998), 240. Figures for January 2002 are from <www.worldbank.org/prospects/pinksheets/pinksheets0202.htm.> All other figures are the yearly average.

other contributing factors. The important point (see table 5.1) is that commodity prices so far have generally declined relative to the prices of manufactured goods.[44]

Thus, for example, despite the ravages that global forests have borne over the past four decades the price of timber has been held virtually constant through the period. This constant price has all but guaranteed continuing overexploitation in nations with limited economic options. Just 20 percent of the earth's original forests remain as large, relatively natural ecosystems (frontier forests). In the poorer regions of the world, these forests remain under assault (under moderate or high threat are 77 percent of the remaining frontier forests in Africa, 60 percent in Asia, and 54 percent in South America).[45] Some forest destruction is a result of agricultural clearing or mining, but that activity too might slow if timber (and other commodity) prices were higher. Rising commodity prices would slow demand, promote recycling, enhance energy efficiency, and accelerate the dematerialization of economies. It would also help to correct economic imbalances between wealthy nations and poorer ones (albeit in highly uneven patterns, and albeit slowly since demand for resources would slow as prices rose).

The good news is that such a shift could in principle be incorporated within existing trade agreements selectively or generically. The necessary data are already available and globalization is now so thoroughgoing that global prices could be pegged (the "could" here being technical rather than political). The most ecologically problematic commodities (e.g., tropical timbers) could follow a different pricing track than ecologically less problematic commodities. The bad news is that such initiatives are not likely given current attitudes in wealthy nations, especially the United States. Moreover, with the possible exception of petroleum producers, commodity producers have been unable to act in concerted fashion so far. Perhaps, then, the central political question of our time is the following: Can the generalized discomfort with globalization, environmental problems, and rising inequality be marshaled into a fundamental compromise akin to the rise of unionization and the welfare state in the age of industrialization?

If there is ever to be a fundamental compromise that parallels the establishment of the welfare state in the era of industrial society, it will need to be global rather than national in scale. The fundamental compromise of electronic capitalism must somehow also address environmental sustainability and human well-being simultaneously. Globalization, contrary to the view of many who would support such change, is not necessarily an enemy of movement in this direction. Global economic integration is both a means of undermining national-scale democracy and the potential institutional basis for the development of some form of global democratic governance.

In other words, globalization based on economism may not be as inevitable and invulnerable as it presently appears to be. Given climate change and the limited future of plentiful energy, continued GDP growth *requires* accelerated dematerialization. Carrying capacity may also ultimately imply some restraints on total global economic capacities—a possibility that would place distributional questions starkly front and center. One simply must assume that many citizens and global leaders will come to see the world in these terms and through anticipation avoid the worst possible futures. To do so they will need, of course, to resolve democracy's dilemma at least in part.

Achieving accelerated dematerialization and reversing rising inequity can delay—maybe even allow us to avoid—the starkest ecological and/or socioeconomic and thereby political deterioration. Rules of the global economic game that are at once ecologically prudent and socially just are in the end in the best interests of all, including the rich in the rich nations. Continual measurement of sustainability limits and well-being outcomes on a comparative basis has the best hope of making this truth widely visible.

The Two Deficits and the Limits of Electronic Capitalism

Even in wealthy countries, many feel economically vulnerable, and polls have suggested that few trust their governments to protect their interests in global trade negotiations.[46] This discomfort may help to create a climate in which democracy's dilemma might be resolved through the establishment of a system of transparent, balanced, and democratic global governance. There are two important points of vulnerability within today's global system (other than a politics that flows from either distributional issues or environmental issues, or a generalized distrust). These may pose a significant challenge to electronic capitalism's initial trajectory.

The two sources of personal insecurity and systemic vulnerability might be called a "democratic deficit" and a "family-time deficit." The democratic deficit is, of course, visible within the present structures of global-scale decision making that pretend that economic and trade politics can be separated from (or should always and automatically trump) environmental and social concerns. This absence of openness was rendered starkly visible, for example, in the choice of Qatar—a venue easily closed to demonstrators—as the site of the 2001 meetings of the WTO. The family-time deficit is the result of economic competitiveness so intense that total work time in one- or two-adult families increases simultaneously with rising productivity. For significant proportions of the population, income and employment security may also decline, even in the face of low unemployment levels. The democratic deficit is underlined in chapters 6 and 8, and the family-time deficit is central to chapter 7. These deficits, when linked with concerns regarding environmental sustainability and global social well-being, could combine to alter the present trajectory of electronic capitalism.

6

Integrating the Three Bottom Lines through Global Governance

It at first seems curious that it is not difficult to envision policy initiatives that might help to redirect globalization—to better balance the three bottom lines on a global scale. It is, however, hard to envision a politics that might put such policies into place or, for that matter, to identify an array of social forces to see any set of effective, noneconomistic policies through to action on a global scale. One political result of this conundrum is a strong contemporary retreat into illusions regarding the potential for politically effective localism without the prior establishment of viable, noneconomistic global governance. Another is widespread cynicism and a sharp decline in political participation and attentiveness. Both are responses to national policy outcomes widely taken to be an inevitable consequence of equally inevitable global-scale economic competition. There is, however, no insurmountable reason (other than this presumption of inevitability) that social and environmental advances could not be made a condition of continued global economic integration.

In stark contrast to today's cynicism regarding the possibilities inherent in politics, at the outset of the first industrial revolution, Marx was confident (though not necessarily correct) regarding the identity of an agent of change. However, and also in stark contrast to today's world, he had no real mental picture of the design of transformation he was sure would come (beyond an end to the private ownership of the means of production). The proletariat, the employees of mass industrial society, were not asked by Marxists how they felt about their purported role in history. Without an institutionalized and democratic transition option, the Marxist transformation was an abysmal failure.

A contemporary politics of change, one might then hypothesize, must be profoundly democratic. It must arise out of a widespread perception of a decline in democratic effectiveness in a context of global economic integration. That is, people need to realize that what is missing is a multidimensional, global democratic decision process, beginning with the development of a genuine transparency in global-scale politics. It must also be widely perceived that enhanced opportunities for diverse, noncommercial, voices are essential at all levels of governance. This emphasis on democracy as a value is not only an apt lesson of history, but necessary because democracy may be electronic capitalism's only remaining noneconomistic core value. Given the challenges of establishing effective democratic practice at a global scale, however, it remains considerably easier to imagine the "what" of more democratic global policies than the "how," the "who," the "when," or the institutional "where" of achieving them.

Wrongheaded pseudoscientific certainty about the "who" of change, with only the vaguest of noble assertions regarding the "what" of change, was a key source of the abysmal failure of Marxism in practice. That is, the absolutism of "actually existing socialism" derived in part from a false certainty regarding the majority status and presumed political inclinations of the industrial proletariat. Marx presumed that industrial workers numbered, or soon would number, upwards of 90 percent of the population. That not-altogether-unreasonable extrapolation from the earliest beginnings of mass industrial society was simply wrong. "Revolution" (which never succeeded in any mass industrial society) was then conducted on behalf of this "agent of change," but was never led *by* that alleged agent. Communist revolutions took place only where the proletarian agent was decidedly not a majority and indeed was not even sufficiently numerous to object to being the agent of history. History itself was allegedly proven, scientifically, to be in need of such an agent. In the end, neither a science of society, nor agency, nor revolution, provides a very promising basis for human affairs.

As social science Marxism was also wanting, but so too is today's economistic (and often hyperempirical) social science. Where historic sweep and an underlying moral sensibility were Marx's strengths, though he would not have admitted to the latter, contemporary social science is too often conducted in a narrow (largely ahistorical) and essentially amoral manner (implicitly presuming that economic growth benefits, or will benefit, the poor and the environment). One of Marx's greatest weaknesses was that he suffered the monumental illusion that a fusion of economic and political power through absorption of the economic realm into the political would make it obvious what values, objectives, and policies were appropriate. His putative proletarian agents in the meantime went their own way and "made deals"—the great compromise of the democratic Keynesian welfare state slowly evolved with no revolution and absent any merger of economy and politics.

Historic compromises took place at the level of the state, the community, and the workplace (through unionization), and through a myriad of life choices by countless individuals. The "agent" in effect chose never to be born—the agents' children and grandchildren became dentists and bureaucrats, salespersons and engineers, managers and movie stars. The terrifying aspect of contemporary society in the age of the democratic dilemma is that the same monolithic outcome that Marx wrongly foresaw has come about the other way around—the economic realm has all but subsumed the political. This new monolith, wherein the media and public discourse are dominated by narrowly defined economic results, is, as we have seen, at the heart of electronic capitalism. The best prospect for change is through the potential openness of a not-yet-dormant democratic ethos and the global-scale politicization of noneconomistic values, such as family and community, nature and environment, and fairness and equity.

The belief in a "science of history and society" was a nineteenth-century intellectual illusion; the retreat into moral neutrality and a tyranny of small questions is a twentieth-century intellectual failing. While there is no single "must" that would alter electronic capitalism once and for all, the overall desirability of a better balance among economic, social, and environmental objectives seems clear. What would seem in keeping with democratic reassertiveness are policy proposals offered in a what-might-be-done spirit, without overconfident assertions regarding who or what groups might take up advocacy of these proposals. Also doubtful are any claims that particular policies are wholly a product of "science." Inevitably policies reflect the values of the proponent. That is as true of the policies proposed in this book as it is of the neoliberal advocacy of the acolytes of economism. It is in this democratic spirit that these final chapters are offered.

Democracy's dilemma necessitates an unrelenting struggle against media-induced intellectual closure. The first what-might-be-done proposition here might, then, appropriately center on a need for increased openness in global decision-making institutions and a need to create forums for discursive interaction. These might include community-based spaces for considering global-scale social and environmental issues, reserved licenses for noncommercial (low-capitalization) media, exclusion (or restraint) of commercial interests in public schools and universities, and radically improved funding for public libraries, including guaranteed low-cost public access to, and a strengthened noncommercial presence on, the Internet. The remaining "what-might-be-done" items follow a plea for interventionist politics at the global scale. Before turning to the particular policy proposals, we also briefly review what has thus far been done to balance global trade and investment expansion with social and environmental protection.

Right-Sizing Politics and Policy in a Global Era

In the preface to the 1975 edition of Polanyi's *The Great Transformation,* R. M. MacIver expressed the hope that by examining economic and social history we might learn "to rebuild the institutional fabric so that we may better withstand the shocks of change." The concomitant expansion of industrial capitalism and development of national governments would seem to suggest a present need to develop a civil society and an institutional fabric of governance at the global level. MacIver also then, impressively for 1975, asserted that the lesson of Polanyi's masterwork was that "such liberal formulas as 'world peace through world trade' will not suffice. If we are content with such formulas we are the victims of a dangerous and deceptive simplification. Neither a national nor an international system can depend on automatic regulants. Balanced budgets and free enterprise and world commerce and international clearinghouses and currencies maintained at par will not guarantee an international order. Society alone can guarantee it; international society must also be discovered. Here too the institutional fabric must maintain and control the economic scheme of things."[1] Today these words are more apt than ever.

Both MacIver's assertion and Polanyi's initial analysis were prescient in many ways. International society has not yet, as MacIver put it, been "discovered." There are small beginnings of a global civil society, and in the environmental realm, as will be detailed shortly, there are limited treaty-based initiatives and organizations. What is lacking are democratically rooted decision and enforcement mechanisms and structures—MacIver's "institutional fabric." In terms of the return of social depredations not unlike those Polanyi so insightfully captured regarding the first transformation, the nearest to protection in the contemporary context is the United Nations' Charter of Human Rights, hardly a match for the narrow economism presently embedded within the WTO, the IMF, and most national governments. Interestingly, much of the today's opposition to economism is self-consciously localist in character. While it does not explicitly reject global social and environmental governance, it pointedly emphasizes initiatives at a small-scale, often bioregional, level. While decentralism and the self-conscious resistance to globalization may help to rally an articulate opposition to globalization, it may also slow the development of global-scale governance initiatives.

This current of political decentralization and distrust of large-scale governance has been strong throughout the history of environmentalism.[2] The classic environmentalist slogan "think globally, act locally" captures this very well and seems to imply that acting nationally, regionally, or globally is probably futile, evil, or somehow beyond human capacities. Such a view, including an advocacy of local economic autonomy, is explicit in the literature of bioregionalism. Mander and Goldsmith describe bioregionalism as "watershed economics," a viewpoint "that advocates economies of self-sufficiency within naturally articulated 'bioregional' boundaries."[3] As Kirkpatrick Sale puts it, "Far from being deprived, even the most unendowed bioregion can in the long run gain economic health with a careful, deliberate policy of self-sufficiency."[4] Clearly bioregionalism is also in keeping with, for example, Lovins's decentralized energy visions; both favor organizing economic and political activity within biologically and geophysically determined local jurisdictions. Bioregionalism is thus the antithesis of electronic capitalism and presumes that it can and should, in effect, be "turned back."

Bioregionalism stresses the importance of knowing the subtleties of, and lovingly caring for, one particular place—learning about that place over a lifetime and through the changes in generations. Again in Sale's words, "The crucial and perhaps only and all-encompassing task is to understand *place,* the immediate, specific place where we live. The kinds of soil and rocks under our feet; the source of the waters we drink; the meaning of the different kind of winds; the common insects, birds, mammals, plants, and trees; the particular cycle of seasons; the times to plant and harvest and forage—these are the things that are necessary to know. The limits of its resources; the carrying capacities of its lands and waters; and places where it must not be stressed; the places where its bounties can be developed; the treasures it holds and the treasures it withholds—these are the things that must be understood."[5] Bioregionalism is thus about localism and rootedness—ecological, cultural, and economic.

Bioregionalism helps to express a deep contemporary need for a more meaningful sense of place, one of several forms of connectedness threatened by (but also potentially enabled by) electronic capitalism. In this spirit, bioregionalists praise "traditional knowledge," which some see as the equal of, or superior to, scientific knowledge. Others, in some of the urban- and regional-planning literature, remind us of the threat to a sense of spatial belonging within a known landscape posed by excessive automobile dependence and urban sprawl. Some also note the environmentally problematic nature of architectural norms like office towers designed without any relationship to climate, positioning and movement of the sun, temperatures or winds—all is overwhelmed by nonsustainable energy use. Many people thus come to lose all awareness of nature in the conduct of everyday lives lived in air-conditioned cars, residences, and office towers (the latter two incorporating indoor parking facilities).

Bioregionalism has two particular strengths, only sometimes weakened by a tendency toward politically naive romanticism. Bioregionalism articulates one of the great potential strengths of local jurisdictions as a seat of environmental protection—detailed knowledge, including multigenerational traditional knowledge, of what is ecologically important in a local region. This strength lies at the heart of environmentalist inclinations to the local and suggests that local authority should not be omitted from environmental decision making. Humans take care of, or wish to take care of, that which we know and love, and we tend to care most for what we know best. However, creating local political and economic institutions that are not consistently overwhelmed by global economic and political forces may, in the world of electronic capitalism, require as a precondition policies that balance economic ends with social and environmental ends at the global scale.

A second strength of bioregionalism might help, in part, to deal with the challenge of overwhelming global political and economic power—much bioregionalist analysis advocates *economic* decentralization and self-sufficiency. It is arguable that to the extent that communities (and nations) are self-sustaining in terms of the vital aspects of their economies (food, shelter, and culture would seem a plausible core), there is the prospect for greater political autonomy. What is not present within the bioregionalist literature, however, is any clear sense of how, politically or in any other way, to slow the rapid movement toward globally organized economies—even, and perhaps especially, in the realms of food and culture (as well as in resources and all forms of technological and manufactured output).

Many bioregionalists are explicit in their opposition to economic globalization. David Morris argues that free trade separates authority from responsibility with serious environmental and social costs, that in effect "we give up sovereignty over our affairs in return for a promise of more jobs, more goods, and a higher standard of living."[6] Also opposed to free trade, Herman E. Daly argues on both economic and environmental grounds that long-distance trade is too energy intensive and that it proceeds in part because the costs of energy (or in California export-agriculture, the cost of water) are heavily subsidized.[7] Daly and John B. Cobb, Jr., while accepting the general logic of comparative economic advantage, also assert that Smith and Ricardo "would have found compelling" the case against free trade "in a world of free capital mobility, demographic explosion, ecological distress, and nation-states unwilling to cede any sovereignty to a world government."[8]

Daly also offers a telling criticism of overdependence on comparative national advantage: "Uruguay has a clear comparative advantage in raising cattle and sheep. If it adhered strictly to the rule of specialization and trade, it would afford its citizens only the choice of being either cowboys or shepherds."[9] He goes on to note that personal fulfillment, community, and nationhood all require economic diversity—in the case of Uruguay, the opportunity to have local banks, medicine, and symphonies, not just ranches. Though few bioregionalists have made the case so far, it might be added that overspecialization imposes additional environmental costs through the excessive concentration of particular extractions from nature and emissions to it. Nature's reproductive and absorptive capacities might generally work better with a large number of small, widely dispersed sawmill or hog operations than with a small number of large ones.

Bioregionalists have also said little about the possible forms of environmental governance appropriate to a world dominated by global economic integration. Simultaneous global economic centralization and local political decentralization are not necessarily impossible, but this pattern is sufficiently challenging that its logic needs to be more fully articulated. Without a clear position of how localism and globalism are to be integrated, bioregionalists have found themselves with rather curious political allies—sometime with economic protectionists, and sometimes with opponents of environmental protection.

Sale's *Human Scale* articulates the central themes of environmentalism and political decentralization and asserts a quintessentially American distrust of government while mourning the failure of American governance: "The plain fact is that government in this country, in all its levels and manifestations, is simply not working. Of course it isn't. It's too big."[10] What is striking is the extent to which decentralist environmentalism and North American neoconservatism are expressed in a common language.

The cover of *Human Scale* reads: "Big government, big business, big *everything*—how the crises that imperil modern America are the inevitable result of giantism grown out of control—and what can be done about it. Sale examines a nation in the grips of growthmania and presents the ways to shape a more efficient and liveable society built to the Human Scale." Sale speaks of a crisis in capitalism and advocates organic agriculture, workplace democracy, worker and community ownership of industry, solar energy, recycling, and increased public transportation expenditures. Yet he prominently and sympathetically quotes then-candidate and arch-antienvironmentalist Ronald Reagan: "I am calling . . . for an end to giantism, for a return to the human scale—the scale that human beings can understand and cope with. . . . It is this activity on a small, human scale that creates the fabric of community, a framework for the creation of abundance and liberty."[11]

The one difference between the two quotations is telling. Sale speaks of growthmania, where Reagan speaks of the creation of abundance. Sale sees political decentralization and "human scale" as a means of achieving environmental protection and the restraint of overconsumption; Reagan uses decentralization to achieve the opposite result—a concentration of wealth and weakened environmental protection. What is also telling is how three movements—the 1960s new left with its emphasis on participatory democracy, the new right with its rejection of "big" government, and environmentalism with its advocacy of environmental assessment, regulatory openness, and public hearings—all assume that they are proffering increased citizen participation and control and a limiting of the power of "faceless bureaucracies." All distrust the structures of government and none thinks clearly about how locally organized governance might effectively contend with globally organized economic structures.

Decentralist environmentalism thus may be politically naive in its refusal to recognize that few, if any, islands of local authority can remain distinctive for long without global social and environmental rule making. Those who yearn for Jeffersonian democracy's modest-scale political jurisdictions forget that those jurisdictions contained within their borders most of their significant economic actors and that those economic actors were of roughly equal size and influence.

Imagining that "human scale" will result in the demise of growthmania or improved environmental protection fails to recognize the extent to which political power is inherent in economic scale. The power to shift investment, employment opportunities, taxable income, and assets from one jurisdiction to another (or simply to forgo expanding or producing within a jurisdiction) is the power to affect, if not determine, policy outcomes. Such power is not always exercised, but in general the larger the scale of economic organization and the smaller the scale of political decisions (and the less diverse the economic options within the jurisdiction), the greater the mismatch in terms of power differential. The full political resources of the most powerful economic organizations are always, of course, used selectively and may take time to mobilize. Environmental protection initiatives thus gained ground in the 1970s, enjoying for a time something of a "motherhood" status, but from the late 1980s economic actors began to take environmental issues more seriously—both in terms of voluntarily taking some positive actions and in terms of mounting a more sophisticated political resistance to effective regulation. Environmental protection has generally lost ground since.

A further compounding factor regarding the local level of governance is often overlooked. Local governments almost always depend on a revenue stream dominated by property taxes. This dependence undermines municipal autonomy with regard to one of the most environmentally important aspects of municipal policy jurisdiction—planning decisions. Planning decisions determine urban form—the shape of the municipality and the mix of buildings—and this in turn contributes powerfully to choices regarding transportation mode, intracity distances traveled, and thereby many aspects of environmental protection.[12] Without regional governance, the shape of urban regions is left to decisions within small municipal governments at the urban periphery. These small governments are typically no match for large developers bearing economic promises and/or political threats. Here again, at the municipal level, limited-scale jurisdictions are less effective at environmental protection, and a mismatch of economic and political scales is again fraught with social and environmental problems.

The notion that local governments are able to protect local environments when national governments, given the structure of global economic organization and trade arrangements, frequently can no longer do so seems spectacularly naive. One reason many environmentalists and others cling to this hope is the widespread, and not unreasonable, perception of how little influence people of ordinary means have at the global level. This is the essence of democracy's dilemma in an age of global economic integration.

It is also important to note in this context that even environmental concepts such as sustainable development are distrusted by many greens, as too far removed from people whose lives are affected by "global ecological planning." As Wolfgang Sachs puts it, "It is inevitable that the claims of global management are in conflict with the aspirations for cultural rights, democracy, and self-determination. Indeed, it is easy for an ecocracy that acts in the name of 'one earth' to become a threat to local communities and their life-styles. After all, has there ever, in the history of colonialism, been a more powerful motive for streamlining the world than the call to save the planet?"[13] Sachs's caution here is not unwarranted, but it should be noted that it could also serve as a rationalization for such unecological local practices as slash-and-burn agriculture or the overharvesting of threatened species using modern technologies such as snowmobiles and fish radar.

The challenge, again, is to establish trade, social, and environmental rules that advance local democracy, cultural diversity, socioeconomic equity, sustainability, and environmental protection. What is needed is a global institutional context that creates and encourages local environmental initiatives rather than undermining them. Internationally, this might include, for example—as will be detailed below—deliberately setting some or all commodity prices on a gradual upward trajectory relative to prices of other goods. Local initiatives and global initiatives are not, of course, mutually exclusive—and indeed are mutually reinforcing. Even partial local economic autonomy might help communities or nations to resist the temptation to accept global economic investment and trade on any terms. However, global action on several fronts (e.g., human rights, labor rights, and environmental protection and social policy minima) is necessary to create the political and economic space to pursue democratic possibilities at the local level. Such initiatives may fall well short of governance, but they almost certainly would require some form of international economic (likely trade-related) sanctions as a means of enforcement.

Before considering these global-scale policy possibilities let us first quickly review present-day global actualities regarding environmental protection in particular. The focus here is on global environmental initiatives because systematic global-scale social policy and economic equity initiatives are essentially, and tragically, negligible.[14] There have, however, been some modest successes regarding human rights, labor rights, and the rights of women and children.[15]

What Has Been Done? An Assessment of Multilateral Environmental Treaties

An array of multilateral and bilateral environmental treaties have been negotiated—indeed, since the late 1970s environmental politics seems to be conducted almost as much at the diplomatic level as at the national level. Major environmental treaties include the Convention on International Trade in Endangered Species of Wild Flora and Fauna, known as CITES (1973, 1979, 1983); the Montreal Protocol on Substances That Deplete the Ozone Layer (1987); the Basel Convention on the Control of Transboundary Movements of Hazardous Wastes and Their Disposal (1989); the United Nations Biodiversity Convention (1992); and the United Nations Framework Convention on Climate Change (1992, followed by the additional agreement in Kyoto, Japan, in 1997). It is thus widely acknowledged that many environmental problems are global in scale and can only be resolved with the active involvement of many, if not most, nations. The question that remains is whether this ad hoc series of international environmental agreements is adequate to the task.

The Montreal Protocol is one of the more comprehensive and effective of these ad hoc multinational environmental initiatives.[16] Nonetheless, there have been instances of inadequate enforcement whereby ozone-depleting substances have been imported into the United States, a signator, for use in automobile air-conditioning systems. There have also been ongoing and significant violations of the Basel Convention, including the export of hazardous wastes from rich nations to poor and inadequate treatment under the guise of recycling initiatives.[17] This treaty, however, has the largest number of signators of any environmental treaty (132), and the Basel Protocol of 1999 (on the tenth anniversary of the original treaty) establishes "a worldwide system for the placing and enforcing of claims arising from the transnational trafficking in hazardous wastes."[18] However, a fund for assisting developing countries with emergencies is based wholly on voluntary contributions, and only time will tell how effectively claims will be generated and resolved.

Enforcement of CITES violations is an ongoing challenge, despite widespread good intentions and efforts, and the poaching of tigers, rhinos, elephants, and bears to supply body parts for export continues in many nations. Some national customs agencies are far more effective than others in blocking shipments, but many are flawed. In several Asian nations medicines using such parts are still widely available on a semiopen basis. The Worldwide Fund for Nature (WWF) and other NGOs are, however, working with Asian traditional medicine communities to develop and promote acceptable substitutes. All in all, one could say that the enforcement record on this and the other treaties identified earlier has been mixed. Some analysts see the record as improving, but these assessments generally exclude or remain generally pessimistic about the greatest challenge—climate warming.[19]

Indeed, perhaps the two most important international environmental treaties are the most notable enforcement failures. Fully ten years after leading the adoption of the Biodiversity Convention, Canada has still not developed an effective system of protecting the habitat of endangered species within its territory. If adequate protection cannot be easily achieved in a vastly wealthy country with a very low population density, what are the prospects for the rest of the planet? A related and notable failure is the International Tropical Timber Organization (ITTO), created to protect tropical wet and dry forest habitats in part through commodity price increases.[20] Neither ITTO, nor the Biodiversity Convention of 1992, has significantly slowed the clearing of tropical forests, nor are there effective means by which the convention can be enforced even for signatory states.

Probably least effective of all are the climate-change agreements. Worldwide, there are still an estimated $200 billion dollars in public money annually going to subsidizing the production and use of fossil energy. The 1992 Framework Convention on Climate Change was signed by over 150 nations at Rio, but it was not ratified by all and was not enforced by many. As Lamont C. Hempel has observed, "By the time the Second Conference of the Parties (COP-2) met in Geneva in July 1996, it was clear that at least fifteen developed nations, collectively responsible for over half of the world's greenhouse gas emissions, were not on course to reduce their emissions levels by the year 2000."[21] Germany and Europe achieved reductions in greenhouse gas emissions for the 1990s, but these resulted in good measure from the deindustrialization (and modernization) of East Germany and Eastern Europe. In the United States and Canada, though reductions were agreed to in 1992, greenhouse gas outputs not only were not stabilized and restored to 1990 levels as agreed, but rose throughout the 1990s, by double digit amounts in both nations.[22] Newer reductions agreed to in Kyoto in 1997 (6% below 1990 levels by 2012) have been even less successful to date, with the United States, the largest producer of emissions by far, flatly refusing to participate.

Many other nations are in violation of both the original 1992 agreement and the Kyoto agreement. Moreover, developing nations continue to be unwilling to commit to any reductions though they may have a reasonable basis for this resistance in terms of equity considerations. Only Argentina and Kazakhstan among developing nations agreed to voluntary reductions prior to COP meetings in Buenos Aires in 1999, and U.S. legislative bodies remain adamant that the U.S. should not agree to reductions without participation from China, India, and other large, poorer nations. OPEC-led price increases for oil in 2000 may lead to some reductions by the 2012 deadline, but at this point it seems already that the Kyoto agreement will be a failure not unlike all previous efforts regarding greenhouse gases.

Overall, then, the pattern seems to be that specific problems—especially those with technical solutions of modest economic cost—have relatively good prospects of success through the treaty route (even in the absence of comprehensive enforcement agencies or structures). Without economic or other sanctions, however, one can generalize that the broader the problem and the more important the economic implications, the more thorough the failure of treaty-based environmental initiatives so far. This is not to suggest that we should disparage the efforts thus far or give up on learning how to engender greater participation and compliance. On the contrary, being mindful of the scale of the challenge of, for example, getting U.S. cooperation with regard to climate change, is the best hope of achieving effective global governance as regards the environment in the long run.

As noted earlier, overfishing remains the norm in the majority of the world's seventeen major ocean fisheries despite any number of treaties. Even treaties with enforcement regimes, such as the North West Atlantic Fisheries Organization (NAFO), have not been notable successes to say the least. Moreover, many international environmental bodies, such as the United Nations Environment Programme (UNEP), are desperately weak. As John McCormick puts it, "The UN system . . . is regarded by INGOs as having only limited influence and power, mainly because its decisions are not binding on member states, but partly because of funding and personnel problems."[23] What is missing in most environmental treaties and in most international environmental agencies are the power and the capacity to enforce the limited rules that have been developed. International and global *economic* arrangements, such as prohibitions against dumping and cross-subsidization, are overseen and enforced more systematically and effectively.

Though environmental agreements may be inadequately enforced, or in some cases not even ratified by signators, economic, trade, strategic, and military-related international agreements and concerns have all been used to overwhelm existing domestic environmental policies. Most notorious in the trumping-by-trade-treaty category is chapter 11 of the NAFTA agreement, which empowers polluters to sue (and, more important, to threaten to sue) national and local governments for even attempting to protect the environment. Also notable in this regard are the provisions of GATT and the WTO, and several noted interpretations of these provisions. Perhaps the most infamous is the ruling in favor of Mexico (supported by other nations) that sections of the U.S. Marine Mammal Protection Act violated GATT trade rules. Specifically, the U.S. could not disallow imports of tuna caught without rules regarding the killing (by-catch) of dolphin (which feed on tuna). U.S. fishers practiced a variety of protections (at 90% effectiveness) at considerable expense and objected to competing in the same market with fishers who did not make such efforts. The trade panel determined that nations may not "impose" environmental protections outside their national territorial jurisdictions and that the product (tuna) was "substantially the same" regardless of the processes involved in its "production."

The dolphin-tuna ruling led directly to the widespread opposition of leading environmental organizations to trade agreements that has continued and broadened since.[24] The ruling was made by three "trade experts" meeting in private and did not allow that the United States was not seeking to prohibit the practices in question, but only to prevent the importation of goods that competed, arguably unfairly, with environmentally superior domestic practices. If generalized, the perspective embodied in this ruling has the potential to always provide trade advantages to firms and nations whose environmental protections are the least adequate. A GATT panel (in 1994), however, ruled in favor of the so-called corporate average fuel efficiency (CAFE) standards, which imposed penalties on European luxury cars exported to the United States because, for economic reasons, these manufacturers did not also sell smaller, fuel-efficient vehicles to improve their averages (as did Japanese and U.S. producers). This ruling may have smoothed the way for the passage (and acceptance by the United States) of the Uruguay Round agreement that created the WTO. WTO panels have since ruled against domestic efforts at environmental protection in a number of cases, most notably regarding the protection of sea turtles.[25]

One might generalize that trade consistently trumps environment within the relatively closed and decidedly economistic settings of trade-treaty dispute-resolution processes. The WTO has so far viewed environmental regulations as disguised barriers to trade and has shown little sensitivity to the enormous—and democratic—political efforts necessary to establish such protections. Nor does the WTO seem to have any knowledge of, or concern for, the decades-long struggle to achieve open and democratic environmental decision making at the domestic level.[26] One might even go so far as to say, and many antiglobalization protesters indeed have said, that democracy itself is threatened by such outcomes. At the least, it is little wonder that fewer citizens have an affinity for domestic civic life.

This effect is compounded by the fact that WTO panel decisions involve a decidedly closed and legalistic process. There have been few if any active involvement opportunities even for well-established and prosperous NGOs, let alone smaller organizations or economically less significant communities and interests. Journalistic coverage of such events, if there is any, often reads like nationalistic cheerleading, as if those in a nation where economic advantage is gained by some firm at a cost to the environment are also advantaged. For the most part media reporting appears only in the business pages of elite newspapers or in law reports and journals. Even keeping track of such matters is thus beyond the means of many citizen organizations, not to mention individual citizens.

Historically, of course, strategic (as distinct from trade) considerations have also trumped domestic environmental concerns. Trade rules, in effect, have only recently been elevated to this lofty status of being considered somehow beyond everyday democratic considerations. An example of strategic concerns trumping environmental health is the case of uranium miners in the U.S. Southwest at the height of the cold war.[27] One case of a strategic treaty trumping environmental and social concerns is the case of low-altitude NATO military overflights of Innu territory in Quebec and Labrador. Frequent low-level training flights have threatened a variety of animal species, including the 600,000 caribou in the George River herd, and thereby to Innu hunting and trapping. A Canadian federal environmental assessment (EA) regarding the issue would not even consider the question of discontinuing the flights.

This "predecision" resulted in the withdrawal of the Innu representatives from participation in the process. Regarding the possibility of discontinuation of the flights, the EA report included the following passage: "Because of commitments to its allies, the Government of Canada could not accept such a recommendation at this time. It follows that those participating in the review ought not to think that the work of the panel could reasonably result in such a termination."[28] In general, the overpowering of domestic decision processes and politics by international trade and strategic obligations stands in marked contrast to the ongoing weakening of international environmental agreements by domestic political considerations.

What this comes down to in the broadest sense is a structured process of globalization wherein internationalism and extraterritoriality are the norm in economic, but not in environmental, matters. WTO disallowed the application of U.S. protection of porpoises and sea turtles on imported tuna and shrimp, but no international body intervenes to prevent the export from the United States of pesticides banned in the United States for domestic sale and use. As Paul Wapner puts it, "In 1992 . . . U.S. companies reported shipping more than two thousand tons of domestically banned pesticides. By 1994, recorded exports of domestically banned pesticides had increased by 46 percent since 1992—equalling nearly nine tons per day. The majority of these exports went to the developing world. . . . Industrialized countries domestically ban certain pesticides to protect their own ecosystems and citizens. When they consume foreign-grown fruits and vegetables or reap financial rewards from banned pesticide exports, they benefit without having to experience the direct, adverse effects of extensive pesticide use."[29] When this "circle of poison" was a celebrated issue in the United States in the early 1980s, considerable concern was raised about pesticide residues on food imported into the United States.[30] Nonetheless, no international rule or agency has disallowed the practice of producing agricultural chemicals for export that are judged unsafe domestically.

One result of this general imbalance is that pesticide poisoning resulting in death is far more common in poorer nations than in rich, despite the fact that only 20 percent of pesticides are used in poorer countries. The overall result of this reality, when combined with WTO rulings, is that trade trumps the environment in both directions. Rich nations can easily export environmental troubles, but not so easily their higher environmental standards. In another related case the Sierra Club of Canada sought court action to require Atomic Energy of Canada Limited (AECL) to comply with Canadian domestic environmental assessment rules with regard to exports of nuclear power stations to China and Turkey. This prompted the president of AECL to remark that it was ironic that no one complains more about extraterritoriality than Canadians, but that in this case we are being told Canadian laws should apply in another country. The possibility of a trade-treaty rule that when there are two different sets of environmental rules in play, the higher standard should prevail escapes those of an economistic bent. Nor are they inclined toward the establishment of global environmental standards.

David Vogel, however, points out some examples where trade realities may help to advance environmental protection.[31] He speaks of a "California effect" where tough standards introduced in California regarding automobile emissions have induced producers in Europe (and elsewhere in the United States and Canada) to produce cleaner cars than they otherwise might have. He also notes that recycling requirements tend to favor domestic firms because there is an economic advantage created for firms that produce near to their markets (and thereby likely involve domestic production facilities). Another example of trade pushing international environmental standards higher is the European attempt to impose strictly determined green labels on imported (and domestic) goods. This would include specific European retailers that now decline to sell wood extracted from old-growth forests in an unecological manner. Very rich markets can, it seems, in selected cases force limited economy-environment balancing on supplier nations and firms.

Global firms may also prefer harmonized (and relatively stable) environmental standards, if they concede that there must be such standards. The International Standards Organization (ISO), a quasi-public but essentially nongovernmental agency, has developed ISO 14000 environmental management standards in an attempt to harmonize how international and domestic firms handle environmental concerns. However, the ISO is itself dominated by global firms, primarily those from wealthy nations.[32] Moreover, adherence to ISO standards is voluntary for firms, and those standards are not generally performance oriented. That is, the emphasis is on the development of managerial decision processes, more than on the control of specific emissions or process inputs.

Regarding the role of the ISO in global environmental governance, Jennifer Clapp has noted that this is an example of the increasing role of market-based, nonstate actors in the establishment of publicly recognized, privately established "hybrid" regimes in international governance. She argues that "while firms are asked [by ISO 14000] to set their own environmental goals and are asked to commit to preventing pollution, none of the codes . . . stipulate that firms must meet specific performance or emissions standards."[33] ISO 14000 calls, for example, for the use of environmental auditors—a management practice that can be highly informative and may result in considerable environmental improvement, but that leaves all management prerogatives open. In the end the process is strictly voluntary and essentially closed to public participation and scrutiny.

Considerable harmonization of environmental and social standards has taken place within the European Union (EU), a process that has gradually evolved since the 1952 creation of the European Coal and Steel Community, the precursor to the European Community, in turn the precursor to the EU. Neither GATT nor the WTO, however, has ever really attempted to understand environmental or social equity standards to be anything other than potential or actual impediments to the free flow of capital and goods—trade. The NAFTA side agreement arguably in principle stands somewhere in between, but in practice NAFTA arrangements have been nearer to WTO-style economism. The small steps taken to acknowledge environmental and social impacts of open capital and goods movement have been more than offset by the powers granted to foreign corporations to sue signatory governments regarding environmental protection initiatives (and to governments to appeal environmental protection initiatives as nontariff barriers to trade).

Nonetheless, the NAFTA side agreement did establish the Commission for Environmental Cooperation (CEC), based in Montreal. The CEC has gained considerable visibility with its annual report on industrial pollution releases by state or province, a list that consistently shows Texas and Ontario at or near the "top" (notably down the list of polluters are New York and California, despite having much larger populations). Beyond this, however, the CEC's effectiveness has been limited. It has not achieved anything even approaching even-handed enforcement of comparable environmental regulations across North America. The result has been a selective (and mercifully limited) environmental race to the bottom led by such jurisdictions as Louisiana and Texas (for the petrochemical industry), Mexico (largely through ineffective enforcement), British Columbia (for the forest industry), and Ontario (since 1995, for any and all industries).

The CEC is funded equally by the three NAFTA nations and has a total annual budget of about $9 million. It is empowered to investigate complaints by individuals or environmental organizations regarding failures to enforce domestic environmental legislation. This capacity was put in place because of fears primarily among influential NGOs in the United States regarding widespread environmental nonenforcement in Mexico. There was a double fear that a pollution haven might be a magnet for relocating industries and that extensive pollution might not be contained on the other side of the United States' southern border. The bottom line regarding what was established to meet these concerns, however, is that the CEC can only act with regard to the alleged nonenforcement of existing domestic laws. It cannot impose even minimal international standards or query existing laws in any way. It cannot impose trade sanctions or fines or penalties of any kind even if nations are found to be ignoring their own laws. It is difficult to imagine a more mild-mannered imposition on national autonomy, especially in comparison with the scale and range of interventions associated with the trade-related provisions of the NAFTA accord.

The CEC has investigated issues in Mexico and one finding did lead to the scrapping of plans for a large pier in Cozumel that threatened Paradiso Reef, a biologically rich site frequented by scuba divers. It has also investigated damage to freshwater fish habitat in British Columbia resulting from power dams (and possibly in violation of existing Canadian law). In total, however, fewer than thirty requests for investigation have been submitted and most have not proceeded to a full investigation. Nonetheless, some actors have recently sought to weaken the rules regarding environmental complaints, so that individuals or citizen groups would first need to provide evidence that substantial environmental harms have already occurred.

The level of evidence required in such a possible provision would effectively exclude all but the most prosperous and technically capable environmental organizations from the process. The proposed changes would also eliminate any possibility of action before the fact, as was the outcome in the case of the Cozumel tourist boat pier. Powerful interests in Canada urged that complainants also be required to establish clear causal links between any alleged environmental nonenforcement and trade. The overall goal of such initiatives is to ensure that CEC is utterly apolitical, a world populated by discrete and expensive lawyers and no one else.

The CEC itself has also in some situations been less than fully transparent and generally lacks "teeth" in terms of enforcement related to its "findings of fact." There is even some anecdotal evidence that the organization lacks sufficient independent power to publish its own commissioned reports.[34] The U.S. presidential election campaign of 1992 involved sufficient public doubts regarding NAFTA (especially from labor and environmental organizations) to lead then-candidate Clinton to propose a special protocol—a campaign promise that led to the NAFTA side agreement and created the CEC. Thus, while NAFTA does not approach the level of social and environmental policy harmonization that the EU has attained, it has at least these very modest provisions.

The principal problem is that the CEC itself is effectively powerless, and decision making remains in the hands of national governments operating within the closed world of diplomacy. Even with highly constrained and circumscribed powers, the inner workings of the CEC proceed largely behind closed doors. There is no North American parliament that parallels the European parliament. In North America, economic integration proceeds apace with no meaningful attempt to ensure the secure establishment of social and environmental minima, or even to monitor and render visible lost ground within these realms.

Trade treaties have thus been primarily designed to accelerate the growth of trade and investment across national borders—in effect, at almost any cost in terms of environment and social equity. But it is too often overlooked by critics of this reality that the very existence of trade treaties and their, albeit limited, enforcement regimes also provide a potential opportunity to promote and even to achieve social and environmental harmonization upward, rather than downward. It is arguable that the EU has accomplished harmonization upward as often as not. The NAFTA Side Agreement on Labor and the Environment shows in principle that there is no technical (as distinct from political) reason why the NAFTA treaty could not contain stronger social and environmental provisions.[35] Only a lack of political will (obviously no small matter) prevents the incorporation of effective environmental regulations and social minima.

A first step toward harmonization upward within NAFTA might involve changes to the CEC. For example, the agency could be empowered to monitor and publicize the evolution of income distribution patterns in North America and to make social policy recommendations should there be significant declines in equity. As regards environment protection, the power to investigate nonenforcement might be strongly confirmed at the political level and then expanded to incorporate the power to take public note of significant, ongoing environmental deterioration or deteriorating environmental standards or capacities within partner nations, or any state or province therein. Moreover, the power granted to corporations to sue governments regarding environmental regulations could be revoked as a violation of democratic processes.

Without such changes, and others touched on below, the potentially positive impacts of expanded trade on environmental protection noted by Vogel and others will not often be realized. Without new rules and structures there is merely a greater capacity for passing the environmental buck—upward from the national level and downward to the provincial and local. Moreover, while some specifically environmental treaties have been reasonably effective, others merely read well, it being understood from the outset by signatories that there is a great deal of room for maneuver with regard to compliance. The ad hoc character of environmental treaty initiatives, as well as the frequent enforcement shortcomings, could be lessened were the evolving global environmental rules linked, at least in some cases, to trade-based sanctions. That is, full participation in treaty-based trading opportunities could require adherence to environmental and, in due course, social policy minima. This step need not apply to all such violations, nor need enforcement involve either full exclusion or be applied precipitously.

Penalties need only apply to industries where trade advantages are gained through environmental noncompliance. It should be noted that this proposal would still be a very long way from adequate global environmental governance as long as environmental agreements are only applicable to nations that have chosen to ratify them. That is, environmental treaty participation could be a condition of trade participation. At the least, the most significant environmental treaties—perhaps CITES, the Basel Convention, the Montreal Protocol, and Kyoto—might be linked to trading regimes. Again, noncompliance at first might only be noted, leaving considerable time for an appeals procedure and the achievement of compliance. At some forewarned point in time, though, a surcharge could be applied to selected relevant commodities and/or products. This modest proposal is in keeping with the trade-sanctions approach of existing trade regimes. The difference lies in the acknowledgment that economy and environment are irretrievably interrelated. It offsets the idea that environmental rules are but disguised barriers to trade. It would begin having us see environmental malfeasance (and ultimately human rights violations and the absence of fair wages) as dangerous and unacceptable means of achieving competitiveness.

Thus, it is important to see that such widely reviled organizations as the WTO have, despite their histories and habits, a positive environmental and social potential. How else, or where else, one must ask, could global environmental and social standards, if the political wherewithal for their establishment were ever generated, be enforced?

Regime Theory, Capacity Building, and Democracy's Dilemma

Two well-established bodies of literature explore the processes by which national and global institutions of environmental and social governance might develop. The literature of capacity building looks at the creation and improvement of governance capabilities at the national level. The concept of capacity building in environmental governance was central to, and given added momentum by, the Agenda 21 action program of the 1992 UN Conference on Environment and Development in Rio.[36] The work of Helmut Weidner, Martin Jänicke, and others has documented the extent to which and the ways in which governmental capacity in environmental policy has been built in numerous nations. Jänicke's most recent volume assesses seventeen nations, bringing the total studied to thirty.[37]

The conclusion of the most recent national environmental capacity-building studies, especially in relation to globalization, is decidedly mixed. Capacities have continued to expand especially in institutional terms, but some global challenges (climate change) and other problems (decreasing biodiversity, deforestation, and sprawl, for example) have increased. As these authors put it "under conditions of economic globalization . . . the restrictive factors that our first study stressed are still highly effective. Accordingly, a *real* shift from end-of-pipe measures or (technology-oriented) ecological modernization to a development path of structural ecologization, let alone sustainable development, is rare."[38] In other words the advances are highly selective; pollution monitoring and abatement by technical means are accomplished in more and more nations, but restraint in energy and materials use and impositions on biodiversity remain limited everywhere.

Regime theory focuses on the global level. Stephen D. Krasner defines regimes as "sets of implicit or explicit principles, norms, rules, and decision-making procedures around which actors' expectations converge in a given area of international relations."[39] Regardless of the discomfort on the part of some analysts with how one knows whether or not a regime actually exists for any specific "area," many analysts agree that one is evolving at the global level for environmental protection.[40] My own view is that if that is the case, a regime is a long way from the governance necessary for effective protection.

Regime theorists are, however, mindful that enforcement capability is lacking at the global level. As Robert O. Keohane puts it, "With the partial exception of the European Union, international organizations are not authorized to enforce rules within the jurisdiction of sovereign states, nor do they usually have the ability to carry out large-scale projects on their own."[41] David Fairman and Michael Ross also point out that capacity building often fails for political (as well as administrative) reasons, in particular because of a lack of environmental concern in nations receiving aid to domestic environmental capabilities.[42] Regime theorists are also mindful of a general inability to assess the outcome of changes to existing regimes or institutional arrangements. As Oran R.Young put it (in a discussion of possible global arrangements for deep-seabed mining): "No satisfactory technique exists for identifying social-welfare functions regarding comparatively simple choices among conventional goods and services, much less one that would suffice to identify community preferences with respect to complex institutional arrangements."[43]

It is my hope that the perspective offered in this book could add something to this literature. The ideological ascendancy of economism might suggest for example that there are likely to be, for want of better terminology, dominant and submissive regimes. That is, while there may be an evolving international regime in the environmental arena, in recent years it has increasingly been eclipsed by the economic and trade regime. The economic regime is dominant because the WTO and the IMF alone among regimes have the capacity to enforce their rules (Keohane); economic concern is far more universal among national elites than is environmental concern (Fairman and Ross); and economic success is thus far (as we have seen) more readily measured than three-dimensional success (Young). It might even be argued that while environment is a submissive regime, virtually no regime exists within international affairs with regard to most aspects of the social dimension.

While an environmental regime has arguably begun to emerge in international affairs since the 1970s, the economic regime embodied in treaties like NAFTA and institutions like the WTO has not only overwhelmed it, but it has in effect limited environmental capacity building at the domestic level. Some specific rulings discussed in earlier chapters have likely discouraged capacity building and the possible emergence of concern. But more important, the imperative of economic competitiveness has helped to tip the political balance away from environmental protection initiatives and social equity improvement at both the international (regime) and domestic (capacity-building) levels. Multidimensional democratic government at the level of the nation-state, borne of the industrial era, has been undermined without the creation of multidimensional governance at the global level.

In effect, regime theory could also serve as a frame for democracy's dilemma. Environmental and social regimes must emerge at the global level with strengths comparable to that of the now-dominant economic regime.[44] Otherwise both balance and democracy are overwhelmed at all levels of governance. But to achieve strong environmental and social regimes, democracy must be strengthened at either the global level (presumably via a rising global civil society) or the domestic level (at least within some key states). However, at the global level "the culture of secrecy in multilateral trade negotiations effectively relegated NGOs and other social movement organizations to outsider status."[45] At the domestic level stronger democracy is necessary to stand up to economistic global pressures, but if anything democracy has been weakened by declines in civil society and community, by the rise of media dominance, and by the very fact of globalization in its present form.

Both effective international environmental and social regimes and improving domestic institutional capacities require a political sea change. They will not, as some (especially some capacity-building analysts) seem to assume, emerge simply because the need arises. We need, contrary to existing trends, to radically enhance democracy at the domestic level in order to create democratic governance at the global level. As David Held argues, "If democracy is to prevail, the key groups and associations of the economy will have to be rearticulated with political institutions so that they become part of the democratic process—adopting within their very *modus operandi,* a structure of rules, principles, and practices compatible with democracy."[46] This includes everything from developing the capacity to subject global corporations to the will of local communities to some form of three-dimensional rule making and even governance through the WTO and other trade bodies. Whether or not this will prove politically possible is unknown.

Part of making such a change possible lies in having some sense of what might be accomplished. That is, enhanced democracy at the level of the nation-state might be possible if we were to resolve at least in part democracy's dilemma—to imagine effective governance without government at the global level. Thus I offer at this point a summary of what might be done were such a not-impossible sea change to occur at some point in the future. I will return both below and in chapter 8 to the matter of the politics, as distinct from the possible policies, associated with global governance.

Four Policies in Search of Global Democratic Governance

Four initiatives that might help to guide electronic capitalism toward environmental prudence and greater social equity are: (1) the establishment of global environmental protection minima—either incorporated in trade treaties, or left in a parallel set of comprehensive environmental treaties but with the addition of trade-based enforcement penalties; (2) the establishment of labor, human rights, and social policy minima perhaps in a comprehensive social equity treaty associated with broadened trade liberalization; (3) some global economic instrument—such as an energy and materials throughput tax (EMTT)—linking global commodity prices (especially for energy and other environmentally problematic commodities such as fish, timber and mining outputs) to global GDP or to the price of manufactured goods (this initiative would slowly but steadily accelerate dematerialization—that is, reduce material and energy throughputs per unit of GDP at a rate faster than the long-term historic average); and (4) the establishment (based on a Tobin tax and/or environmental and social noncompliance penalties and/or the EMTT) of a fund to finance technical aid and economic incentives that allow and accelerate environmental treaty compliance in poorer nations.

Such initiatives might not in and of themselves be sufficient to create an environmentally and socially benign globalization, but each would help to establish a world that performs in terms of three bottom lines rather than one. Without such steps, trade and economic considerations will continue to trump social and environmental considerations almost every time and may continue to the point where the economy itself is visibly dysfunctional. With such steps, or some other better set in the same spirit, the full array of everyday business and consumer decisions would move both economy and society in a positive direction well before social pain and ecological damage reaches the rich in rich nations. Such initiatives, however, require that decision makers relearn how to think beyond this quarter's balance sheet. They have to really understand that the permanently poor buy few goods and services and that ecological diversity and sustainability are essential to the quality of life. What is required is a broad and explicit recognition that economistic forms of globalization impose many negative social and environmental pressures and outcomes, both subtle and cruel.

The intention of the first two interventions is, of course, to continually raise the environmental and social "bottom" and to thereby constrain tendencies to "race" in that direction. In the environmental realm the well-intentioned attempts at this, through global treaty-based initiatives, have thus far been unevenly enforced. The challenge is to democratically and persistently delineate and enforce a comprehensive set of global environmental standards. One approach might be to require that international corporations comply everywhere with the standards of their nation of origin. If multinational corporations were to simply seek "flags of convenience" for subsidiaries, or to work through "renegade" suppliers, more elaborate rules would be necessary. Some especially progressive MNCs now voluntarily take responsibility for their suppliers; the challenge is to lift others to this standard.

Another approach would be to hold firms everywhere to the environmental standards of the set of nations where the firms' global sales are the highest. There are, of course, many ways to dodge such initiatives—for example, firms producing and selling wholly within poorer nations might avoid compliance altogether if this approach were used. The best option is to establish an array of global standards and to tie OECD trade access to signing on to all or most of the environmental treaty "package." The best enforcement tool for participants for case-by-case noncompliance might be the imposition of some form of "environmental noncompliance export duty."

In similar fashion, the second intervention, social minima, might involve universal economic rights in nations participating in trade regimes, and include such matters as the outlawing of slavery, limits on child labor, the establishment of minimum workplace standards, and an enforceable right to establish trade unions and to engage in the collective withdrawal of labor. It would not be hard to draw up a longer list; one need only reread the economic history of the nineteenth and early twentieth century in Europe and North America. In the long run, however, there should also be exploration of a universal minimum-wage system, possibly scaled to the level of national economic development (GDP per capita). This latter provision would encourage a continually improving floor on this aspect of global competitiveness. The scaled minimum wages need not be so generous as to retard global investment in the poorest nations. There is much room for "scaling" here. Even 10 percent or less of a European minimum wage would be a vast improvement in many locations. Such wage standards might only apply to production for export (though that would hopefully in turn put upward pressure on all wages).

In contrast, at present there are inadequate social protections of even a most basic sort, though there have been some significant gains through the efforts of human rights activists—Amnesty International and the International Labor Office, among others.[47] Overall, some have argued that international investment and global trade integration will tend to improve basic human rights and labor protections. Statistical analysis by Jackie Smith, Melissa Bolyard, and Anna Ippolito, however, has cast doubts on this assumption, concluding that "we could not replicate the positive association . . . found between the presence of transnational corporations and human rights practices."[48] These authors also quote prominently the doubts of David Trubeck regarding the need to explicitly establish social welfare rights in international law rather than simply assuming that general economic improvement will automatically enlarge the social welfare of all citizens.[49]

This is in keeping with the views of Robert McCorquodale and Richard Fairbrother, who conclude their detailed reflections on the relationship between globalization and human rights with the view that "economic globalization . . . simultaneously creates opportunities and presents challenges for the international protection of human rights."[50] The general point here is that there is no automatic "trickle down" even for basic human rights, let alone for economic equity and social policy improvement. But, and this is a crucial distinction, economic integration *can* be taken as a window of opportunity in all matters fundamental to human well-being. Here, one should be clear, is a middle ground between those who reject globalization out of hand and those who blithely assume in the face of evidence that global economic integration will somehow magically improve the lives of all in lock step with gains in global GDP.

Increasing the relative price of energy and materials through an EMTT (the third intervention) would, as noted previously in some cases, simultaneously promote: reuse and recycling, energy efficiency, improved public transportation, reduced urban sprawl, reductions in some pollutants, wilderness protection, resource sustainability, and other forms of ecological modernization. It would also accelerate the development of industrial ecology, the preservation and adaptation of historically significant buildings (and some insignificant ones as well), and, in general, more environmentally intelligent consumer decision making. An EMTT might also be used to provide some of the funds necessary for the fourth intervention.

One important key to the success of the energy component of an EMTT is that it be applied to all energy sources, not just carbon-based energy. Virtually all energy use imposes some environmental costs. It is not an impossible task to develop a scale for different energy sources to adjust the basic tax according to overall impacts. Such a scale, however, would (once one got past the most benign of renewable energy sources) be highly contested politically and inevitably arbitrary to some extent. This does not preclude trying, and indeed there are domestic social science and policy precedents as well as the evolving science of life-cycle assessment to which to turn.[51] What is to be avoided in this undertaking is a "headline-of-the-day-based" selection of one environmental impact over others. Were that approach to be taken, the unintended environmental consequences of such a tax might exceed the gains (though this risk is low given that all energy sources carry impacts). In brief, the evaluation method underpinning the tax must be comprehensive. Specifically, climate change is not the only issue to be considered, nor is nuclear energy necessarily a bogeyman. The simplest solution to such concerns and complexities would be to apply an even-handed tax on all energy, excluding only the most benign sources.

Clearly, however, this third intervention is crucial. An EMTT would simultaneously promote ecological modernization, wilderness protection, sustainability, and pollution reduction—without imposing anything by way of a global environmental enforcement bureaucracy. If such a tax were widely in place, detailed environmental treaties would "only" need to deal with especially threatening and intractable problems. As noted, this tax could conceivably be a source of funding for possible experiments in global environmental and social policy harmonization. We are, of course, a long way politically from the latter possibility (social policy minima). However, it should be noted that such initiatives might also be of considerable environmental benefit if directed at, for example, the promotion of family planning by choice through gender equity in educational opportunities, or global reductions in infant mortality.

The fourth intervention requires little elaboration. The political pressures on behalf of long-term, global-scale environmental concerns are relatively stronger within wealthy nations than poorer ones, but "foreign aid" has systematically lost ground for some time now. Moreover, in poorer nations, low wages and poor working conditions and a willingness to ignore ecological and sustainability concerns are widely perceived to be the leading competitive advantage. The initiatives toward greater global equity and environmental protection put forward here are as likely to find their way onto the agenda in wealthy nations as in poorer ones. Technical and financial incentives will be necessary to effectively marshal global participation. The possible funding sources identified above for this suggested intervention are meant to be those that could impart social and/or environmental benefits within both collection and expenditure processes.

In sum, these are proposals without a politics. In that sense it might be argued that they are impractical. But on another level they are thoroughly rooted in an imaginary but not impossible future, one less economistic than the present. We are otherwise left to assume that the imbalances of contemporary globalization are inevitable because the cult of impotence so widely practiced in today's world is the only alternative. The proposals are also practical in the sense that they would not require large-scale government and bureaucracy at the global level and so would help to circumvent democracy's dilemma.

Global Governance Policy Possibilities

The overarching objective of the four interventions is improved environmental sustainability (dematerialization) and global social equity—globally harmonizing environmental protection and social equality no less than we have globally integrated trade and investment. The use of economic instruments such as these avoids both ineffective "trickle-down" assumptions and overly bureaucratized global quasi-government. Most important, these instruments are adaptive—they can be introduced gradually, outcomes can be measured, and levels can be adjusted. These particular instruments are far from sufficiently fleshed out here, but they can be designed to reward nations and firms that are "ahead of the curve" and should encourage others to act in imaginative ways. Ongoing measurement, study, and review of outcomes would probably be needed, but these could be done by international agencies, NGOs, and scientific bodies—micromanagement by a global government should be unnecessary.

One possible additional initiative in the environmental realm is the wider entrenchment of the precautionary principle within international environmental and trade agreements. Protectionism in environmental guise can arise through this principle, but I am not convinced that many actual cases have been convincingly demonstrated. For example, "proof of safety" based on industry-funded short-term toxicity tests on animals is generally inadequate as a basis for overturning hard-won national regulatory rules. Such a low standard disallows long-term health effects, most ecological and biodiversity considerations, moral and religious considerations (which will only increase with advances in molecular biology), and ethical considerations regarding, for example, the humane treatment of animals. It also disregards the need for multigenerational evidence regarding reproductive and mutative effects and conveniently disregards a long history of fraudulent science or the normal industry practice of selectively releasing scientific findings.

At the very least, if our global future is to be a democratic one in any meaningful sense of the term, all "trade-panel" decisions that can potentially trump domestic regulation(s) ought to be conducted in public with generous intervenor funding to ensure the effective participation of nongovernmental, noncorporate actors. All this has been widely discussed, but I would go further. It does not seem unreasonable that if trade panels are empowered to override national environmental laws and regulations, the executive leadership of the global overseeing bodies should be much more publicly accountable, and even perhaps (ultimately) directly elected. Those national environmental laws and regulations have been achieved, after all, in the face of all the domestic economic and political power that can be mustered by powerful economic interests. Even if so-called bootlegger-baptist (environmentalist-protectionist) coalitions are involved in establishing some environmental regulations, it would not seem unreasonable that the burden of proof lie nonetheless on the side that is, after all, challenging (domestic) *democratic* decisions. If unwarranted protections were achieved from time to time, this would ultimately be demonstrable.

The fear of protectionism disguised as environmentalism is ironic, given that those who advance such assertions often do not even admit that the use of child labor to produce exported goods is an unfair trade practice. The International Labour Organization suggests that such practices, and worse, are commonplace. Indeed, in the world of trade treaties and relations there has so far been almost no collective willingness to act within the social realm. The possibilities for additional initiatives are thus almost infinite. Several specific possibilities are offered here that put the four interventions suggested above into a wider perspective. That is, perhaps the best way to see the four interventions set out above as relatively practical initiatives is to begin to imagine more dramatic possibilities.

Why not, for example, make advanced medicines and communications technologies available at lower prices in the poorest nations so long as resale into more prosperous nations is prevented? Some steps have been taken regarding the former in particular cases, but far more could be done. The logic of such initiatives is obvious enough, but why not take more radical steps toward a truly global society? Why not, for example, establish modest pensions for the poorest of global citizens, perhaps paid out of a global energy and material throughput surtax? Such pensions might at the outset involve only one-time payments at age sixty or seventy to impoverished citizens in the very poorest nations (where precious few live that long). A third possibility might be to increase the availability of "microloans" to poor individuals in both poor and rich nations. All studies of such expenditures suggest that it would be difficult to achieve more three-dimensional (social, economic, and environmental) payoffs per dollar of social investment.

These few additional initiatives are merely suggestive of what might be possible were we to widely presume that while economic integration and economic growth are a good thing, they are not necessarily and automatically so. The net positive value of what is now widely assumed to be progress must be demonstrated in three-dimensional terms. To the extent that success is only one dimensional, initiatives must be established that guide the ever-more-integrated global economic system toward balanced, multidimensional success. Economic growth must come to be understood to be more a means than an end.

Electronic capitalism exists in its present inequitable, undemocratic, and ecologically unsustainable form in part because global-scale governance can appear, or easily be made to appear, as an even more frightening prospect. Full-blown global *government* is understandably frightening because at present even national, state, and municipal governments appear to be beyond influence, often seemingly already too complex to be governed both effectively and democratically. It is also widely presumed, on both the right and the left, that the larger the scale of governance, the less the prospect for influence by "everyday citizens." At a global scale the left fears undue "corporate" control, the right fears undue "foreign" influence—in both cases the concern is that the predominant influence will be in the hands of "others." Ironically, such feelings run highest in nations whose influence within the global context is highest, most particularly the United States. I will return to this concern in chapter 8.

In essence, it is simply not widely appreciated that as the global economy approaches comprehensive integration, global governance already exists—and it is not made less problematic by the fact that it is one-dimensional governance. Indeed, democratic failure at the national and subnational level is in large part of function of global governance by default. It is the governance of trade treaties that pretend that everything that is not trade is a "side" issue that can be all but ignored. In effect, the absence of explicit and open multidimensional global governance creates implicit, and effectively closed, global governance. The economic authority of trade agreements and "everyday" business arrangements and influence has effectively swallowed "the political" throughout the world. As we have seen, noneconomic values are marginalized; private, individual, and short-term needs overwhelm public, collective, and long-term needs.

The democratization of electronic capitalism—and the creation of a greener, fairer globalization—is thus an enormous political challenge. Above and beyond the justifiable general unease with more explicit global-scale governance, the real political challenge lies in reversing the domination of culture generation and political life by global corporations and the electronic media. This combination of factors has, as we have seen, contributed to a pervasive and growing political cynicism rooted in a sense of, and a growing reality of, citizen powerlessness. Effective change will not come quickly. It will take time for an increasingly global citizenry to learn how to hold national governments to delivering concerted multidimensional action on the global stage. It might, however, take even longer to develop effective global-scale citizen and organizational cooperation across cultures, languages, and perspectives in order to somehow achieve concerted action more directly.[52] This discussion will be taken up again in chapter 8.

It will take time for those aware of the need for change to appreciate that everything about economic globalization is not necessarily negative and that economic protectionism may be as great a danger as unbridled globalization. It will take time and insight to resist the many and varied calls for isolation and/or ethnic and national chauvinism from both the right and the left. In the meantime, there is another dimension of social and political life at the opposite end of the spectrum from the forums of the global political economy within which positive change may ensue. Indeed, as will be seen in chapter 7, a fundamental change in the way many people in wealthy nations think about everyday life—work, family, and community—may already be underway. This potential change may even ultimately help to tip the political balance to a more benign form of electronic capitalism.

7

Community, Work, and Meaning: Everyday Life as Politics

While the integrated global economy, essentially rooted in an economistic quasi-polity, carries a glaring democratic deficit, at the personal level in many nations including the most successful, another deficit is increasingly visible: a family-and-community-time deficit of dangerous proportions. Putnam and others have demonstrated a worrisome, even alarming decline in community, democratic, and organizational participation. Moreover, the rising divorce rate in the most successful economies is equally troubling. Both changes are coincident with the rise of the mantra of global competitiveness and ongoing reengineering. The media-fed pressure to consume and a hardest-working-nation-takes-all global competition (which draws all family members into the job market, encourages overtime and shift work, and requires frequent job changing) combine to continually accelerate the pace of everyday life. Stress and depression are increasingly taken by most people to be a normal part of life in today's world.

However, many others—especially perhaps among those who have gotten passably near to "winning the game"—are stepping back and doubting the hectic, highly competitive, consumer-oriented life that electronic capitalism deems desirable. It is yet possible that this will also be taken by many to have been one of the personal lessons of the September 11 attacks. Regardless of this possibility, as we will see, reduced work time had already reentered the political agenda in many nations (especially in Europe). The achievement of work-time reductions (WTR, as it has come to be called) may not automatically result in more time for family and community life, but it at least makes those options possible. Those who campaign for WTR may or may not have doubts about global economic integration, or worry about environmental sustainability, but they do know that their own lives are not nearly as good as they might be and that the answer may not be more work and goods, but less and fewer.

Electronic Capitalism's Hidden Vulnerability: Success

There is perhaps an unspoken fragility about electronic capitalism (as distinct from often-noted fragilities of capital flight, tax avoidance, income disparities, and the possibility of a "race to the bottom" in wages, social policy, and environmental protections). This chapter largely puts aside the often-noted fragilities and focuses on possibilities that may arise from economic success. Away from the world of global governance, amid our everyday lives, new perspectives and options are arising for many at the personal, and even spiritual, level. As noted, many people in both poor and rich nations face increased personal pressures rooted in accelerated competitiveness. In the rich nations increasing numbers are finding ways to, in effect, trade money and stress for time, community, and creativity. Voluntary early retirement, for example, is increasingly commonplace. In Europe, the view that money is time is taking hold at both the personal and the policy level.

The pressures that underlie such changes are not of course universally felt, but there are nonetheless signs that change processes are in motion. Change in this realm can occur incrementally or rapidly. Most importantly, it can occur with or without government involvement and with or without any visible social or political movement. It can arise at particular workplaces, or at the level of the family or individuals. Government or corporate initiatives need not necessarily be involved, though they would be affected were WTR to catch on for large numbers of people. It is also possible that in some economic circumstances governments and corporations would establish policies that encourage such change (as they already have in much of Europe). Alternatively, they may vigorously resist such change—especially in the face of full employment and/or the demographic challenges of an aging population.

Regardless of the view of governments or corporations, a shifting sense of work and meaning may be effectively resolved for some only with a reordering of their personal time allocations and life priorities. The option of significant reductions in work time or arrangements arises out of such things as prosperity, uneven economic development (which creates low-cost housing options away from major centers of economic growth), the norm of two-earner families, the wide availability of flexible work arrangements, and advanced telecommunications. For many, the impetus for change arises out of the squeeze placed on family life by universal (two-parent) breadwinning, long-distance commutes, involuntary overtime, shift work, career instability associated with downsizing, and around-the-clock commerce. For others it arises out of a sense of the fundamental pointlessness of devoting more and more time to marketing, promotion, and sales, and less and less to either the actual production, or even the enjoyment, of goods.

Ironically, while today's ever-rising tide of hype has thus far effectively promoted rising consumption, it has also provoked a reaction in some people—for example, a greater frequency of postmaterialist values. Indeed, green thinking itself evolves often in a context of economic prosperity.[1] Prosperity and accelerated, but essentially nonproductive, work options may contribute to a loss of meaning in the work experience and in such a context, overconsumption and hype could come to be fundamentally counterproductive. Alienation from ordinary employment experiences is compounded for some by an ever more obvious disconnect between wealth and what most people experience as hard work. This disconnect has been blatant in the case of teenage pop stars, youthful dot.com billionaires, professional athletes (who work at playing), lottery winners, and some stock market day-traders. When faced with the realization of how unlikely such possibilities actually are, those alienated by more mundane employment experiences may opt to both work and consume less. The game having been lost before it began, many may choose to free more time for spiritual, family-centered personal fulfillment—or to pursue their dream regardless of the material consequences.[2]

Shifting Opinion on Work and Consumption?

Recent surveys found that while 89 percent of 4,000 Americans agreed that "buying and consuming is the American way," 82 percent also agreed that "Americans buy and consume more than we need." The ambivalence could not be more comprehensive. When asked what would make their lives more satisfying, the largest proportion (66%) said "if I were able to spend more time with family and friends," the next-largest proportion

(56%) chose "if there was less stress in my life," and the third-highest proportion (47%) chose "if I felt like I was doing more to make a difference in my community."[3] A very high proportion (88%) believe that "protecting the environment will require most of us to make major changes in the way we live." In contrast, very low numbers selected more materially oriented "lifestyle" options. But it is difficult to identify what would cause significant numbers of individuals to actually alter their everyday patterns toward more fulfilling lives.

While the option of merely continuing with a vaguely unsatisfying, but materially secure existence will remain the norm, more may opt for radical personal change. A trigger for personal change for many is illness. For others, it is the gradual choice of a systematic strategy to attain a modest level of economic security and actually accept that level as sufficient once achieved. This perspective is often simply a recognition earlier in life than has been the norm that there are satisfaction limits to the relentless pursuit of careers in public and private bureaucracies, especially bureaucracies increasingly unable to engage in a mutual sense of loyalty and personal connectedness. One downsizing experience too many may be the trigger (and one such experience is enough for some). Generally, the more prosperous (and equitable) an economy (and the more modest frugality is encouraged by public policy), the more people might in the future opt for money-time trade-offs in some form.

Amy Saltzman has documented many cases of voluntary downshifting in the United States—people who transformed their notion of success through, for example, turning down promotions or shifting to less pressured occupations. She also reports a number of polls that indicate some shift in attitudes toward work and leisure. In the 1980s work was seen as "the important thing" by a solid majority, but in the 1990s leisure eclipsed work by 41 to 36 percent. A separate 1989 survey also found that 82 percent of women and 78 percent of men "said that they would choose a career path with flexible full-time work hours and more family time, but slower career advancement, over one with inflexible work hours and faster career advancement."[4] More recently, in Norway studies on the willingness of full-time employees to reduce working hours and wages (by modest amounts) found that a majority reported they would be willing to make such a shift if the broader result would be a lower rate of unemployment.[5]

Ironically, then, the ever-more-intense push to work and consume, and ever-increasing "productivity" (which inevitably results either in more products or fewer people involved in producing them), may have the potential in some contexts to slow consumption voluntarily. Economic "man," in the end, may be less universal than economists have assumed. Lifelong work and infinitely expandable material needs could prove to be a characteristic particular to mass industrial society and ill-suited to an age of hypercommunication, automation, and frequent downsizing.

Even a genuine return to spirituality (broadly defined) is not impossible—the less materialistic, value-focused, classical and medieval outlooks may be more suited to the emerging age than is the modern perspective. Today's electronic megahype may someday be understood to have been akin to Shakespeare's "protesting too much." That is, the very need for extreme product promotion and obsessive competitiveness may mask an emerging change in the dominant underlying view of existence, and may signal an emerging perspective that recognizes the rich possibilities associated with a sense of material sufficiency. At the same time that fevered promotion and consumption may itself encourage a waning inclination to satisfy human needs in exclusively material ways.

As improbable as it may seem at present, the ever-increasing volume and variety of commercial hype could provoke a counterintentional and counterintuitive outcome. The modest, but infinitely repeated, goal of each producer to sell additional units of branded output could in combination render most such initiatives relatively ineffective in time. Consumer resistance and ad saturation are already well known to the advertising industry, but it is not beyond possibility that such tendencies could rise to a more conscious and generalized level. In effect, time itself might become a more highly valued "commodity." The "acquisition" of time is attainable only through the intelligent restraint of consumption, and perhaps radical selectivity regarding place of residence (away from high-cost centers of more highly paid employment opportunities).

Related to this possible shift in the worldview underlying everyday workplace and consumer habits is another emerging ironic shift, also embedded in human psychological complexity. It has been astutely observed that boredom may be more frequent in fast-paced than in slow-paced societies. Mark Kingwell calls this latter tendency "develocitization."[6] That is, most people who have flown before now readily become restless and bored while flying at 700 miles per hour at 35,000 feet, or even while waiting too many seconds for a modem to download (at a speed of information transfer that was staggeringly fast, even miraculous, only a few months before). This easy habituation to the acceleration of seemingly everything parallels the rising indifference to consumerist hype, however creative and clever. In this second altered perspective the time necessary to partake of simple, slow (and thereby low-cost-per-hour) pleasures rises in value. A world of accelerated (and insecure) work and high-speed media could come to seem meaningless by comparison with quieter, slower times and spaces.

These possibilities may even contain the seeds of future social change, a way of distancing oneself from the monolithic tendencies of electronic capitalism at the personal, family, and workplace level without significant change at the global political level. The often-noted pace of modern life (not unrelated to its instability and underlying hypermaterialism) already propels many toward life choices such as downshifting, job sharing, early retirement, time out, and alternative modes of personal fulfillment. Popular books on these themes are increasingly commonplace and include such self-explanatory titles as *Simple Abundance; Something More: Excavating Your Authentic Self; What's the Rush?; The Simple Living Guide;* and *Your Money or Your Life?*.[7] They all contain advice regarding slowing down, making do with less, being less materialistic, getting to what is important in life, and finding meaning in one's everyday existence. Works by Sarah Ban Breathnach, for example, have attained number 1 status on the *New York Times* bestseller list, and another group publishes a magazine titled *Simple Living: The Journal of Voluntary Simplicity.*[8]

The contemporary lack of meaning arising in part in today's workplaces emerges from several sources. One source is the uncertainty and insecurity associated with continuous reengineering and globally oriented task deployment and redeployment. Employees may perceive incessant change as a lack of loyalty and appreciation on the part of employers. Not surprisingly, such attitudes are increasingly reciprocal, and the constant drain of high-quality employees is accelerated by globally available, Internet-based employment information and services. Another contemporary source of workplace discomfort is the isolation from coworkers and customers in technologized workplaces such as call centers, electronic retail outlets, and highly automated production facilities. Also important, and less and less often fulfilled, is a human need to directly and physically participate in the production of products that are beautiful, important, or useful. These sources of meaninglessness are arguably exacerbated by the impositions on nature associated with the largely automated production of ever-fewer essential products, and from the general failure of electronic capitalism to distribute output equitably (removing the sense that output is meeting real and important human needs).

Similarly, the sense of a too-rapid pace of life derives from develocitization, from employment of virtually all adult family members, from the increase in overtime for both hourly and salaried employees (regardless of whether unemployment is high), from increases in travel time to and from work, from hours lost to television viewing that were once used in family and community activities, and from the driving pace established in every workplace by global competition. Indeed, professional or management status is now widely conferred by employers to control hours and payment to job categories that were once regulated more strictly by contractual rules. Continuous (as distinct from total) work-time rules have also been considerably extended even in high-risk occupations such as truck driving. As Juliet Schor puts it, after presenting evidence that leisure time in the United States has sharply declined in recent decades: "one of capitalism's most enduring myths is that it has reduced human toil."[9] The overall result is the beginnings of a rising preference for reduced work time.[10]

These tendencies may be reinforced by a number of other trends, including the increased physical separation of work and residence, a change that may throw the two modes of existence (home and work) into sharper contrast. But the prospects for actual change (as distinct from widespread psychological discomfort) may depend on an end to the decades-long abdication of government in the realm of innovative and meaningful WTR regulation. Inaction in this realm is in stark contrast to an ongoing political obsessing regarding the value of family life. Endless political rhetoric about "values" and "family values" may in part be a collective sublimation of the widespread alteration of everyday life (including longer work hours, increased employment insecurity, and increased commuting times and distances). The stresses related to those changes manifest themselves primarily in dysfunctional and apolitical ways so far (from high divorce rates to road rage to increases in compulsive gambling and depression), but it would seem not impossible that the personal and family stresses inherent in electronic capitalism might be redirected toward public policies that require, encourage, or permit reductions in work time.

Generally, work-time reductions are primarily an issue in the wealthiest nations and political pressures for WTR policies are greatest when unemployment rates are high. Actual work-time pressures are, however, greatest when unemployment rates are low (as in Japan in the 1980s and the United States in the late 1990s). It is important here to recall that the new global economic order has produced low unemployment only in selected times and places (Japan and the United States in the 1980s, the United States since the mid-1990s, and only recently in Great Britain, Denmark, and the Netherlands, for example). All recently show some signs of softening and Japan in the 1980s in some ways predated electronic capitalism, being more statist in orientation, for example, than the current norm. High unemployment, as noted in chapters 1 and 2, has thus far been endemic or nearly so in nations as diverse as Spain, Russia, France, Germany, Indonesia, and Australia. Governmental WTR initiatives have been most appealing so far for their potential to reduce unemployment and have often been instinctively resisted by business as threatening of productivity and competitiveness despite the fact that they may lower the cost of social programs and thereby taxation.

However, unemployment is not the only logic for reductions in work time—especially, for example, reductions in involuntary overtime. Electronic capitalism, even when unemployment is low, favors short-term contracts, as well as benefit-free, part-time work, even in rich countries in prosperous times. Part-time, temporary, insecure work offers little by way of social identity or security. At the same time in such circumstances many others are working harder and longer than ever. The quality of family and community life thus suffers simultaneously from overwork and underemployment. John Gray sees the work-based realities and patterns of contemporary life as politically and economically central: "Global *laissez-faire* is not a conspiracy of corporate America. It is a tragedy—one of several that have occurred in the twentieth century—in which an hubristic ideology runs aground on enduring human needs that it has failed to comprehend. Among the human needs that free markets neglect are our needs for security and social identity that used to be met by the vocational structures of bourgeois societies."[11]

The larger irony in this is that, despite the endless rounds of downsizing, there remains something unnecessary about much of what presently passes for work. The greatest potential in the productive capacities of electronic capitalism has thus far been missed—many more people could be freed from long hours of repetitive, meaningless employment. Our economy has so far only, in effect, replaced tedious industrial work with tedious and pointless marketing and retail work. A considerable percentage of today's employees are devoted to the task of selling us things we do not otherwise even imagine we need. The best way to resolve some of these tensions, and to realize the full potential of the new productive and communicative capacities, may lie in part in a mix of voluntary, contractual, and societywide reductions in work time. The real challenge of today's society is to find ways to gradually reduce the need for pointless and tedious work and to share high-quality creative and meaningful employment opportunities more widely.

Productivity and production inexorably advance, yet family structure, environmental quality, community integration, a societal sense of security, sources of social identity, and a sense of meaning and purpose are slowly being undermined. The hopeful thing about this situation is that the same advances in productivity also contain the seeds of truly fundamental change. There is the possibility for reaping truly meaningful benefits, leading toward a collective future fundamentally different from the past. Those changes, I am convinced, may increasingly center on society's understanding of work itself.

Work and Meaning: Cultural Portents of Change

It is difficult of course to anticipate the future place of work in society, but the possibility of fundamental change does exist, though as yet largely unseen. One curious sign of change is that it is becoming increasingly less obvious what is play and what is work. As noted, today's media-dominated economy delivers some of its highest economic rewards to those who merely play very well—at basketball, tennis, soccer, golf, baseball, or music—or play at being someone else with cameras rolling. Others earn vast sums for being "personalities," playing at being themselves. Craft and mass industrial society also rewarded skillful players, but electronic capitalism has taken play-as-work to a level unique in human history. Play ("entertainment") has become a central segment of the economy as a whole. Sports franchises are valued at many hundreds of millions of dollars, individual athletes are paid tens of millions annually, and countless billions are invested in stadiums and arenas. The U.S. film industry produces one of the nation's most important global exports, so important that U.S. trade negotiators pretend, or actually believe, that Hollywood's output is a commodity like any other, having nothing to do with "culture."

One reason for the very great rewards associated with play-as-product is that, especially as digital reproduction advances and secures a global market, replication and delivery costs (as distinct from production costs) approach zero. That is, once initial investments are recovered each additional sale is almost 100 percent profit (presumably shared in some way between the media corporation and the "artists")—thus very small increments of improvement in product salability are worth a very great deal. That explains why better baseball players make millions and only slightly lesser versions never escape charter-bus runs through medium-sized communities and soon turn to construction work. But none of this explains why countless billions are spent on entertainment, rather than on nicer homes, additional goods, or time off. Why has play become one of electronic capitalism's leading products? The answer may say something important about contemporary society.

My admittedly not easily demonstrable speculation on this point is that many people in wealthy societies semiconsciously recognize that much of what passes for work and output is unnecessary, not just tedious or sometimes unpleasant, but fundamentally pointless. It may be exhausting, well remunerated in some cases, and necessary from the employer's standpoint, but it has little if any value beyond that. Neoliberalism fixates on and scapegoats the public sector, but clearly vast areas of the private sector are tremendously "overbuilt" as well. Many may vaguely sense the underlying possibility of fundamental change from the very pervasiveness of the hype that consumes our lives and the deepening clutter in our basements and attics. Nonetheless, we continue to work out of habit (or because we fear a complete disconnect from work) and continue to make not-very-necessary purchases because we have the money.

Thus we so intently watch others at play in part because we sense that our hectic working and consuming are no longer really necessary (other than to help keep the economy going). What was a means to survival has become an end in itself. We sense that if all that is produced and consumed were really needed, people would not need to work so hard at convincing us to buy more. We know, but generally do not acknowledge even to ourselves, that much of what we do for a living is unnecessary. Often, we would prefer to be doing something else, but do not know how to find, or lack the courage to seek, more balance and meaning in our lives. In fact, we all could be playing more and working less, but most of us can only manage to do the next best thing—celebrate (and repetitively observe, and even dwell on the lives of) those who at least appear to play especially well.

There are other, also admittedly obscure and counterintuitive, signs of a societal need to fundamentally rethink work and meaning. There are many other manifestations of this widely felt (but not understood) need to work less and play more. All are obsessive, the latter two noted here now bordering on societal addictions. Three such manifestations are the contemporary fixation on welfare cheating, compulsive consumption, and a widespread and growing obsession with gambling. None of these warrants extensive analysis here, but each is worth brief elaboration.

In the 1990s one political issue with particular resonance in the United States and Canada was welfare spending. In the United States, a Democratic administration enacted a draconian rollback of welfare eligibility, and many individual states went further. There were many reasons for these actions, some of which were altogether sensible. Welfare has, for example, proven to be a multigenerational habit for some. However, when the welfare cutbacks were first enacted there were often insufficient employment opportunities to absorb both those already looking for work and those who were pushed into looking. Overall, it might be hypothesized that part of both the appeal of welfare and the general hostility toward welfare recipients is the growing pointlessness of much work. Some of the hostility is thus a projection of the fear that what we ourselves do is unnecessary. We also fear that we ourselves could end up on welfare when our employer installs electronic robots or outsources production to some distant corner of the globe. We deny that fear by resenting those who avoid the increasingly pointless hours we spend at work. What we overlook is the possibility of reduced work time for all implicit in both involuntary unemployment and nonproductive (e.g., hype-oriented) work.

Compulsive consumption habits, the second item on the list, are obvious to even the casual observer. We North Americans, for example, devote on average more than 25 percent of our work time to financing our means of going back and forth to work. Moreover, consumer debt has never been higher, even at the peak of prosperity. Many voluntarily work overtime despite already having little time to enjoy the things they have already acquired. Thousands of road accidents result from people driving and talking on the telephone simultaneously. Billions of dollars are spent on precooked food not so much as a convenience, but in many cases because work hours for all family members are so long that no one has time to shop, let alone cook. A poor diet and obsessive eating have meant that nearly half of North Americans are overweight.

Obsessive gambling affects up to 10 percent of the population, mostly (but not exclusively) among those of low to moderate income. There are many psychological explanations for such behavior, but there are also many social explanations. One is an intense wish to escape from unsatisfying work lives. Another may reflect a wider indifference to the acquisition of additional possessions than we usually recognize. This indifference renders the remote possibility of transforming one's circumstances more appealing and meaningful than the consumption opportunities actually available.

Even if some of the above is an overinterpretation of contemporary trends, these aspects of contemporary life collectively suggest that a fundamental rethinking of the meaning of work may be in order. In my view, such a rethinking would render visible the greatest positive potential of the surge in productivity and production associated with computers, automation, and globalization. Productivity is so high—and the potential for further gains so great—that we can and should consider the possibility that "work" in the usual sense might come to occupy a greatly diminished proportion of our lives. Such a shift might also have the potential to reduce contemporary excesses in consumer demand and to redistribute both work and consumption opportunities. Some of us, and ultimately everyone, would in effect trade money and goods for more time to enjoy what we already have. The change could be largely voluntary, though it might also be noted that certain public policy disincentives could be removed (through changes in taxation or the establishment of a legal right to refuse involuntary overtime, for example).

Rethinking Work and Everyday Life

Work serves an array of functions. Most people are healthier and happier with lives that balance work and play rather than with lives utterly dominated by one or the other. Yet increasingly work displaces play. Few people are able to significantly adjust their work patterns on an individual basis (by taking less money for less work) without risking their economic futures. The cost of entry into professional employment of all kinds has become, in most cases, more intensely competitive. This is also true—irony of ironies—regarding careers in the world of play. One need only consider the number of hours basketball legend Larry Bird spent practicing foul shots, or the age at which and the intensity with which golf champion Tiger Woods began a life oriented toward sports. Career success is increasingly determined in childhood (or rooted in one's capacity to gain admission to and to pay for an elite education), and continuing success presumes that there are few pauses until one's career is completed.

There is, of course, great joy in work. Doing something well that is important to others is central to what gives life meaning. The implications of work as a source of meaning are profound, since today's work patterns are constantly shifting and for many are even less stable than was the norm in industrial society. In this, Rifkin was largely right: whole categories of work will be radically altered or rapidly eliminated—bank tellers and travel agents, for example, may go the way of elevator operators. Rifkin was wrong, however, in assuming that there would never again be enough work. While this outcome might have seemed plausible in the early 1990s, it now seems improbable. In any case, it is important to understand that a declining "need" for human labor is not something to be feared, something inevitably thrust on hapless individuals by a merciless system of automation and globalization. On the contrary, though this view will not be easily recognized, a declining need for human labor is a profoundly positive possibility inherent in today's productive capacities.

The possibility that more of us might spend less of our lives in routine tasks is cause for celebration. The challenge is psychological and social in that we have come to define ourselves in terms our jobs and will not easily accept the changes that are now possible for the first time in history. The challenge is also political because what might be called a work-and-spend syndrome is crucial to the present functioning of electronic capitalism.

Nonetheless, a gradual reduction in, and redistribution of, work time on a global basis makes sense environmentally, socially, and even economically. The challenge is to find ways to make this change more widely appealing. As noted, a substantial majority of us will say that we want more time for family, friends, and community (and we doubtless do), but few actually take up the, albeit limited, opportunities that do exist. The perceived costs of doing so are bound up with a relationship between work and meaning that evolved within mass industrial society.

Our sense of the functions of work remains rooted in survival and reproductive instincts. This is as true of developing computer software as it is of hunting and agriculture. Those basic functions remain with us despite the differentiation and specialization of social and economic organization. Work is also still inseparable from our sense of identity. In the age of settled agriculture, the first piece of information humans would seek about other humans came down to "where are you from?" only because it could be presumed in most cases what one "did." With mass industrial society that primary question evolved into "what do you do?" That evolution reflected the differentiation and specialization of modern societies. Even today, it is also an implicit question about class and education. Work (and class) is who we are and the primary way we begin to understand who others are. It is little wonder that involuntary job loss can alter human behavior, and even personality. Our "job" is how we connect to society and essentially determines how we see ourselves.

With the transformations of the industrial revolution a clearer division arose between public (work) and private (home) as socially distinct spheres. As transportation evolved (and work weeks shortened), the physical distances between home and work typically expanded. Industrial workplaces demanded something new of humans: routinized behavior and total commitment. There was, and remains today, little possibility of truly divided loyalties—in the early days of the industrial revolution those who felt them often perished. Thus within a generation or two identification with one's work was thoroughgoing for most people. In the later part of the nineteenth century the notion of a "job" evolved for many, especially the middle classes, into the notion of a career, a lifelong calling for which one prepared from one's early years. It became normal for professionals to expect to remain in their calling all their lives, following ever-longer periods of preparation. The sense of identity with, and commitment to, one's chosen work grew even deeper.

Work became who we were, the basis not only of a relatively secure livelihood but also of how we connected to a complex, hyperspecialized, and finely gradated society. Most people in a modern society can rank perhaps a thousand distinct occupations, and the rankings accorded to each by all societal members are remarkably consistent, given the spectacular variations in vantage point that exist. Work provides us with a way to fit into society as a whole and, arguably, the larger the society (and the more globalized), the more important this sense of connection becomes. Work (and to a lesser extent family) is how we are assured that we are a part of entities larger than ourselves—enterprises, nations, even a species. As our ability to directly provide for ourselves declined (in the transitions from hunting and gathering to agriculture to industrial society), this connection became a key psychological underpinning of our existence. Citizenship and the welfare state have also counted for something in this regard but are hardly any longer as reassuring as secure employment, wealth, or access to land.

Work, then, provides our most important sense of connection to community and society. It is the primary basis of our sense of stability and security, as well as a major source of self-esteem and meaning. Work also provides a daily opportunity for social interaction and it structures one's day, week, year, and life. Through work we come to feel a sense of tired satisfaction at the end of each day and the expectation that we may eventually "achieve" retirement. Through work we measure our progress in life one day at a time and one (career) step at a time. Life is comprehensible and organized. For all of these reasons involuntary job loss, and even retirement without anticipation and planning, can be devastating.

When such losses are commonplace, as in the early 1990s, the downsized may feel less singled out, but also far more fearful that they will never again reconnect. Retirement is feared in part because it is life's last ritualized step prior to institutional care and/or death. When retired or unemployed, some even dwell on the fact that the enterprise where they worked thrives in one's absence, just as the birds will sing and the rains fall after one is dead and buried. The next step for humankind may only come when more of us can recognize that all of this is an artifact of mass industrial society. It is not inherent in being human and it may no longer be a viewpoint appropriate to electronic capitalism.

The word *job* derives from the word *gob* (a small bit). A job prior to mass industrial society was a task, as in the phrase a "job around the house." The trend within electronic capitalism toward temp or contract work is in effect a partial return to a preindustrial meaning of employment. So too are increases in university teaching on a course-stipend basis, increases in self-employment, freelancing, and consultancy, and finely tuned part-time seasonal, daily, and weekly scheduling in the retail sector. The terms and conditions of work in these areas are often unfair—part-time work is often involuntary and primarily a means whereby employers avoid paying health, retirement, and other benefits to a growing proportion of their employees. Organization of these pools of "gob" workers is made possible (or less expensive to employers) through computerization of scheduling.

These trends are, of course, part and parcel of the growing gap between rich and poor, but they also provide opportunities, for some, for more varied and interesting lives. They may also provide a means of learning to develop a sense of self outside the world of work. One "is" a musician or writer, but one's job right now is "doing" office temp or construction work. It is also plausible that this restructuring of work, especially in combination with an overall reduction in average work time, could contribute to a resolution of the increased domestic challenges associated with de-gendered work opportunities.

Such shifts—combined with computer networking and telecommuting—could promote the reintegration of family, community, and work more typical of preindustrial existence. It is even possible to imagine the restoration for some of the sense of security inherent in small-scale agriculture or the satisfaction inherent in craft production. What was lost two centuries ago could be reborn. The ongoing restructuring of work relations could produce a growing decline of the "organization man" mentality rather than the personal devastation commonplace in the mass downsizings of the early 1990s.[12] Reduced work time could even render the anonymous "crowd" typical of mass industrial society a little less "lonely."[13]

The key to a positive transition in the character and meaning of work lies in the more equitable distribution of work, a general reduction in work time, and a gradual pace to such shifts. Unemployment is simply unnecessary. Most of the time it is the result of deliberate policies, a cheap means of controlling inflation and discouraging employee assertiveness. Work time (and wage levels) could be fine-tuned on a different basis. Downsizing in the face of competitive pressures or declining demand could be disallowed in favor of reduced overtime, reductions in annual bonuses in a system that allocates a proportion of incomes on this basis, accelerated early retirement, or systematic reductions in the length of workdays or workweeks.

Europe is moving in this latter direction. Japan in its heyday had a bonus system. But, these issues aside, the overall evolution of electronic capitalism could be spectacularly positive if it led to *globally* redistributed employment opportunities linked to the gradual trading of income increments for increased leisure in wealthier nations. Such changes could be in part at least achieved on a highly decentralized and largely voluntary basis—nation by nation, workplace by workplace, occupation by occupation, or one person at a time.

Downsizing or Downshifting

Heilbroner once penned a lovely phrase characterizing work over "most of the past" as having been "an onerous imperative of existence." He anticipated that "this importunate and exhausting predominance of work is certain to be markedly diminished in the not too distant future. By 1980—or by the year 2000—a work week of 30 hours, even of 20 hours, is by no means unimaginable."[14] This view was plausible at the time, but as it turns out, has not been achieved thus far. It could be argued, however, that now is the best time in history to recapture many of the positive aspects of life lost with the onset of the industrial revolution, in the aftermath of the horrors of everyday nineteenth-century life that Heilbroner, Polanyi, and others have described. The human condition has risen spectacularly since that time, but since the 1940s gains in leisure time have been arrested. We are now in effect trading the time we once collectively spent on family and community pursuits for an accelerating flow of goods.

The dawn of environmentalism provides another logic for proceeding with reductions in work time. André Gorz, writing twenty years after Heilbroner, was one of the first to link an environmentalist perspective and the then-emerging possibility of automation resulting in sharply reduced work time. In 1983, he stated baldly that "the micro-electronic revolution heralds the abolition of work." He also spoke of a thirty-hour week and of a less competitive, more relaxed way of life with work lives of 10,000 to 20,000 hours: "Twenty thousand hours per lifetime represents 10 years' full-time work, or 20 years' part-time work, or—a more likely choice—40 years of intermittent work, part-time alternating with periods for holidays, or for unpaid autonomous activity, community work, etc."[15]

Clearly the world envisioned by Heilbroner and Gorz in the 1960s and 1980s respectively, and greeted with alarm as inevitable by Rifkin in the 1990s, has not arrived and does not threaten to arrive automatically or imminently. What did emerge, and continues today in many large European nations, has been (in some nations) increased unemployment, general increases in part-time and contract work, and perhaps small declines in the average age of retirement. Also significant more recently, in selective locations, has been an employment boom in the so-called new economy—computers and software, advertising and marketing, biomedical research and telecommunications. Another reason that a shorter workweek has not arrived within the time frame they predicted both Heilbroner and Gorz understood very well.

Both writers were concerned about protecting the right to work. Both were also convinced that the market system required the near universality of a connection to the production system through employment. Regarding the right to work, Gorz concluded that the "guarantee of an income independent of a job will only bring freedom if it is accompanied by *the right to work for everyone;* that is, the right to participate in the production of society."[16] Heilbroner worried that work would "become more of a privilege than a necessity" and noted that "the market system has always taken for granted one self-evident social phenomenon: a mass participation in the economic process." He also concluded that "in the foreseeable economies of genuine abundance and technological mastery, the market mechanism appears to have a declining functional relevance." "For most of us," he further opined, "this may appear as a disturbing conclusion."[17] Markets, he might have said, function best in providing an effective means of attracting and allocating scarcities of goods, skills, and capital. Heilbroner stopped short of asking whether there might be any level of abundance at which a significant proportion of the population might simply elect to work less.

Gorz concluded that automation and abundance would undermine capitalism, but—in contrast to Heilbroner's caution and ambivalence—he greeted the prospect with unbridled enthusiasm. For Gorz, the reason automation, abundance, and the market are incompatible has to do with the structure of workplaces—that is, with social relations between employers and employees. The "fundamental aim of keeping full-time work as the norm" is, in Gorz's view, "to maintain the relations of domination based on the work ethic." In his words, "If . . . work took up only 30 hours or less per week, it would become just one activity among others which were equally important or more important."[18] Neither Gorz nor Heilbroner paid much attention to the potential for global-scale expansion of consumption. Nor, curiously, did either say much about the opportunities for additional consumption that might be presented by additional free time (assuming that sufficient money were available). Gorz, however, did consider the bizarre notion of paying people to consume. This, needless to say, has not caught on either. Indeed, the global economic system has thus far proven far more adaptive than either Gorz or Heilbroner imagined. And it has been vastly better at generating new employment opportunities than Rifkin or other early critics of globalization and downsizing imagined.

The 1990s resurgence of employment and economic opportunities in the United States led some there to ask whether the business cycle might be in suspension, an assertion as improbable as Gorz's imagined abolition of work. That resurgence was enough, however, to suggest that a review of the recent history of employment patterns might be useful. The massive expansion of the state from the late 1930s onward allowed mass industrial society to continue to expand, to overcome a tendency to produce "too efficiently," resulting in uneven consumption and massive cyclical downturns. Public spending softened the downturns and public debt sometimes helped to revive stagnant economies. In short, public spending on transfer payments and public-sector employment helped to created economic stability and resiliency. The 1930s were not repeated in part because we created mixed economies. The cycles continued, of course, but were softened considerably until the late 1970s. Ongoing structural employment declines in manufacturing were softened by the continued expansion of the public and retail sectors. Thereafter, slow growth in wages was softened by the rapid trend to multi-income families.

Two other developments were masked through the golden period of mass industrial society (from the end of World War II until the 1970s). The trend toward shorter workweeks, highly visible in the early days of industrial society, was slowed after World War II. The forty-hour week attained totemlike status and thereafter productivity increments went to higher wages, profits, and public-sector spending, but not to increased leisure time. With the rise of electronic capitalism, reductions in work time returned, but they were neither shared nor gradual. They returned in the form of downsizing, forced and semiforced early retirements, and the rapid expansion of insecure, underremunerated, part-time and temporary work. At the same time there was political reaction within economic and political elites to the public sector that had sheltered mass industrial society from both cyclical downturns and structural underemployment. In part, this was a response to the economic stagnation that followed rising oil prices in the 1970s, combined with a determination to continue to improve the relative position of the already rich. Neoconservatives recognized that the welfare state was particular to the politics of mass industrial society. This recognition was at once apt and brutal.

The expansion of the welfare state appears to be at an end. Freer global trade allows low-end wages in wealthy nations to stagnate, and in that context generous welfare-based transfer payments might be owing to a considerable minority of the employed population. There has been little, if any, political constituency for such an outcome. Moreover, shorter-term unemployment insurance payments were suited to the cyclical (and temporary) unemployment of mass industrial societies, not to the downsizing typical of electronic capitalism. Rising inequality was thus the norm of the 1980s and early 1990s. The massive economic expansion of the later 1990s saw lower unemployment and longer hours for many, but only rarely any restoration of the loss of relative income shares for low- and middle-income earners. Americans took over from the Japanese as having the most hours of work per person per year, but many still feel vulnerable to job loss, even when unemployment is low.[19] The experiences of the early 1990s had undone resistance to longer hours and to lower wages. Electronic capitalism's restoration of the American dream thus came without undue attention to universal opportunity, or any attention to the time necessary to enjoy the rebirth. As Saltzman puts it, the hard-earned beautiful front porches of the 1990s were empty most of the time.[20]

WTR and Sustainability: An Emerging European Sensibility

European green parties have long advocated reduced work time as a means of integrating economic, social, and environmental policy. More recently, as Europe lagged behind North America in the reachievement of low rates of unemployment, bold policy initiatives have been adopted. These initiatives are at the center of a widespread desire in much of continental Europe to differentiate itself from the neoliberal focus of the Anglo-American democracies. The question faced by Europeans has been how to achieve acceptable levels of employment in the face of global competition, including radical tax reductions and reengineering in the United States and Canada, without either radically weakening social programs to attract investment or pushing the unemployed into low-wage jobs. The answer, which may or may not be successful in the long run, is work-time reduction.

The most visible initiative has been France's Aubry Law, legislated in June 1998 by the Socialist-led, left-green government of Lionel Jospin. Effective January 2000 (January 2002 for firms with fewer than twenty employees), the thirty-five-hour workweek is the new national standard and all hours above that level are considered overtime.[21] Firms that reduce work time, and hire new employees proportionately, will have their payroll taxes reduced. Much of the cost of that reduction is recaptured by the government from forgone unemployment insurance and other social-benefit costs. Additional aid is available to firms that, for example, hire a high proportion of young or long-term unemployed workers. Details regarding wage adjustments or increased flexibility in the organization of workplaces and work patterns were left to workplace or sectoral bargaining. This latter step was a compromise with employers (following intense opposition) and could result, when combined with the governmental incentives, in little or no cost to employers in some settings. In general, it should be noted that a workplace-by-workplace approach to work-time reduction is feasible in a European context in part because a high proportion of employees are unionized.

Anders Hayden, a leading advocate of work-time reduction, summarizes the early results of the French initiative this way: "In May 1999 the

French government released an assessment of the first 11 months of negotiations. A total of 4,076 workplace agreements had introduced workweeks of 35 hours or less, reducing work hours of 1,142,427 employees and generating a positive employment effect of 56,767 jobs—42,834 new jobs and 13,933 layoffs avoided. (By August the job-creation total had grown significantly, to 118,433 based on 14,615 agreements.) Employers and employees had opted for a diverse range of options, ranging from shorter workdays to additional holidays on an annual basis. Most agreements also covered managers, who often saw work time above 35 hours per week accumulate in 'time banks,' to be taken later as time off." Estimates of the overall employment generation associated with the initiative range from 250,000 to 450,000 jobs. Again in Hayden's words, "Critics originally claimed the 35-hour law would scare away investment and actually destroy jobs. As it turned out, 1998—the year following the announcement of the law—was the best year for job creation in France out of the last 30, with 350,000 private-sector jobs created."[22]

France's initiative has thus far been the boldest, but there has been a good deal of activity on work-time reduction throughout continental Europe. In Germany, change has come directly through collective bargaining. The most widely noted such agreement in Germany was that achieved at Volkswagen in 1993, when weekly hours were cut from 36 to 28.8 hours, saving about 30,000 jobs. Pay cuts for the 20 percent cut in hours ranged between 11 and 15 percent.[23] That is, hourly rates increased but not nearly as much as hours were reduced. Again, it must be noted that this agreement and those in many other sectors have been achieved with no public policy action; the standard German workweek remains at 48 hours, where it has been for much of the past century. One problem widely debated in Germany regarding the initiatives negotiated so far is the considerable increase in work-time flexibility that employers have extracted in exchange. That is, shorter work time has been traded for employer flexibility regarding both Saturday work and greater short-term variability in scheduling. Some agreements even have annualized hourly totals with scheduling highly variable within that limit.

One problem with employer-controlled flexible work time that has been discussed in Europe is that it may undermine one of the prime objectives of work-time reduction—greater family stability and greater opportunity for community involvement. The best prospect for adjustment in this regard is the wide reachievement of very low levels of unemployment. In that context employers would likely become more mindful of employee concerns on a one-on-one basis for fear of losing effective employees to more adaptable and cooperative employers. Other approaches might see, for example, contractual or even legislated protection of some minimum number of weekends off per year for employees with some minimum level of seniority.

Whereas the recent French initiative is the boldest on the part of a large European nation, the Netherlands has made perhaps the longest and most thoroughgoing work-time reductions. In 1970 employees in the Netherlands worked 1,800 hours on average (the equivalent of forty-five 40-hour weeks per year). By 1995 this had declined to 1,397 hours per year on average, a decline equivalent to an astonishing ten 40-hour weeks per year per employee. Part time work had become the norm for many, most often by choice. Most dramatic, however, is the outcome in terms of unemployment: in 1999 the Dutch unemployment rate was even lower than that in the United States at 3.4 percent. In 1984 Dutch unemployment stood at 12.2 percent; following a steady fall for a decade and a half, it was 5.5 percent in 1997 and 4.3 percent in 1998.[24] Economic change in the Netherlands dates from the historic Wassenaar agreement that saw employers accept work-time reductions and employees accept wage moderation aimed at the restoration of profitability in Dutch firms. The other key to change in the Netherlands has been the promotion of "long" part time in national legislation that requires that employers provide (proportionately) the same benefits to part-time as to full-time employees. Only 6 percent of Dutch part-time employees would prefer full-time work, and many employees have a guaranteed right to opt for part-time work.

The expansion of part-time employment in North America has taken place under very different rules and patterns. In North America, part-time employees would often prefer to be full-time employees and any adoption of part-time work, or even an expression of interest in it, can reduce chances of career advancement. Moreover, North American firms extensively utilize both part time and overtime to cut down on the number of employees for whom they must pay payroll taxes and to avoid having more (full-time) individuals eligible for benefits. The overall outcome is employment practices that are not only frequently oppressive and antifamily, but that may be dangerous and lead to a widespread combination of overwork and underemployment. This in turn, as noted, leads to public and private expenditures (and attendant environmental costs) that would otherwise be far less necessary. Lifestyle consequences include the extensive use of highly packaged instant meals, and numerous short "escapes" rather than a smaller number of more extended vacations. Another result of extensive overtime is increased intolerance of the unemployed among industrial workers and increasingly obsessive consumerism, both as psychic compensation for overwork.[25]

Other challenges would probably occur with the transfer of work-time reductions from Europe to North America. Many parts of the United States currently have considerable labor shortages. Work-time reductions, it would seem, might exacerbate such problems. That is not certain, however. The right working conditions might lure additional people into the labor market on a limited basis. Retired professionals might take part-time work if they could easily adjust their work commitments to their leisure preferences (taking the winter or summer off, for example). One employer in the U.S. Midwest found that he could attract employees in the face of low unemployment by matching a short factory shift to the hours of the school day and thereby eliminating the need for childcare. It has also been found in general that employees that have an additional free day per week have a lower rate of absenteeism and higher productivity during the hours they do work. This latter outcome has provided a gain for some European employers who have made the shift to reduced work time.

Also worth mentioning here is the Danish use of sabbaticals throughout the economy. Denmark, like the Netherlands, has achieved very low unemployment essentially without neoliberal deregulatory and "shrink-the-state" initiatives. Since 1994 there has been a job-rotation system in Denmark that allows working individuals, with employer consent, to opt for up to one year away for educational leave, family leave, or sabbatical leave. Employers must hire a replacement from the ranks of the unemployed. The employee then receives temporary income from the government (at a 60% rate without an approved educational objective). The additional cost to the government is not large; it just pays a benefit on a different basis to a different person—to someone who is voluntarily, and usually with a goal beneficial to the economy, taking time out rather than to someone whose time out is involuntary. In 1996 there were 121,000 people utilizing this scheme in a nation whose total workforce was 2.8 million.[26] The Danish scheme would appear to have two positive social effects in addition to those pertaining to work-time reductions: it could reduce the number of people who are frequent long-term users of unemployment insurance, and it could increase the number of people who can quickly adapt their skill sets in tune with rapid technological change.

All of this is not to say that reduced work time in and of itself would lead directly, immediately, and automatically to social (and environmental) improvement. Reduced work time also carries some potential environmental and social risks. These concerns are discussed in the next section. Overall, the hope is that what might emerge in continental Europe is an alternative sensibility. This would be a distinctive version of electronic capitalism where consumerism is somewhat restrained through stronger environmental standards and more sustainable, less auto-centric urban forms, and where work-time reductions improve social life (and further restrain consumerism). In Europe unionization may continue to be a significant political force and social programs may be just a little less vulnerable to globalization's tax-reduction pressures. It is far from certain, of course, that such an alternative model can compete with North America, where such a sensibility has been largely overwhelmed. The prospects are better, however, if Europeans come to be more fully comfortable with enjoying the wondrous wealth they have already achieved and leave to North America for now the less sustainable, high-stress, and antifamily excesses of the twenty-four-hour economy.

WTR: Some Risks and Possibilities

Environmentally, reduced work time has considerable positive potential. First, pressures to extract resources beyond sustainable levels, or to allow polluters to engage in "job blackmail" with equanimity, would decline if reduced work time were to reduce normal levels of unemployment. Second, significant environmental problems associated with time-related burdens on infrastructure could be mitigated in part through greater variability in work-time patterns (reduced peak loads mean fewer power plants and highways would be needed). Third, reduced work time may involve for some a conscious choice of additional time over additional money and goods. Moreover, a societal inclination to reducing work time is easily linked to societal concern about sustainability and equity at the level of political ideas—reducing work time is about sharing available work when difficult economic times arise. It might even ultimately come to be associated with recognition that certain levels of output and consumption are sufficient, all things considered.

On a more everyday level, appropriate personal environmental behaviors are often a function of time. That is, "convenience" is often environmentally problematic—from the excessive packaging in prepared and fast foods to opting when pressed for time for driving rather than walking, cycling, or using public transit. Time constraints also encourage the use of the dryer or dishwasher rather than the clothesline or sink. Composting and recycling are also time consuming, as is dealing with weeds and pests organically in backyard gardens. Reduced work time does not ensure virtuous environmental behavior, but it may render it a more likely choice.

Perfection and universal compliance in these behavioral matters is neither likely, nor likely necessary. There would be a considerable net reduction in energy and materials use if a higher proportion in wealthy nations walked or cycled just on nice days or hung out the laundry while the dishwasher was doing the dishes. People would be more fit and the sheets and towels would smell fresher. Of course, many people cannot change behaviors owing to age or infirmity. But a combination of increased opportunities associated with work-time reductions and a modest shift in price and tax incentives and other market signals, in the spirit of the policy suggestions in chapter 6, would promote (rather than require) environmentally appropriate behavioral change.

A more fundamental shift might, however, eventually come to be a conscious choice for some, however modestly at first: the choice of time over money. Change at this level cannot be forced; it may even be more likely without policies that somehow mandate reductions in work time. A focus on opportunity structures that allow and gently encourage individuals to alter their own work patterns is vastly preferable—one size need not fit all. Work-time policy should focus on making overtime voluntary, on enhancing voluntary partial early retirement opportunities, on delivering equivalent (pro-rated) benefits to part-time employees, and on ensuring that tax and other incentives do not disadvantage those who might opt for time rather than money.

Without enhanced opportunities for time-money choices, goods will continue to be consumed (at a considerable environmental cost) both out of necessity (to create time) and in an often-futile attempt to compensate for a vaguely hollow, overworked existence. Too much that too many wish to do will continue to be put off to a future that may not arrive in time to be all that "golden." But enhanced environmental protection and sustainability is not, as noted, a certain result of wide reductions in work time. It may even be the case, for example, that electronic capitalism will deliver high incomes and consumption to a considerable proportion of the population through stock market speculation. Or while some voluntarily reduce their work time, others may take up the slack voluntarily (or not so voluntarily if wages fall or if the work shed in wealthy nations is transferred to poorer nations with super-low wages that permit an even higher output of goods).

Another environmentally pertinent question is the following: In what ways might WTR alter consumption patterns and habits? The environmental impacts associated with postindustrial human play could be as environmentally problematic as industrial-age work, even if total work time were to decline. At the least, reduced impacts are not an automatic result of increased leisure as some early analysts, including Gorz, implied. More free time could mean more motorized travel—and thereby more energy consumption and air pollution. Or more time could be used to apply more pesticides and fertilizers to ever more "perfect" lawns. Or more time might mean more opportunity to go hunting for ever scarcer wildlife, or to drive off-road vehicles through mountain streams, just as the television ads suggest would be the most fun ever.

More free time, combined with telecommuting from places where housing costs are low, might even help to induce a return to larger families and thus increased human populations in wealthy (high-consumption) nations. There is no assurance that significant numbers of individuals would spend their additional time growing more of their own food and thereby using less packaging and shipping. They might spend all day with mindless multimedia and still only have time to pop an unhealthy frozen dinner into the microwave. In brief, the list of environmentally doubtful ways to use additional time is almost endless—WTR is far from a sure way to environmental nirvana.

There are, however, some reasons for thinking that environmentally preferable behaviors would be taken up by more than a small minority. First, there would be some loss of income relative to what might have been earned had long hours continued. Many would seek lower-cost options, and higher energy prices and/or the EMTT were it to come to be would keep the cost of environmentally doubtful (less sustainable) options high compared with less problematic options. Less energy- and materials-intensive pleasures—including better meals, family and community activities, nonmotorized recreation, and in some cases electronic communications—would be less expensive. It is also arguable that such pleasures are inherently superior when time is a less significant factor in the equation—"slow" food, freshly picked, simply tastes better.

All of this is part of a persuasive environmental logic for WTR as, on balance, a step forward. But there is a deeper rationale as well. Indeed, a case can be made that only the incorporation of declining work time into an environmentally informed vision of an alternative future can make such a vision politically feasible. What might otherwise seem a postindustrial version of medieval asceticism will not motivate popular demand for political and social change in poor nations or rich. In the face of unprecedented productive capacity and the ever more effective (and invasive) selling of material consumption, there is almost nothing less likely. The opportunity to attain the time to enjoy both material and nonmaterial pleasures, however, alters the equation considerably. Ironically, it has some potential to place, on balance, an asceticism of denial on the side of an overwork-consumerist lifestyle. From this larger perspective, work-time reductions are part and parcel not just of *an* alternative to electronic capitalism as presently practiced, but are far and away *the* most politically viable alternative.

Few individuals are prepared to forgo the bounty of contemporary societies; indeed all too few can do more than hope to acquire their fair share of that wealth. There is no widely popular inclination to living modestly other than as part of a trend toward slowing down the pace of life. Even an EMTT would only likely be politically salable as part of a tax shift that saw equivalent reductions in, for example, income or property taxes. There is, however, a considerable potential cross-class appeal to freeing the time to enjoy what many in wealthy societies already have. Especially appealing would be policies that permit individuals to make such choices at suitable times in their lives or in their family situations. That is, there is an enormous potential appeal, for example, to the Danish policies of creating opportunities for extended leaves for retraining or Dutch policies that extend benefits and promotional opportunities to those who elect some reduction in work time. Also potentially appealing might be industry-specific initiatives to make overtime beyond some modest limit strictly a matter of choice. Changes of this sort are, however, just the tip of the iceberg in terms of what might ultimately be possible.

Arguably, the greatest potentials of electronic capitalism lie in three realms: the freeing of human existence from many tedious and repetitive work requirements, the potential to alter the geographic connection between workplace and residence, and the creation of low-cost worldwide instantaneous, interactive, multichannel communications. The full potentials of all three may be constrained within the present economistic model of electronic capitalism and potentially enhanced by a model that places greater emphasis on environmental protection, distributional equity, and work-time reduction. While manufacturing requires fewer and fewer employees per unit of output, the radical improvement of productivity is essentially lost to most individuals if tedious manufacturing work is simply replaced by tedious, and ever more expansive, retail and sales work. Equally futile is the continuous use of all productivity gains to produce nonsustainable goods, rather than applying them to a mix of relatively dematerialized economic gains and enhanced leisure.

Similarly, disconnecting work and residence might be of substantial benefit to families if family members are at home *and* not constantly working. Relocating within a manageable-scale community, or to a wilderness, or to a more urban existence only makes sense in terms of quality of life if one has the time to enjoy the pleasures the new location offers. There are real environmental risks associated with a widespread physical detachment of work and residence, but the worst of them involve residential dispersal *combined with* frequent long-distance commutes. Greater freedom from physically going to the office on an everyday basis gains little environmentally (and socially in terms of family-time deficits) if it is replaced by traveling vast distances for more extended stays on a less frequent basis.

Full utilization of the potential of global broadband communications also requires time and so is in competition with both work and an enhanced family and community life (though it might also enhance both). There is really no technical reason why virtually all recorded information cannot ultimately be available virtually anytime and anywhere. Access may only be on a shared basis in poorer communities and societies rather than directly in each household, but there is no technical reason that access should not approach universality. There are, of course, environmental concerns with availability at this level but also enormous potential sustainability gains associated with equipment updates that replace chips rather than full computing units. The greatest challenge to this vision of a communicative future may lie in our present time constraints and media fixation. Without the redistribution of both time and media power, the possibilities for uploading information will not be as widely distributed as the capacity to download. Without a time-intensive broadly distributed input capability, noncommercial information of all kinds will likely continue to be drowned by commercially dominated information.

Clearly the Internet, even a commercial version, will foster interesting new possibilities for global-scale virtual communities. However, the potential for real family and community restrengthening may only begin to be realized through a restabilization of residential patterns (made possible in part through more extensive telecommuting to connect with multiple and changing employers) and an increase in free time. The combination of global (largely virtual) social and political networks and stable, active, interactive local communities could provide some political counterbalance to the staggering power of global-scale economic organizations. Both forms of community require more time and personal energy than is presently available to most citizens, rich or poor.

The Rebirth of Community within a Global Political Economy

Much of the political potential for work-time reduction lies in the fact that change could be gradually tailored to the economic circumstances of nations, firms, or families. Increases in unemployment may bring the issue to the fore politically, while prosperous times may open additional individual opportunities. Opening the possibility of fundamentally changing one's relationship to work may bring consideration of the excesses of electronic capitalism down to the personal level as nothing else can. Moreover, opportunities for change are open to individuals at varying income levels (above the minimum), especially if the change they make involves a residential shift to a relatively low-cost setting (away from locales where housing costs alone require high-paying employment). Environmentally, shifts of this type would increase use of underutilized buildings and infrastructure.

To the extent that a proportion of the population might detach their lives even in part from organizations that demand more of their lives than they are prepared to give, electronic capitalism might be rendered less monolithic. This is a possibility with real potential for long-term change, one of the few that exist outside of global-scale environmental and social governance. It is a long-term prospect because the potential to continually enhance labor productivity is almost unlimited. Indeed, ameliorating crises of overproduction and market saturation will require one of three things: employing an ever-higher proportion of the population in unsatisfying retail employment (the more excessive, the less satisfying), or downsizing workforces (thereby exacerbating overproduction), or acceding to wider opportunities for reduced work time. Whatever the choice, more space outside the world of global-scale production and consumption may arise or be created.

There will always be a potential for local-scale economic activities within which individuals can organize their lives at a different scale and pace. All production cannot be globalized. In some sectors local-scale production has significant advantages, including—in some cases—potential political advantages. While political and administrative decentralization combined with economic globalization enhances the formidable political power of corporations, *economic* localization can in part offset such power. While large corporations have considerable advantages in producing globally branded products in technologically advanced, globally organized, capital-intensive production systems, room remains nonetheless for local production on a selective basis. Those products where local production might be competitive with global-scale production include three of the essentials of human life—food, shelter, and culture. Shelter and municipal infrastructure, for example, almost inevitably has a locally organized component, in part because buildings and infrastructure must be serviced and maintained where they are and because the portability of many building materials is limited.

Food is, however, the economic sector within which political resistance to global-scale production has been most persistent. Moreover, on a purely practical level, as noted, many locally produced foods taste better and have higher nutritional value owing to their freshness (and need not be laced with preservatives). The taste test applies to fresh produce, baked goods, beer, and restaurant meals made fresh from local ingredients. Increasingly, in this age of mad cow disease, genetically modified crops, and imported residues of domestically banned pesticides, people are only comfortable knowing personally the producers of the food they eat. It is also no accident that fast food is generally unhealthy food (only fat-and-sugar-dominated foods lend themselves to factory-based, centralized production, freezing, and extended transport). Global corporations have, of course, a cost edge in some parts of the food industry, but they face inherent disadvantages that are not easily overcome so long as any capacity to discriminate survives among consumers. It is thus no accident that fast food advertising targets children too young to understand nutritional issues. Obtaining good food takes time and proximity—from the growing to the cooking and presentation.

Culture may seem a rather surprising inclusion here in a list of what might not be readily globalized. Culture, as we saw in chapter 3, is at the heart of media-dominated electronic capitalism and is a "product" replicated at low additional cost per unit—virtually free, once produced, for billions of electronic replications. But globalized electronic cultural replication is inherently political and is, inescapably, a threat to religions, to languages, to communities, to education, and to all forms and aspects of local and national cultural autonomy. Indeed the more that global media intrude and dominate, the more refreshing and appealing local live performance will seem. Live theater, which speaks to the history of a particular locale (and perhaps in the local language or dialect), resonates by helping people to feel rooted. Live musical performance is inevitably better in some ways; like fresh-baked bread and homemade soup, it communicates more fully with more of one's senses. The visual arts can capture and convey a sense of one's locale, and be part of what seems special about a locale to visitors. Globalized cultural homogenization will thus always provoke the ongoing creation of its opposite.

If there is a lesson in the Napster, electronic music-swapping, phenomenon, it is that cultural interest is universal and could alone come to occupy in healthy ways a considerable proportion of whatever time is freed by work-time reductions. Napster and its successors are not just about listening, but also about offering personal preferences and about building endlessly complex cultural subcommunities. This is analogous to the evolution of global chat groups on an endless variety of topics. It would be problematic were such virtual communities to substitute for real communities, but they are more likely to be a complement and, as with endless electronic chats among teenage friends, the actual constantly becomes virtual and vice versa. It is only a step from putting forward one's musical preferences and chatting with like-minded virtual communities to creating music and stories and visuals that are offered first virtually and at some point more directly and personally. Virtual and actual communities are only in conflict if time is at a severe premium. Both are worthwhile pursuits and if both are to be, as they say, all that they can be, work in the sense of wage labor in the pursuit of mass production and perpetual consumption of corporate output cannot forever occupy the overwhelming proportion of human lives.

A great irony in maintaining local cultural distinctiveness, food as cuisine, and shelter as a durable and locally informed art form is that resisting homogenization can create a willingness to bear the additional costs of non–mass production. Ironically, in many cases the long-term result of such an outcome is frequently not impoverishment, but prosperity (through, for example, expanded exports and tourism). The citizens of Prague have for a thousand years through good times and bad invested in and cared for their public buildings (and the public facades of many private buildings) as a distinctive art form. They have also often chosen musical ability over mass production and industrial development, even through Nazi occupation and communist totalitarianism. They now have an economy that is not as wealthy as some in Europe, but that generates considerable employment, investment, and foreign currency earnings (tourism alone generated more than 25 percent of GDP throughout the 1990s).

The cathedrals of Europe were not produced as investments, nor is great literature, but what products of today are likely to result in comparable total revenue (not necessarily to the producing organization even if it still exists) a millennium after they are produced? What, if anything, has appreciated more in value over long periods of time than fine art or high-quality, hand-made musical instruments? Work in such a context has a completely different meaning, as it does, in a different way, when one produces a fine meal from one's garden or an intellectual product offered at little cost via the Internet. As we develop the capacity to meet everyday basic needs using less labor, it is hard to imagine that these possibilities will not become more appealing, more visible, and more a central part of our everyday lives.

Creative production will not supplant electronic capitalism. It often does not produce much income to individual producers, and the accrued economic value of art and craft-built "products" depends on long-term global economic growth. But the direct economic payoff is secondary, of course. Great buildings, art, food, literature, and music provide a sense of self and a sense of community, collectively and individually. Enduring buildings, cities, and products are also more environmentally sustainable precisely because they last—the extractive costs are paid only once for centuries of use. Preserved wild nature (or complex rural settlements not overwhelmed by industrial-scale agriculture and/or extraction) now increasingly play the same kind of role, or could as fewer and fewer such spaces remain. Creating or preserving such possibilities for the future is how we can pay back those of earlier centuries who labored so hard and long, and who have unknowingly opened this possibility to us now for the first time in human history.

These considerations regarding work alter and complicate the ever-accelerating extraction, production, and "productivity" of the contemporary economy and may, implicitly at least, fuel the sense of personal discomfort felt by many. The realization that there is much more to life than economic output also fuels a sense of deficit regarding the time necessary for family and community. For some individuals and families these discomforts can be resolved at the personal or workplace level. However, the full realization of the positive potentials of electronic capitalism—the freeing of most humans from lifetimes of labor—is bound up with the extent to which these possibilities are in harmony with resource sustainability, social justice, and environmental quality. Solutions at that level require some resolution to democracy's dilemma. Some proposals are offered in the concluding chapter.

8

Global Politics One Nation at a Time

Adjustments in work time and patterns help us to confirm to ourselves that life is much more than production and consumption, but more is needed to resolve democracy's dilemma. Solutions at the global scale are especially needed. In particular, as outlined in chapter 6, established and enforced social and environmental minima are essential. How might these minima come to be established and in what forum?

The need is clear, but no magical agent will spring from the Internet fully functional and conscious. Nor is a social force likely to spontaneously and naturally arise from within the existing structures of global socioeconomic life. Moreover, no existing institution or set of institutions seems at present eager to provide the necessary auspices. There is no avoiding a need for a considerable shift in global political forces. The 1999 attempt at a Seattle Round of WTO talks (and most events related to global trade and economics) revealed, of course, some change in political context from that which went before. What might be called the "stealth phase" of global electronic capitalism would appear to have passed. But it is terribly easy to make such protests appear illegitimate, and some among the protestors seem to relish that role.

Perhaps a more significant sign of the nascent emergence of a global civic politics is the widespread refusal *in the marketplace* to eat foods containing materials from transgenic crops. It will likely prove exceedingly difficult to deny consumer choice in an economic system whose founding principle and leading self-proclaimed virtue is consumer choice. It may be especially difficult to deny choice regarding products that for profit purposes must be sufficiently distinctive to have obtained patent protection.

Another sign of emergence is the systematic split between Europe and North America on a number of issues, including those relating to the precautionary principle, climate change, and sustainability. There is apparently, then, no avoiding a future that features a heavy dose of global environmental politics. Nevertheless, while humanized globalization is possible in policy design terms, there is no point in pretending that it will be easily achieved in political terms. The policies that might render the global economy greener and more equitable thus far lack both an obvious agent and an obvious stage. One initial observation worth making is that domestic politics in Europe and North America will likely prove decisive to the outcome.

However, the evolution of a more environmentally and socially benign globalization *is* possible. There are significant political forces that, for example, favor the spread of trade union rights. These forces were still sufficiently strong even in the United States to have seen then-President Clinton advocate, in Seattle, the inclusion of trade union rights within the rules of the WTO. This kind of approach is crucial. Since full-blown sovereign government at the global scale is all but excluded, and global jurisprudence is still decidedly weak, enforcement must be tied to something. The something that comes nearest to having teeth is continued access, or priority access, to global trade. This, of course, implies a prior challenge to entrench a commitment to environmental protection, social policy minima, human rights, and trade union rights *at the global scale,* especially in the domestic politics of the nations with whom all others wish most fervently to trade. This commitment is not there at present.

Short of adoption of significant measures in a global context, however, positive changes on environmental or social fronts may evolve a few nations at a time. A shift to energy and materials throughput taxes might gain ground in the domestic politics of more nations were it crafted to replace other forms of taxation. Ecotaxation has already gained considerable ground in European policy and political circles.

Moreover, hasty retreat from all global-scale initiatives is not essential. Even such seemingly radical initiatives as global minimum wages may have a potential to gain wide public support, even conceivably from forward-thinking global corporations that have goods to sell to those whose wages might rise (or who might find less resistant customers for their goods in rich nations if their profit margins were less outrageous and less obviously earned on the backs of the world's poor).

Support for multilateral economic justice would also be rendered more substantial if more effective democracy were to gain purchase in more poor nations. Crucially, few nations in the developed world can openly oppose the spread of democracy or advances in the rule of law. This is a window of opportunity. Indeed such steps are widely perceived to make for a more stable investment climate. Within a more democratized context, environmental NGOs, for example, might be strengthened globally and noncompliance with environmental treaties thereby made more visible and salient.

Globally effective environmental organizations cannot be impossibly far away or the ever-expanding range of environmental treaties would not have been signed in the first place (even if in some instances they are primarily meant to provide the appearance of action). And again, the real trump card for environmental activism may prove to be—of all things—consumer sovereignty. It requires a great stretch of ideological contortion for firms to claim to be at the service of consumers and to deny, in the age of universal websites and 1-800 numbers, the possibility of food labeling and consumer information regarding what people are eating.

Where Is the Global Middle Ground?

All in all, then, the political prospects for resolving democracy's dilemma are daunting but not hopeless. But where are the international and global institutions that might be pressed to adapt, to serve as the site of global democratic governance? Obviously the United Nations could play a part. But could, for example, the WTO be charged with additional duties? In its brief history, this particular organization has been largely devoid of social and environmental policy capacities or inclinations. WTO officials have been neither democratic nor open, though there have been some discernible shifts in that regard.[1]

The best reason to seek to involve this organization is that trade-based sanctions, as noted, may be the best noncompliance option, though the world is still a long way from a politics that would support such possibilities. This is no basis, however, for dismissing them for the whole of the world's future. If the general analysis of this book is correct, the democratic deficit of electronic capitalism could eventually push global politics in directions that would legitimate such thinking, even in Washington, London, and Ottawa. Continued economic integration all but requires political integration of some sort, and it is impossible to foresee what forms that integration may take.

The NAFTA debate and the WTO both pretended that economic integration carries few, if any, social and environmental consequences. Those consequences are, however, too real to be ignored. While they are less straightforward than many of globalization's critics claim, they do and will systematically affect the everyday lives of most of the creatures living on the planet, including, perhaps indirectly, even rich humans in rich nations. In 1998 global trade in goods and services had reached 5.3 trillion U.S. dollars. At this scale it is impossible that significant and universal social and environmental effects would not result and will not increase in the future. It is also difficult to imagine that ongoing economic integration at this scale would not eventually generate demands for global democratic governance in some form. To assume otherwise is to concede that future generations will accept a monolithic and undemocratic world. If there is not the political wherewithal to accomplish change, to resolve democracy's dilemma at least in part, through such institutions as the WTO, then the level of political change achieved must be judged inadequate to the task.

Needless to say, other global institutions must also evolve and participate in the process of change. The bottom line is that neither open and democratic global governance, nor unfettered corporate rule, is an inevitable consequence of electronic capitalism. An accommodation nearer to the former than the latter may ultimately be achieved. The present challenge is to create greater political space for a middle ground regarding global integration. That middle ground is forclosed by any presumption that trade, investment, and economic growth should always trump other considerations and that trade can be isolated from environmental and social outcomes.

Competitiveness-at-all-costs, so dear to the monopoly media of electronic capitalism, also creates uncompromising opponents of global economic integration. Thus far media emphasis on the violence attendant on antiglobalization demonstrations has discouraged the parallel development of a politics of fundamentally altered globalization, as distinct from a politics oriented toward antiglobalization. In some political contexts, there is also a danger that well-intentioned resistance to globalization could be joined by those who would see us revert to narrow and dangerous forms of protectionism. The hope is that cooler heads, those that regard global economic integration with both doubts and enthusiasms that are equivocal and balanced, will be able to modify its worst excesses through a democratized global political integration.

To this end politically progressive opponents of globalization need to be reminded of many things, including (1) the positive effects that global economic integration might have in discouraging war (nations will hesitate to bomb their own economic assets, not to mention their customers); (2) the upward pressures on wages in poorer nations that economic integration might foster, especially if it were achieved through altered trade rules; (3) the technology transfer that investment may help to accelerate, including environmental protection technologies; (4) the positive educational and human contact potentials inherent in some of the new communications technologies; (5) the hope that increased communication and interaction might ultimately help to reduce racial and ethnic hatreds and suspicions; (6) the fact that humankind still requires additional economic growth and that trade integration may contribute to it, however unevenly thus far; and (7) the fact that accelerating automation and productivity open a possibility all but unknown in human history—the possibility that we may create the material basis (though not necessarily the social wisdom) to avoid lifetimes dominated by work.

On the other hand, those who assert that economic growth through unidimensional global economic integration can cure all ills need to reflect on the improbability that (1) employees will feel any appreciable loyalty to employers that show no loyalty to them; (2) wages can be kept low in poor nations or driven downward in rich ones without losses in consumer confidence (and capacities); (3) many citizens and customers will simultaneously believe that consumer choice in marketplaces is an important right *and* that all products need not be comprehensively labeled; (4) social programs can be undermined politically by perpetual tax cuts without some of those costs (such as health care and training) being borne by corporations; (5) keeping people in jail is cheaper than, for example, improved early childhood education; (6) continuous downsizing might not undermine corporate memory and effectiveness; (7) even the rich can always avoid drinking the water, eating, and breathing; and (8) there are not already such excesses of both work time and hype that some of one's best employees might not simply opt out of the overemployment and overconsumption game.

Some have of course reflected on such matters and are prepared to adjust both personal and corporate behavior accordingly. Many corporations are open to change toward more sustainable production practices, especially when such practices advance their economic bottom line but even sometimes when they do not. Some come to such conclusions from having had highly publicized run-ins with environmental organizations, others from a calculation that their corporate reputation as an enlightened firm is worth considerable environmental expenditure. On the other hand, there is also considerable profit in environmental rapaciousness, and almost always some firm somewhere is prepared to engage in it.

The relative optimism of ecological modernization theorists is worth mentioning here. They essentially argue that "environmental interests can no longer be ignored and increasingly make a difference in organizing and designing production and consumption."[2] That is, while we may be a long way from achieving environmental sustainability and social well-being, many nations are gaining ground on some ecological fronts as they are growing economically. Modern economies are becoming more ecologically efficient and can, at least potentially, continue to do so under conditions of globalization.[3]

One such theorist, Arthur Mol, in assessing this prospect, argues that the practices of the wealthy nations will find their way into transnational practice "owing to the more advanced environmental regimes and experiences of developed countries, their generally greater interests in the construction of international environmental regimes, and their more powerful position in international negotiations."[4] One can only hope that this proves to be the case over time. As Mol is well aware, there are interests in both rich and poor nations that would prefer to use globalization to weaken environmental regimes rather than to advance their spread to a global scale. I would agree that the balance of interests in this regard is yet to be resolved.

The best prospects for achieving a world where trade, production, and consumption continue to expand are through global measures, rules, and practices that steadily advance social equity and that harmonize environmental protection upward. Such a historic compromise is more likely as noneconomistic research and communication advances, and especially *if* democracy is enhanced at the domestic level. There is, in any case, every prospect of a widening realization that local, state, and national democracy will not and cannot flourish in a fundamentally undemocratic (economistic) system of global governance. As the fall of communism demonstrated, the obvious cannot be ignored forever, even under conditions of restrained information flow and the absence of democratic institutions. Global economic integration ultimately requires global democratic governance.

National Sovereignty as Global Governance

As was the case with Mark Twain, the demise of the nation-state is much exaggerated. The nation-state remains the residence of democratic politics, such as it is in a global media age. National states still exist and their demise, as Matthew Paterson notes, is greatly exaggerated sometimes out of neoliberal desires for a virtual end to government or leftist defeatism. In his words, "State action to manage what can still be called 'national economies' is still possible, both individually and collectively."[5] The emphasis in this book has, of course, been on "collectively." Just as freedom is arguably the recognition of necessity, global governance can still arise through political practice in nation-states. It must also be understood that effective national sovereignty now, in an age of global integration, requires cooperative regional and global governance. Even without September 11 and the events that have followed, this should have been plain enough.

No nation can remain an island in a rising global sea. At times in recent decades the United States has taken a lead on the development of international environmental treaties. Of late, it has been the leading point of resistance. It has also more consistently resisted an expanding role for the United Nations and the evolution of a world court. To achieve a "California effect" writ large, it is crucial that the United States see its way through to a global, participatory, political leadership role that parallels its economic leadership role. One can only hope that more Americans will take to heart British Prime Minister Tony Blair's assertion, post–September 11, that national self-interest and the mutual interest of like-minded nations are now the same thing.

David Held speaks of a new institutional complex of global scope and cosmopolitan conceptualization "given shape and form by reference to a basic democratic law, which takes on the character of a government to the extent, and only to the extent, that it promulgates, implements, and enforces this law. But however its institutions are precisely envisaged, it is a future built upon the recognition that democracy within a single community and democratic relations between communities are deeply interconnected, and that new organizational and legal mechanisms must be established if democracy is to survive and prosper."[6] National democracy requires global governance, as we have seen, but global governance in turn depends on the revitalization of the democratic histories, ideologies, habits, and structures of those of the world's nation-states that are privileged to have them.

In a world where even area codes dissolve into 1-800 numbers and .com designations of unknown locale, the meaning of borders and sovereignty, governance and citizenship must change. No national objective of consequence can be successfully pursued autonomously even at present (let alone future) levels of global economic, transportation, communications, investment, and trade integration. David Held and Anthony McGrew state this as clearly as is possible. Globalization, they say, has been going on for centuries, but today it is genuinely different in both scale and nature. This, however, "does not signal the end of the nation-state or the death of politics. But it does mean that politics is no longer, and can no longer be, based simply on nation-states."[7]

Environmentally, the globe has always been integrated, but the collective human capacity to affect that environment at a global scale is a result of the increasing scale and integration of economic activity. All of this is obvious. What somehow, almost inexplicably, has been less than obvious is the possibility that willful impotence regarding global poverty, and environmental and social deregulation, could be overcome through linking trade opportunities to global social, environmental, and human rights standards. That is the essence of global governance, and it can be achieved through existing nation-states acting in concert.

Thus, one must conclude, even limited global governance has to be accomplished primarily through the vehicle of the democratic politics of existing states. Democracy's dilemma is real. The idea of full-blown global government is flawed in principle. The challenge is to achieve global governance through the cooperation of effectively democratic national governments. The rejection of globalization, the undoing of trade treaties, protectionism, and extreme localism are all understandable but mistaken objectives. The need is to tie environmental protection, social equity, human rights, and (ultimately) democracy to global economic integration—to make them conditions of economic participation. Achieving that will require a reborn civic activism at all jurisdictional levels and strong democracy indeed.

Toward Enhanced Domestic Democracy

Democracy in many nations has declined in recent decades, even as it has been nominally established in more and more settings. However, the task of creating global governance requires that democracy be enhanced considerably. Some of the dimensions of the decline have been explored throughout this book. At this point it may be useful to recall some of the ways democracy might be enhanced, especially in the wealthy nations. Global governance requires national democracies effective enough to see preferences for environmental protection and social equity through the fog of the cult of impotence. These preferences are not necessarily as strong as green theorists might prefer, but they are decidedly stronger (one must hope) than the dominant economic forces of globalization have provided thus far.

Democracy at the domestic level might be significantly enhanced by (1) media reform that establishes and protects a multiplication of voices; (2) the continued development and wide communication of a social science that is multidimensional rather than economistic; (3) radical campaign finance reform that allows effective political communication to be accomplished without the need for vast fundraising and that all but excludes large contributions from unions, corporations, or individuals; (4) significant progress on the reduction of average total work time within families at least to the level that was normal prior to the decline in civic participation; and (5) a wider appreciation of the need for global governance rooted in restored democracy at the level of the nation-state. The final item on the list implies a wide understanding of the distinction between global governance and global government. It perhaps also suggests, as touched on above, that the antiglobalization movement should focus more on a concerted campaign for democratic guidance for, than on flat-out resistance to, global economic integration.[8]

Nor need the task at hand threaten capitalism itself. The central challenge is to find ways to guide a global economy toward desirable and necessary social and environmental behaviors without bureaucracy or government at the global scale. Comprehensive global bureaucracies are rightly resisted politically and likely unnecessary. This is the heart of democracy's dilemma, but it can be resolved. An environmentally and socially benign (or even beneficial) globalization does not require global government. The essential tool of environmental and social governance could be the market itself, albeit a market in motion under modestly, but genuinely, revised rules—one possible set of which was sketched in chapter 6. Such initiatives add little to the vast complex of rules that guide investment, production, and trade. Market actors adapt, often brilliantly, to the existing set and would do so in response to an enhanced set. Democratically achieved transparent and adaptive changes in the guidance structure of global trade integration would short-circuit, or at least limit, the potential for a social and environmental race to the bottom.

Such new rules will not, however, be adopted without prior acceptance within the OECD nations, especially in North America. This in turn requires a wider understanding that economic primacy carries profound obligations, more profound than we ordinarily assume. No one else can veto so easily the effective integration of environmental and social objectives into global trade rules and patterns. The OECD nations are the markets in which all others wish especially to trade. Not just all nations, but all firms operating everywhere. Those firms, mostly rooted in OECD nations (and especially the United States), can be made to obey new rules and to participate in new structures, and to do so throughout their global operations, bringing all their suppliers with them. Global firms are not transnational unless OECD governments acting in concert allow them to be. The OECD has already taken some initial steps, establishing guidelines concerning corporate responsibility for human rights and consumer protection. Accepting comprehensive corporate transnationalism is clearly but another form of disingenuous impotence.

Irony of ironies, the route to global governance lies in making the wealthy nations more democratic. These nations are the source of the trade rules that permit the undermining of their own environmental and social legislation. These nations allow the importation of goods produced by labor that has little opportunity to unionize in working conditions outlawed for more than a century within their own borders. Participating in the collective global imposition of gradual change outside their borders would be less an imposition on the sovereignty of other nations than the protection of their own. Moreover, only the wealthy nations can reward democratic effectiveness in the poorest nations with increased economic and technological aid and/or debt forgiveness. Without a commitment to global-scale change, achieved democratically in the wealthy nations, there will be no such change.

Green Politics as Global Politics

One possible future would see green parties foreshadowing multilevel governance and operating at three or more levels: local, national, and global. In intensely majority-oriented electoral systems such as that in the United States, it might make sense to emphasize municipal efforts in the first instance. But the larger challenge is the development of a globalist orientation that permeates each green party at the national level. Green ideas are one of the few perspectives other than neoliberalism that exist in most nations. They are especially strong in virtually all wealthy nations, though of course are a long way from power with but a few exceptions. They need not obtain power at the national level to gain considerable influence.

Most green parties already make an articulate case against economism and for sustainability as a comprehensive integration of economic, social, and environmental objectives. They could also articulate the possibility of guiding economic integration through global governance. This would not require a rejection of a local or bioregional orientation. In some matters the planet as a whole *is* a bioregion, but as I have tried to argue, the possibility of local initiatives depends on the creation of some social and economic minima at the same scale at which economic activities are organized. Local innovation in social and environmental matters can flow more freely when one's locality or nation cannot easily be played off against all others by global-scale economic organizations.

Another possibility is the establishment of a separate World Environment Organization. This could most easily be achieved by an integration of the many small secretariats associated with each of the many multilateral environmental agreements.[9] This organization might also subsume UNEP and might potentially provide a focal point for, and encourage the continuing emergence of, environmental NGOs with a global focus. However, increased effectiveness may require advances in green politics at the national level in many nations, in addition to linkages between this possible organization and the WTO to develop effective enforcement opportunities.

Global capitalism itself, as Theodore J. Lowi observes, requires social order.[10] He also argues that an approach to order built on security (welfare) is no more expensive than one built on insecurity (police capacity) and is a good deal more humane. This is every bit as true at the global as at the national and local level. As T. H. Marshall observed in 1950, the emergence of the welfare state changed our very conception of what it means to be a citizen, creating a social dimension that was rights based. Hartley Dean observes that this reconceptualization can readily be expanded to accommodate an environmental dimension.[11] Both can be expanded to the global level, however partially and gradually at first. As Dean also observes, environmental citizenship is global citizenship and carries with it new obligations as well as rights (limits to personal consumption and obligations to reduce waste perhaps, as well as rights to clean air and water and to the ongoing existence of wild nature).

Toward Multilevel Citizenship

Global governance, then, both requires and provides a further foundation for strengthened democracy at the national and subnational levels. It ensures that equity, environmental, and social policy essentials are not traded off for national economic gain, and that competitiveness is confined to the realm of economic efficiency and creativity as regards production, products, and services. Minimalist global governance also implies a universally shared sense of global citizenship. A truly global media could help to build that sense. There is no technical reason why, in a 500-channel universe supplemented by the Internet, world music, and world literature, everyone could not have access to genuine expressions of all cultures and viewpoints unfiltered by the global media entities that provide the technical aspects of their delivery.

What has been missing is a widespread willingness to really hear and understand what others have to say. Citizenship to this point in history has been many things, but one of those things has been a link to a particular territory and history (and less and less, in an era of mass travel and extensive immigration, to a particular culture). But what else is citizenship? It is a sense of fellow feeling, an acceptance of duties, obligations, and loyalties, as well as some expectations regarding opportunities and protections. In a global economy set in a more and more vulnerable global ecological framework, is it not possible that this sense of citizenship could evolve into a widely and simultaneously felt sense of global citizenship?

Even prior to increased global concern with terrorism, Held wrote: "Our world is a world of *overlapping communities of fate,* where the fate of one country and that of another are more entwined than ever before."[12] So many things that were said before have now taken on new layers of meaning. One simply has to trust that the process in which the world comes to feel, and be, one is not necessarily a bad thing in the long run.

Over recent decades environmental politics has broadened our collective horizons considerably. As a result, many now think within a more extended time frame—of long-term resource needs and the rights of generations yet unborn. We have also extended our horizons in all manner of ways to the needs and health and comfort of other living species, both singly and in terms of their myriad interactions. Environmentalism and globalization have arisen concurrently, perhaps not altogether accidentally. Just as being green broadens our horizons in time and across species, it perhaps also implies—given globalization in all its meanings—feelings and assumptions akin to citizenship crossing all human borders and both human and nonhuman distinctions. Perhaps we will soon, in a sense we are yet to discover, become both citizens of nations and citizens of the earth.

Notes

Chapter 1

1. Bill McKibben, *The Age of Missing Information* (New York: Penguin Plume, 1993).

2. Alan Frizzell and Jon H. Pammett, *Shades of Green: Environmental Attitudes in Canada and around the World* (Ottawa: Carleton University Press, 1997).

3. Charles Lindblom, *Politics and Markets* (New York: Basic Books, 1977).

4. Eric Helleiner, *States and the Reemergence of Global Finance: From Bretton Woods to the 1990s* (Ithaca: Cornell University Press, 1994); Linda McQuaig, *The Cult of Impotence* (Toronto: Penguin, 1999).

5. See, for example, Murray Dobbin, *The Myth of the Good Corporate Citizen: Democracy under the Rule of Big Business* (Toronto: Stoddart, 1998); William Greider, *One World, Ready or Not* (New York: Simon & Schuster, 1997); Hans-Peter Martin and Harald Schumann, *The Global Trap* (Montreal: Black Rose Books, 1997).

6. George Soros, "The Capitalist Threat," *Atlantic Monthly* 279 (February 1997), 47.

7. James Goldsmith, *The Trap* (London: Macmillan, 1994), 17.

8. Bruce O' Hara, *Working Harder Isn't Working* (Vancouver: New Star Books, 1993); Anders Hayden, *Sharing the Work, Sparing the Planet: Worktime, Consumption & Ecology* (Toronto: Between the Lines, 1999).

9. This point was first brought home broadly by the Brundtland report: World Commission on Environment and Development, *Our Common Future* (New York: Oxford University Press, 1987).

10. Friedrich A. Hayek, *The Road to Serfdom* (Chicago: University of Chicago Press, 1944).

11. Robert H. Frank and Philip J. Cook, *The Winner-Take-All Society* (New York: Penguin, 1995); Jeremy Rifkin, *The End of Work* (New York: Putnam, 1996); Greider, *One World;* John Gray, *False Dawn: The Delusions of Global Capitalism* (London: Granta Books, 1999); Martin and Schumann, *Global Trap;* McQuaig, *Cult of Impotence;* Dan Schiller, *Digital Capitalism: Networking the Global*

Market System (Cambridge: MIT Press, 1999); Benjamin R. Barber, *Jihad vs. McWorld: How Globalism and Tribalism Are Reshaping the World* (New York: Ballantine Books, 1995).

12. Martin and Schumann, *Global Trap,* 63–64. The concern with tax havens is shared by Susan Strange, *The Retreat of the State* (New York: Cambridge University Press, 1996), 62–65.

13. Frank and Cook, *Winner-Take-All,* 17.

14. Frank and Cook, *Winner-Take-All,* 46.

15. United Nations Development Programme, *Human Development Report 1999* (New York: Oxford University Press, 1999).

16. Schiller, *Digital Capitalism,* 209.

17. Herman E. Daly, "Free Trade: The Perils of Deregulation." in Jerry Mander and Edward Goldsmith, eds., *The Case against the Global Economy and for a Turn toward the Local* (San Francisco: Sierra Club Books, 1996), 231.

18. For examples see Schiller, *Digital Capitalism,* 36–37.

19. Barber, *Jihad vs. McWorld,* 224.

20. Barber, *Jihad vs. McWorld,* 295.

21. Julian L. Simon and Herman Kahn, eds., *The Resourceful Earth* (Oxford: Blackwell, 1984).

22. Simon and Kahn, *Resourceful Earth,* 423.

23. Simon and Kahn, *Resourceful Earth,* 181.

24. Simon and Kahn, *Resourceful Earth,* 302.

25. Aaron Wildavsky, *Searching for Safety* (New Brunswick, NJ: Transaction Publishers, 1988).

26. David Vogel, *Trading Up: Consumer and Environmental Regulation in a Global Economy* (Cambridge: Harvard University Press, 1995), 259.

27. Vogel, *Trading Up,* 268.

28. John McMurtry, "The Global Market Ideology: Anatomy of a Value System," in Ted Schrecker, ed., *Surviving Globalization: The Social and Environmental Challenges* (London: Macmillan, 1997), 181.

29. McMurtry, "Global Market Ideology," 181.

30. McMurtry, "Global Market Ideology," 181–182.

31. John Gray, *False Dawn,* 2.

32. Gray, *False Dawn,* 235.

33. Gray, *False Dawn,* 2.

34. Kenichi Ohmae, *The End of the Nation State: The Rise of Regional Economies* (New York: Free Press, 1996).

35. See Robert Paehlke, "Environment, Equity, and Globalization: Beyond Resistance," *Global Environmental Politics* 1 (February 2001), 1–10, as well as Ronnie

D. Lipschutz, *Global Civil Society and Global Environmental Governance* (Albany: SUNY Press, 1996).

36. Robert Putnam, "Bowling Alone: America's Declining Social Capital," *Journal of Democracy* 6 (January 1995), 65–78.

37. Seymour Martin Lipset, *Political Man: The Social Bases of Politics* (Garden City, NY: Doubleday Anchor, 1963), 262.

38. Lipset, *Political Man,* 263.

39. See, for example, Robert Blauner, *Alienation and Freedom: The Factory Worker and His Industry* (Chicago: University of Chicago Press, 1964).

40. Robert Putnam, *Bowling Alone: The Collapse and Revival of American Community* (New York: Simon & Schuster, 2000).

41. Gray, *False Dawn,* 234.

42. Robert Paehlke, "Spatial Proportionality: Right-Sizing Environmental Decision Making," in Edward A. Parson, ed., *Governing the Environment* (Toronto: University of Toronto Press, 2001), 73–123.

Chapter 2

1. A description of environmental damage at midnineteenth century is found in George Perkins Marsh, *Man and Nature: Physical Geography as Modified by Human Action* (Cambridge: Harvard University Press, 1965).

2. Karl Polanyi, *The Great Transformation* (Boston: Beacon Press, 1957), 78.

3. Polanyi, *Great Transformation,* 78.

4. Polanyi, *Great Transformation,* 79.

5. Polanyi, *Great Transformation,* 83.

6. Robert L. Heilbroner, *The Making of Economic Society* (Englewood Cliffs, NJ: Prentice-Hall, 1962), 84–85.

7. Quoted in Heilbroner, *Economic Society,* 85.

8. Heilbroner, *Economic Society,* 76.

9. Heilbroner, *Economic Society,* 82.

10. Heilbroner, *Economic Society,* 88.

11. Heilbroner, *Economic Society,* 102.

12. Heilbroner, *Economic Society,* 102–104.

13. Polanyi, *Great Transformation,* 175–176.

14. See, for example, Marshall Sahlins, *Stone Age Economics* (Chicago: Aldine-Atherton, 1972).

15. Regarding homelessness see, for example, Dennis P. Culhane, "The Homeless Shelter and the Nineteenth-Century Poorhouse: Comparing Notes from Two Eras of 'Indoor Relief,'" in M. Brinton Lykes, Ali Banuazizi, Ramsay Liem, and Michael

Morris, eds., *Myths about the Powerless: Contesting Social Inequalities* (Philadelphia: Temple University Press, 1996), 50–71. Numerous winter-related homeless deaths have occurred in Toronto and other Canadian cities since the mid-1990s.

16. Matthew Josephson, *The Robber Barons: The Great American Capitalists, 1861–1901* (1934; reprint, New York: Harcourt, Brace and World, 1962), 453.

17. Susan Strange, *The Retreat of the State: The Diffusion of Power in the World Economy* (Cambridge: Cambridge University Press, 1996), 3.

18. Thomas F. Homer-Dixon, *Environment, Scarcity, and Violence* (Princeton: Princeton University Press, 1991.

19. W. Stanley Jevons, *The Coal Question* (rpt. New York: Augustus M. Kelley, 1965).

20. See, for example, Ernst von Weizsäcker, Amory B. Lovins, and L. Hunter Lovins, *Factor Four: Doubling Wealth, Halving Resource Use* (London: Earthscan, 1998).

21. See Naomi Klein, *No Logo* (Toronto: Knopf Canada, 2000).

22. See, for example, Richard T. Pascale, *The Art of Japanese Management* (New York: Simon & Schuster, 1981); Charles J. McMillan, *The Japanese Industrial System* (New York: deGruyter, 1984).

23. Robert Putnam, *Bowling Alone: The Collapse and Revival of American Community* (New York: Simon & Schuster, 2000).

24. Bill McKibben, *The Age of Missing Information* (New York: Penguin Plume, 1993), 118.

Chapter 3

1. Daniel Bell, *The Coming of Post-Industrial Society* (New York: Basic Books, 1976), 112.

2. Bell, *Post-Industrial Society,* ix.

3. Bell, *Post-Industrial Society,* 117.

4. Antonia Zerbisias, "The Scary Truth Is out There," *Toronto Star* (May 14, 2000), E16.

5. Michael Moore, *Downsize This: Random Thoughts from an Unarmed American* (New York: HarperCollins, 1997).

6. Michael Kesterton, "Social Studies," *Globe and Mail* (December 1, 1999), A24.

7. Alan Durning, "Asking How Much Is Enough," in Lester R. Brown, ed., *State of the World 1991* (New York: Norton, 1991), 162. In *The Limits to Satisfaction* (Toronto: University of Toronto Press, 1976), William Leiss, places the total number of ads seen by age twenty-one at 350,000 (p. 82). That figure, from the 1970s, is obviously well below current numbers of exposures.

8. Durning, "Asking How Much Is Enough," 162, with supplementary data from Michael Carley and Philippe Spapens, *Sharing the World: Sustainable Living & Global Equity in the 21st Century* (London: Earthscan, 1998).

9. Leiss, *Limits to Satisfaction,* 92.

10. Leiss, *Limits to Satisfaction,* 90.

11. Stuart Ewan, *Captains of Consciousness: Advertising and the Roots of the Consumer Culture* (New York: McGraw-Hill, 1976), 206.

12. Ewan, *Captains of Consciousness,* 208.

13. Ewan, *Captains of Consciousness,* 208–209.

14. Durning, "Asking How Much Is Enough," 162.

15. Carley and Spapens, *Sharing the World,* 141.

16. Fred Hirsch, *Social Limits to Growth* (Cambridge: Harvard University Press, 1976).

17. Leiss, *Limits to Satisfaction,* 115; Juliet Schor, *The Overworked American: The Unexpected Decline of Leisure* (New York: Basic Books, 1991).

18. Paul L. Wachtel, *The Poverty of Affluence: A Psychological Portrait of the American Way of Life* (Philadelphia: New Society Publishers, 1989), 125.

19. Regarding Canadian concerns early in the process of media consolidation see, for example, *Report of the Special Senate Committee on Mass Media,* 3 vols. (Ottawa: Queen's Printer, 1970).

20. Michael Parenti, *Democracy for the Few* (New York: St. Martin's Press, 1995), 165.

21. Edward S. Herman and Robert W. McChesney, *The Global Media* (London: Cassell, 1997).

22. Parenti, *Democracy,* 165.

23. Parenti, *Democracy,* 170.

24. A notable exception to the minimalist coverage of climate warming in the electronic media is the excellent program *What's Up with the Weather?* This program was shown on PBS in April 2000 and was produced by WGBS Boston (available on videotape via <www.wgbs.org>).

25. *Adbusters,* the magazine that seeks to "beat the archetypal mind polluters at their own game," is available from <subscriptions@adbusters.org>.

26. Sharon Beder, *Global Spin: The Corporate Assault on Environmentalism* (White River Junction, VT: Chelsea Green Publishing, 1997).

27. Regarding the famous British court case brought by McDonald's against protestors, see John Vidal, *McLibel* (London: Macmillan, 1997); also see Naomi Klein, *No Logo* (Toronto: Knopf Canada, 2000), 387–396.

28. Anthony Downs, "Up and Down with Ecology—the 'Issue-Attention Cycle,'" *Public Interest* 28 (Summer 1972), 38.

29. Downs, "Issue-Attention Cycle," 50.

30. Quoted in Zerbisias, "The Scary Truth."

31. Bill McKibben, *The Age of Missing Information* (New York: Penguin Plume, 1993), 26.

32. McKibben, *Missing Information,* 62.

33. McKibben, *Missing Information,* 156.

34. McKibben, *Missing Information,* 65.

35. Robert Putnam, *Bowling Alone: The Collapse and Revival of American Community* (New York: Simon & Schuster, 2000).

36. Robert Putnam. "Bowling Alone: America's Declining Social Capital," *Journal of Democracy* 6 (January 1995), 65–78.

37. William Kornhauser, *The Politics of Mass Society* (New York: Free Press, 1959).

38. Putnam, "Bowling Alone," 75.

39. Putnam, "Bowling Alone," 75.

40. All figures in this paragraph are from <www.commoncause.org> in May 2000; the environmental policy contribution data are from the "Common Cause Series (on the website) about the Impact of Big Money in Politics" and "Some Like It Hot!"

41. "E-Commerce Seen as No Boon to Small Business," *Globe and Mail* (July 29, 1999), B12.

42. Dan Schiller, *Digital Capitalism: Networking the Global Market System* (Cambridge: MIT Press, 1999), especially chapters 1 and 2.

43. Thomas J. Courchene and Colin R. Telmer, *From Heartland to North American Region State: The Social, Fiscal and Federal Evolution of Ontario* (Toronto: Centre for Policy Management, 1998), 276.

44. Robert L. Heilbroner, *The Making of Economic Society* (Englewood Cliffs, NJ: Prentice-Hall, 1962), 234.

45. C. Wright Mills, *The Sociological Imagination* (New York: Grove Press, 1961).

46. Schiller, *Digital Capitalism,* 151.

47. Schiller, *Digital Capitalism,* 171.

48. See Hal Niedzviecki, *We Want Some Too: Underground Desire and the Reinvention of Mass Culture* (Toronto: Penguin, 2000); Nelson George, *Hip Hop America* (New York: Penguin, 1999).

Chapter 4

1. John Elkington, *Cannibals with Forks: The Triple Bottom Line of 21st Century Business* (Stony Creek, CT: New Society Publishers, 1998).

2. John Robinson and Jon Tinker, "Reconciling Ecological, Economic and Social Imperatives: A New Conceptual Framework," in Ted Schrecker, ed., *Surviving Globalism: The Social and Environmental Challenges* (London: Macmillan, 1997), 73.

3. Robinson and Tinker, "Reconciling Imperatives," 74.

4. Robinson and Tinker, "Reconciling Imperatives," 77.

5. Robinson and Tinker, "Reconciling Imperatives," 80.

6. Michael Carley and Philippe Spapens, *Sharing the World: Sustainable Living & Global Equity in the 21st Century* (London: Earthscan, 1998), 111.

7. Robinson and Tinker, "Reconciling Imperatives," 84.

8. William Greider, *One World, Ready or Not* (New York: Simon & Schuster, 1997), 47.

9. Greider, *One World,* 193.

10. John Gray, *False Dawn: The Delusions of Global Capitalism* (London: Granta Books, 1998), 235.

11. Robert Paehlke, "Environmental Politics, Sustainability and Social Science," *Environmental Politics* 10 (Winter 2001), 1–22.

12. Putnam is not convinced that "repotting" explains much of the decline in social capital because, overall, there is not a notable increase in residential shifts in the same time frame. However, it is possible that employment shifts have increased and that these shifts frequently require complex commuting patterns for one or more family members. Such changes could undermine both family and civic lives as thoroughly as, or more thoroughly than, changes in residence.

13. Robert Goodland, "Growth Has Reached its Limit," in Jerry Mander and Edward Goldsmith, eds., *The Case against the Global Economy* (San Francisco: Sierra Club Books, 1996), 208.

14. Goodland, "Growth Has Reached Its Limit," 209.

15. Peter Weber, "Safeguarding Oceans," in Lester R. Brown, ed., *State of the World 1994* (New York: Norton, 1994), 41–60; see also Lester R. Brown, Christopher Flavin, and Hilary French, eds., *State of the World 2001* (New York: Norton: 2001), 47.

16. Goodland, "Growth Has Reached Its Limit," 209.

17. Eville Gorham, Seventh Annual Sheperd Lecture at Trent University, Peterborough, Ontario (October 7, 1999).

18. Norman Myers, "Tropical Rainforests," and Robert Paehlke, "Coral Reefs," in Robert Paehlke, ed., *Conservation and Environmentalism: An Encyclopedia* (New York: Garland (now Taylor & Francis), 1995), 153–154 and 645–647.

19. Eville Gorham, 1999 Sheperd Lecture.

20. John Kenneth Galbraith, *The Affluent Society* (New York: New American Library, 1958), *Economics and the Public Purpose* (Boston: Houghton Mifflin, 1973), and *The New Industrial Society* (New York: New American Library, 1967).

21. Andrew Hacker, *Money: Who Has How Much and Why* (New York: Scribner, 1997).

22. The larger problem in this regard would appear to be increased intranational inequality; though some poor nations are still losing ground, some have gained relative ground recently. See Frances Stewart and Albert Berry, "Globalization, Liberalization, and Inequality: Expectations and Experience," in Andrew Hurrell and Ngaire Woods, eds., *Inequality, Globalization, and World Politics* (New York: Oxford University Press, 1999), 150–186.

23. Linda McQuaig, *The Cult of Impotence* (Toronto: Penguin, 1999), 256–257.

24. Aaron Wildavsky, *Searching for Safety* (New Brunswick, NJ: Transaction Publishers, 1988).

25. For further discussion on this point see Robert C. Paehlke, "Environmental Values and Public Policy," in Norman J. Vig and Michael E. Kraft, eds., *Environmental Policy,* 4th ed. (Washington, DC: Congressional Quarterly Press, 2000), 80.

26. Carley and Spapens, *Sharing the World,* 140.

27. For a variety of comparative health statistics see United Nations Development Programme, *Human Development Report 2000* (New York: Oxford University Press, 2000).

28. Helen Epstein, "Life & Death on the Social Ladder," *New York Review of Books 45,* no. 12 (July 16, 1998), 26–30; Peter Townsend and Nick Davidson, eds., *The Black Report on Inequality in Health* (London: Pelican, 1982); Richard G. Wilkinson, *Mind the Gap: Hierarchies, Health, and Human Evolution* (New Haven: Yale University Press, 2001); and the classic: Stewart Wolf and John G. Bruhn, *The Roseto Story: An Anatomy of Health* (Norman: University of Oklahoma Press, 1979).

29. Epstein, "Life & Death."

30. In the late 1980s both the elder George Bush and Margaret Thatcher suddenly realized that they had always been environmentalists. Bush, to his credit, was able to evidence a Sierra Club membership card, though he said little in this regard about his eight years as vice president.

31. See Robert Paehlke, "Guilty Until Proven Innocent," *Nature Canada* 9 (April/June 1980), 18–23.

32. For good background on this issue see Jason Van Driesche and Roy Van Driesche, *Nature Out of Place: Biological Invasions in a Global Age* (Washington, DC: Island Press, 2000).

33. See, for example, the special issue of *Scientific American* on "The End of Cheap Oil" (March 1998). Offsetting this prospect in part are such options as hydrides and oil sands.

34. Robert Goodland and Herman Daly, "Poverty Alleviation Is Essential for Environmental Sustainability," mimeo. (Washington, DC: World Bank, February 11, 1993), 3.

35. Goodland and Daly, "Poverty Alleviation," 3.

36. See, for example, Robert Paehlke, "Eco-History: Two Waves in the Evolution of Environmentalism," *Alternatives: Perspectives on Society, Technology and Environment* 19 (September/October 1992), 18–23.

37. See Robert Bullard, "Environmental Justice Movement," in Robert Paehlke, ed., *Conservation and Environmentalism: An Encyclopedia* (New York: Garland Publishers (now Taylor & Francis), 1995), 250–254.

38. Jeremy Wilson, *Talk and Log: Wilderness Politics in British Columbia, 1965–96* (Vancouver: University of British Columbia Press, 1998).

39. See, for example, John H. Bodley, ed., *Tribal Peoples and Development Issues* (Mountain View, CA.: Mayfield, 1988).

40. Goodland and Daly, "Poverty Alleviation," 17.

41. Goodland and Daly, "Poverty Alleviation," 19–20.

Chapter 5

1. Marina Fischer-Kowalski and Helmut Haberl, "Sustainable Development: Socioeconomic Metabolism and Colonization of Nature," *International Social Science Journal* 158 (1998), 573–587.

2. Fischer-Kowalski and Haberl, "Sustainable Development," 582. The three measures are not, of course, equally precise. The difference in precision would not, however, be so great if common definitions were widely accepted. Well-being could be defined as a combination of accurately kept social and health statistics such as mortality and morbidity, education, and perhaps minimum income levels. Environmental data are probably somewhat less precise, but could improve with a reasonable level of effort.

3. Fischer-Kowalski and Haberl, "Sustainable Development," 583. See also Donella H. Meadows, Dennis L. Meadows, and Jørgen Randers, *The Limits to Growth* (New York: Universe Books, 1972).

4. Fischer-Kowalski and Haberl, "Sustainable Development," 583.

5. Ernst von Weizsäcker, Amory B. Lovins, and L. Hunter Lovins, *Factor Four: Doubling Wealth, Halving Resource Use* (London: Earthscan, 1998).

6. Fischer-Kowalski and Haberl, "Sustainable Development," 584.

7. Robert Prescott-Allen, *The Wellbeing of Nations: A Country -by-Country Index of Quality of Life and the Environment* (Covelo, CA.: Island Press, 2001).

8. UNDP, *Human Development Report 2000* (New York: Oxford University Press, 2000), 157.

9. UNDP, *Human Development Report 2000,* 149.

10. UNDP, *Human Development Report 2000,* 157–160.

11. UNDP, *Human Development Report 2000,* 150.

12. UNDP *Human Development Report 2000,* 151.

13. UNDP, *Human Development Report 2000,* 152.

14. UNDP, *Human Development Report 2000,* 186.

15. UNDP, *Human Development Report 2000,* 157–160. (See especially note c on pp. 157 and 160.)

16. Bruce Bradbury and Marcus Jäntti, *Child Poverty in Industrialized Nations* (September 1999); other studies have also been done annually by Bruce Bradbury et al., including *The Dynamics of Child Poverty in Industrialized Countries* (2001). All are available through the worldwide web at <unicef-icdc.org>.

17. Amartya Sen, *Choice, Welfare, and Measurement* (Oxford: Blackwell, 1982).

18. Michael Carley and Philippe Spapens, *Sharing the World: Sustainable Living & Global Equity in the 21st Century* (London: Earthscan, 1998), 140.

19. Bob Deacon, "Social Policy in a Global Context," in Andrew Hurrell and Ngaire Woods, eds., *Inequality, Globalization, and World Politics* (New York: Oxford University Press, 1999), 211.

20. Carley and Spapens, *Sharing the World,* 161.

21. Carley and Spapens, *Sharing the World,* 160.

22. Frances Stewart and Albert Berry, "Globalization, Liberalization, and Inequality: Expectations and Experience," in Hurrell and Woods, 159.

23. Stewart and Berry, "Globalization, Liberalization, and Inequality," 181.

24. Stewart and Berry, "Globalization, Liberalization, and Inequality," 173.

25. Stewart and Berry, "Globalization, Liberalization, and Inequality," 184.

26. Stewart and Berry, "Globalization, Liberalization, and Inequality," 185.

27. Stewart and Berry, "Globalization, Liberalization, and Inequality," 186.

28. Carley and Spapens, *Sharing the World,* 161.

29. For numerous sources and additional discussion see Robert Paehlke, "Environmental Politics, Sustainability and Social Science," *Environmental Politics* 10 (Winter 2001), 1–22, and Robert Paehlke, "Environmental Sustainability and Urban Life in America," in Norman J. Vig and Michael E. Kraft, eds., *Environmental Policy,* 5th edition. (Washington, DC: Congressional Quarterly Press, 2003), 57–77.

30. Even erosion induced by agricultural or forestry practices not only has ecological effects on streams and rivers but also results in energy and materials use associated with additional harbor-dredging requirements.

31. Albert Adriaanse, Stefan Bringezu, Allen Hammond, Yuichi Moriguchi, Eric Rodenburg, Donald Rogich, and Helmut Schütz, *Resource Flows: The Material Basis of Industrial Economies* (Washington, DC: World Resources Institute, 1997), 15. This study was copublished with the Wuppertal Institute, the Netherlands Ministry of Housing, Spatial Planning and Environment, and the National Institute of Environmental Studies in Tsukuba, Japan.

32. Adriaanse et al., *Resource Flows,* 14.

33. Kenneth Arrow, Bert Bolin, Robert Costanza, Partha Dasgupta, Carl Folke, C. S. Holling, Bengt-Owe Jansson, Simon Levin, Karl-Göran Mäler, Charles Perrings and David Pimentel, "Economic Growth, Carrying Capacity, and the Environment," *Science* 268 (April 28, 1995), 520–521.

34. Adriaanse et al., *Resource Flows,* 14.

35. President Reagan began reducing public expenditures on all things environmental (including energy conservation) as soon after arriving in Washington in 1980 as was administratively feasible. Regarding mid-1980s dismantling of energy conservation initiatives in Canada, see David B. Brooks and Brian Kelly, "Canada Pulls the Plug on Energy-Saving," *Globe and Mail* (March 20, 1986), A7.

36. Adriaanse et al., *Resource Flows,* 16.

37. Von Weizsäcker, Lovins, and Lovins, *Factor Four,* 242–243.

38. Von Weizsäcker, Lovins, and Lovins, *Factor Four,* 242.

39. Discussed in a presentation by Jochen Jesinghaus at the International Political Science Association meetings in Quebec City (August 3, 2000).

40. Regarding the relative openness of North American governments regarding the environment, see Robert Paehlke, "Cycles of Closure in Environmental Politics and Policy," in Bob Pepperman Taylor and Ben A. Minteer, eds., *Democracy and the Claims of Nature* (Lanham, MD: Rowman & Littlefield, 2002), 279–299.

41. Mathis Wackernagel and William Rees, *Our Ecological Footprint: Reducing Human Impact on the Earth* (Philadelphia: New Society Publishers, 1996).

42. Carley and Spapens, *Sharing the World,* 9.

43. The reporting mechanism using three dials was suggested by the International Institute for Sustainable Development (Winnipeg, Manitoba) at the International Political Science Association meetings in Quebec City (August 3, 2000).

44. World Resources Institute, The United Nations Environment Programme, The United Nations Development Programme, and The World Bank, *World Resources: A Guide to the Global Environment, 1998–99* (New York: Oxford University Press, 1998), 240.

45. World Resources Institute, *World Resources,* 187.

46. This is in keeping with findings that international governance agencies are generally more trusted than national governments. See Pippa Norris, "Global Governance and Cosmopolitan Citizens," in Joseph S. Nye and John D. Donahue, eds., *Governance in a Globalizing World* (Washington, DC: Brookings Institution, 2000), 155–177.

Chapter 6

1. R. M. MacIver, Introduction to Karl Polanyi, *The Great Transformation* (Boston: Beacon Press, 1957), xi.

2. This and several paragraphs that follow are adapted from Robert Paehlke, "Right-Sizing Environmental Decision Making," in Edward A. Parson, ed. *Governing the Environment* (Toronto: University of Toronto Press, 2001), 73–123.

3. Jerry Mander and Edward Goldsmith, eds., *The Case against the Global Economy and for a Turn toward the Local* (San Francisco: Sierra Club Books, 1996), 471.

4. Kirkpatrick Sale, "Principles of Bioregionalism," in Jerry Mander and Edward Goldsmith, eds., *The Case against the Global Economy and for a Turn toward the Local* (San Francisco: Sierra Club Books, 1996), 482.

5. Sale, "Principles of Bioregionalism," 472.

6. David Morris, "Free Trade: The Great Destroyer," in Jerry Mander and Edward Goldsmith, eds., *The Case against the Global Economy and for a Turn toward the Local* (San Francisco: Sierra Club Books, 1996), 219.

7. Herman E. Daly, "Free Trade: The Perils of Deregulation," in Jerry Mander and Edward Goldsmith, eds., *The Case against the Global Economy and for a Turn toward the Local* (San Francisco: Sierra Club Books, 1996), 229–238.

8. Herman E. Daly and John B. Cobb, Jr., *For the Common Good* (Boston: Beacon Press, 1989), 210.

9. Daly, "Free Trade," 231.

10. Kirkpatrick Sale, *Human Scale* (New York: Coward, McCann & Geoghegan, 1980), 422.

11. Sale, *Human Scale,* 417 (quoting then-candidate Ronald Reagan).

12. For elaboration see Robert Paehlke, "Environmental Sustainability and Urban Life in America," in Norman J. Vig and Michael E. Kraft, eds., *Environmental Policy* (Washington, DC: Congressional Quarterly Press, 2003).

13. Wolfgang Sachs, "Neo-Development: 'Global Ecological Management,'" in Jerry Mander and Edward Goldsmith, eds., *The Case against the Global Economy and for a Turn toward the Local* (San Francisco: Sierra Club Books, 1996), 251.

14. There have been some modest media-oriented campaigns designed to embarrass individuals or corporations engaged in the global garment trades, especially regarding child labor and less-than-subsistence wage rates combined with high prices for goods.

15. See, for example, Margaret E. Keck and Kathryn Sikkink, *Activists beyond Borders* (Ithaca: Cornell University Press, 1998).

16. A good discussion of the agreement on CFCs and high-level ozone is Karen T. Litfin's *Ozone Discourses: Science and Politics in Global Environmental Cooperation* (New York: Columbia University Press, 1994). See also Edith Brown Weiss and Harold K. Jacobson, eds., *Engaging Countries: Strengthening Compliance with International Environmental Accords* (Cambridge: MIT Press, 1998).

17. Jennifer Clapp, "The Illicit Trade in Hazardous Wastes and CFCs: International Responses to Environmental 'Bads,'" in H.Richard Friman and Peter Andreas, eds., *The Illicit Global Economy and State Power* (Lanham, MD: Rowman & Littlefield, 1999), 91–123; Jennifer Clapp, *Toxic Exports* (Ithaca: Cornell University Press, 2001).

18. "Ten Years of the Basel Convention and beyond," in *Common Ground: A Triannual Report on Germany's Environment* (Berlin: Federal Ministry for the Environment, Nature Conservation and Nuclear Safety, February 2000), 9.

19. Weiss and Jacobson, *Engaging Countries.* See also Lawrence E. Susskind, *Environmental Diplomacy* (New York: Oxford University Press, 1994); William C. Clark, "Environmental Globalization," in Joseph S. Nye and John D. Donahue, eds., *Governance in a Globalizing World* (Washington, DC: Brookings Institution, 2000), 86–108.

20. Michael Ross, "Conditionality and Logging Reform in the Tropics," in Robert O. Keohane and Marc A. Levy, eds., *Institutions for Environmental Aid* (Cambridge: MIT Press, 1996), 167–197; see also June D. Hall, "International Tropical

Timber Association," in Robert Paehlke, ed., *Conservation and Environmentalism: An Encyclopedia* (New York: Garland, 1995), 367–368.

21. Lamont C. Hempel, "Climate Policy on the Instalment Plan," in Norman J. Vig and Michael E. Kraft, eds., *Environmental Policy,* 4th edition. (Washington, DC: Congressional Quarterly Press, 2000), 297.

22. See Robert B. Gibson, *Voluntary Initiatives and the New Politics of Corporate Greening* (Peterborough: Broadview Press, 1999).

23. John McCormick, "International Nongovernmental Organizations: Prospects for a Global Environmental Movement," in Sheldon Kamieniecki, ed., *Environmental Politics in the International Arena* (Albany: SUNY Press, 1993), 140.

24. David Vogel, "International Trade and Environmental Regulation," in Norman J. Vig and Michael E. Kraft, eds., *Environmental Policy,* 4th edition. (Washington, DC: Congressional Quarterly Press, 2000), 353–354. Note that Vogel is generally sympathetic to the expansion of trade and feels that this will not result in net environmental decline.

25. David Vogel, "International Trade and Environmental Regulation," 350–369.

26. See Robert Paehlke, "Democracy, Bureaucracy and Environmentalism," *Environmental Ethics* 10 (Winter 1988), 291–308, as well as William A. Shutkin, *The Land That Could Be* (Cambridge: MIT Press, 2000).

27. Stewart Udall, *The Quiet Crisis* (New York: Avon, 1963).

28. Canadian Environmental Assessment Agency, *Military Flying Activities in Labrador and Quebec: Report of the Environmental Assessment Panel* (Ottawa: Minister of Supply and Services, 1995), 79.

29. Paul Wapner, " Environmental Ethics and Global Governance: Engaging the International Liberal Tradition," *Global Governance* 3 (May-August 1997), 222.

30. David Weir and Mark Schapiro, *Circle of Poison* (San Francisco: Institute for Food and Development Policy, 1981).

31. David Vogel, "International Trade and Environmental Regulation," 366.

32. Jennifer Clapp, "The Privatization of Global Environmental Governance: ISO 14000 and the Developing World," *Global Governance* 4 (1998), 295–316.

33. Clapp, "Privatization," 299.

34. I was one of a group of U.S., Canadian, and Mexican academics engaged to produce part of a North American State of the Environment report that considered the economic, social, and environmental effects of NAFTA. The chapters were completed, reviewed, modified, and edited, but the study was not published in anything like the original form.

35. Richard Kiy and John D. Wirth, eds., *Environmental Management on North America's Borders* (College Station: Texas A & M University Press, 1998).

36. Robert O. Keohane, "Analyzing the Effectiveness of International Environmental Institutions," in Robert O. Keohane and Marc A. Levy, eds., *Institutions for Environmental Aid* (Cambridge: MIT Press, 1996), 13.

37. Helmut Weidner and Martin Jänicke, eds., *Capacity Building in National Environmental Policy* (Berlin: Springer-Verlag, 2002). The earlier volume was published in 1997, also by Springer.

38. Weidner and Jänicke, *Capacity Building,* 410.

39. Stephen D. Krasner, "Structural Causes and Regime Consequences: Regimes as Intervening Variables," in Stephen D. Krasner, ed., *International Regimes* (Ithaca: Cornell University Press, 1983), 2.

40. Oran R. Young, *International Cooperation: Building Regimes for Natural Resources and the Environment* (Ithaca: Cornell University Press, 1989). See also, for example, Keohane and Levy, *Institutions for Environmental Aid,* and Peter M. Haas, Robert O. Keohane, and Marc A. Levy, *Institutions for the Earth: Sources of Effective International Environmental Protection* (Cambridge: MIT Press, 1993).

41. Keohane, "Analyzing Effectiveness," 12.

42. David Fairman and Michael Ross, "Old Fads, New Lessons: Learning from Economic Development Assistance," in Robert O. Keohane and Marc A. Levy, eds., *Institutions for Environmental Aid* (Cambridge: MIT Press, 1996), 29–51.

43. Young, *International Cooperation,* 222.

44. The evolutionary process is thoroughly documented in the two-volume Social Learning Group study: *Learning to Manage Global Environmental Risks* (Cambridge: MIT Press, 2001).

45. Robert O'Brien, Anne Marie Goetz, Jan Aart Scholte, and Marc Williams, *Contesting Global Governance* (New York: Cambridge University Press, 2000), 138.

46. David Held, *Democracy and the Global Order* (Stanford: Stanford University Press, 1995), 251.

47. See, for example, Margaret Keck and Kathryn Sikkink, *Activists beyond Borders,* as well as Anthony Woodiwiss, *Globalization, Human Rights and Labour Law in Pacific Asia* (New York: Cambridge University Press, 1998), and Ellen L. Lutz and Kathryn Sikkink, "International Human Rights Law and Practice in Latin America," *International Organization* 45 (Summer 2000), 633–659. See also the ILO website <www.ilo.org>.

48. Jackie Smith, Melissa Bolyard, and Anna Ippolito, "Human Rights and the Global Economy: A Response to Meyer," *Human Rights Quarterly* 21 (February 1999), 219.

49. Smith, Bolyard, and Ippolito, "Human Rights and the Global Economy," 207.

50. Robert McCorquodale and Richard Fairbrother, "Globalization and Human Rights," *Human Rights Quarterly* 21 (August 1999), 763.

51. See Pace University Center for Environmental Legal Studies, *Environmental Costs of Electricity* (New York: Oceana Publications, 1991), and Robert Paehlke, "Towards Defining, Measuring and Achieving Sustainability: Tools and Strategies for Environmental Evaluation," in Egon Becker and Thomas Jahn, eds., *Sustainability and the Social Sciences* (London: Zed Books, 1999), 243–263.

52. Some positive possibilities in this regard are discussed in Ronnie D. Lipschutz, *Global Civil Society and Global Environmental Governance* (Albany: SUNY Press, 1996), and Pamela S. Chasek, ed., *The Global Environment in the Twenty-First Century* (New York: United Nations University Press, 2000).

Chapter 7

1. See, for example, Samuel P. Hays, "From Conservation to Environment: Environmental Politics in the United States Since World War Two," *Environmental Review* 6 (Fall 1982), 6.

2. See the discussion that follows and especially note 11.

3. Michael Carley and Philippe Spapens, *Sharing the World: Sustainable Living & Global Equity in the 21st Century* (London: Earthscan, 1998), 146–147.

4. Amy Saltzman, *Downshifting: Reinventing Success on a Slower Track* (New York: HarperCollins, 1991), 17.

5. See the extended discussion on this point in Carley and Spapens, *Sharing the World*, 134–167.

6. Mark Kingwell, *Dreams of Millennium* (Toronto: Viking, 1996).

7. Sarah Ban Breathnach, *Simple Abundance Companion* (New York: Warner Books, 2000); Sarah Ban Breathnach, *Something More: Excavating Your Authentic Self* (New York: Warner Books, 1998); James Ballard, *What's the Rush?* (New York: Broadway, 1999); Janet Luhrs, *The Simple Living Guide* (New York: Broadway, 1997); Joe Dominguez and Vicki Robin, *Your Money or Your Life?* (New York: Viking Penguin, 1992).

8. The journal is available from <www.simpleliving.net>, a website that also offers online discussion groups on 28 different topics and is a contact point for 475 local, live study groups and circles.

9. Juliet Schor, *The Overworked American: The Unexpected Decline of Leisure* (New York: Basic Books, 1991).

10. This is expressed in books such as Bruce O'Hara, *Working Harder Isn't Working* (Vancouver: New Star Books, 1993) and others mentioned in this chapter, as well as in new public policies in many European nations (discussed below).

11. John Gray, *False Dawn* (London: Granta Books, 1998), 217.

12. William H. Whyte, Jr., *The Organization Man* (New York: Doubleday Anchor, 1956).

13. The allusion is to David Reisman, *The Lonely Crowd* (New Haven: Yale University Press, 1961).

14. Heilbroner, *The Making of Economic Society*, 234.

15. André Gorz, *Paths to Paradise* (London: Pluto Press, 1985; first published 1983), 41.

16. Gorz, *Paths to Paradise*, 40.

17. Heilbroner, 234–235.

18. Gorz, *Paths to Paradise,* 35.

19. Regarding the extension of the 1990s employment insecurity beyond the period of high unemployment, see Stanley Aronowitz and Jonathan Cutler, eds., *Post-Work* (New York: Routledge, 1998), 91.

20. Saltzman, *Downshifting,* 13.

21. Anders Hayden, *Sharing the Work, Sparing the Planet* (Toronto: Between the Lines, 1999), 135.

22. Hayden, *Sharing the Work,* 138.

23. Hayden, *Sharing the Work,* 144.

24. Hayden, *Sharing the Work,* 149.

25. Personal communication in interview with Canadian Auto Workers staff member, February 24, 2001.

26. Hayden, *Sharing the Work,* 155, combined with OECD employment statistics.

Chapter 8

1. Robert O'Brien et al., *Contesting Global Governance* (New York: Cambridge University Press, 2000), 109–158.

2. Arthur P. J. Mol, *Globalization and Environmental Reform* (Cambridge: MIT Press, 2001), 203.

3. Mol, *Globalization and Environmental Reform,* 114.

4. Mol, *Globalization and Environmental Reform,* 151.

5. Matthew Paterson, "Globalization, Ecology and Resistance," *New Political Economy* 4 (1999), 131.

6. David Held, *Democracy and the Global Order* (Stanford: Stanford University Press, 1995), 237–238.

7. David Held and Anthony McGrew, "Globalization," *Global Governance* 5 (October-December 1999), 484.

8. Robert Paehlke, "Environment, Equity and Globalization," *Global Environmental Politics* 1 (February 2001), 1–10.

9. This is discussed in Frank Biermann, "The Case for a World Environment Organization," *Environment* 42 (November 2000), 22–31.

10. Theodore J. Lowi, "Think Globally, Lose Locally," in Guy Lachapelle and John Trent, eds., *Globalization: Governance and Identity* (Montreal: University of Montreal Press, 2000), 38.

11. Hartley Dean, " Green Citizenship," *Social Policy & Administration* 35 (December 2001), 491.

12. David Held, "Democracy and Globalization," *Global Governance* 3 (September-December 1997), 264.

Index